The Challenge of
Front-Line Management

The Challenge of Front-Line Management

Flattened Organizations in the New Economy

Ronald R. Sims,
John G. Veres III,
Katherine A. Jackson,
and Carolyn L. Facteau

QUORUM BOOKS
Westport, Connecticut • London

Library of Congress Cataloging-in-Publication Data

The challenge of front-line management : flattened organizations in the new economy /
Ronald R. Sims . . . [et al.].
       p.   cm.
    Includes bibliographical references and index.
    ISBN 1–56720–373–6 (alk. paper)
       1. Supervision of employees.   2. Industrial management.   3. Middle managers.
    I. Sims, Ronald R.
    HF5549.12.C427   2001
    658.4'3—dc21   00–032818

British Library Cataloguing in Publication Data is available.

Library of Congress Catalog Card Number: 00–032818
ISBN: 1–56720–373–6

First published in 2001

Quorum Books, 88 Post Road West, Westport, CT 06881
An imprint of Greenwood Publishing Group, Inc.
www.quorumbooks.com

Printed in the United States of America

The paper used in this book complies with the
Permanent Paper Standard issued by the National
Information Standards Organization (Z39.48–1984).

10 9 8 7 6 5 4 3 2 1

Contents

Acknowledgments

Ronald R. Sims. I extend special thanks to my wife, Serbrenia, and to my children, Nandi, Dangaia, and Sieya, who provide ongoing support and encouragement, and to a very special friend and mentor, Herrington Bryce, who continues to challenge me to learn and grow.

John G. Veres III. I would like to dedicate this work to Frances M. and John G. Veres, Jr., and to Beth, Erin, John Jozef, and Olivia Veres, who have all taught me much and put up with more; to Wiley Bolyes and W. O. Jenkins, who taught me most of what I know about my discipline; and to the employees of the Center for Business, past and present, from whom I learned to manage at least tolerably well.

Katherine A. Jackson. I would like to dedicate this book to Nancy Jackson, a parent and educator who nurtured my early leanings toward an academic life; to Curtis Jackson, who fostered in me an appreciation for the practical; and to John G. Veres III, who hired me and nominated me for the Lucy B. Hall Award for Excellence.

Carolyn L. Facteau. I would like to thank my husband, Jeff, who is always there to support and encourage my efforts; my children, David and Katherine, for the constant joy they bring to my life; and my parents, Ralph and Sally Lehr, for teaching me by example the value of setting high goals but remembering that family should always be the highest priority.

Ronald R. Sims. I wish to acknowledge the administrative support of the College of William and Mary. The final and most deserved acknowledgment is for my co-authors. Without their professional and personal involvement in this project, this book would not exist.

John G. Veres III, Katherine A. Jackson, and Carolyn L. Facteau. We wish to acknowledge the assistance of Carmen Moa-Rovera, who suffered bravely in manuscript preparation; Cindy Forehand, whose insightful editorial comments proved invaluable; and Ronald R. Sims, for displaying the drive needed to shepherd this work to completion.

Chapter 1

Understanding the Front-Line Manager's Job

INTRODUCTION

Marston Technologies is an international computer manufacturing company with 10,000 employees in 20 countries. Teresa McCullough and Larry Washington are employees in one of the company's largest facilities. Both have been with the company approximately four years. This morning, while attending a computer training program, their manager, Stan Lawrence, gave Teresa and Larry a big shock. He asked both of them if they would like to become front-line managers (FLMs). Stan explained that two of the FLMs in different parts of the company were being promoted and that he needed two new FLMs. Stan also stated that he felt Teresa and Larry would make good FLMs because they both (1) were highly recommended by their current FLMs, (2) knew the job, and (3) knew people in the two departments that were losing the FLMs. Stan asked both of them to think it over and let him know their decisions the next day. Later, Teresa saw Larry at lunch and they began discussing the possibilities of the new jobs. Both of them agreed that they had never given much thought to being an FLM. They wondered just what the job of FLM would entail.

If you are like Teresa and Larry, you want to learn what being an FLM means. Managing on the front line is a challenging and sometimes taxing activity. FLMs are responsible for the work of others as well as their own work. They must solve problems, make decisions, and take action. They experience pressures from top- and middle-level managers, their employees, and an ever-changing world of work and society. FLMs never seem to have enough time to get their work done.

On the other hand, managing in the trenches is also a very exciting and rewarding experience. FLMs can experience a real sense of accomplishment when their work team is cooperating and performing effectively. Knowing that you have helped your employees develop their knowledge, skills, and abilities (KSAs) as well as other characteristics can be satisfying. Helping to create an environment that employees find rewarding also provides satisfaction.

Managing is an increasingly important activity in today's society, as the role of the FLM continues to grow in organizations. How can you become an effective FLM? Experience is one answer. You can be placed in an FLM position and learn from your successes and failures. However, experience is not the only answer. A systematic study of management can also help your performance. By studying concepts that FLMs have found helpful, you can prepare yourself to meet the challenges of an FLM's job. While study alone cannot make you an effective FLM, it can help you profit from your experience. Learning from the trials and successes of other FLMs can make you an effective FLM more rapidly.

You are about to begin a systematic study of management on the front line. This book will introduce you to the challenging and rapidly changing world of FLM. This chapter defines the FLM, the FLM process, and the basic skills and roles FLMs must perform and provides an overview of major challenges facing today's organizations and the FLMs in those organizations.

WHAT IS AN FLM?

When you talk to people in today's organizations, you get a variety of descriptions of the FLM's job. You find that FLMs perform many different activities and face different problems. The FLM job can differ greatly from one organization, or even one department, to the next.

These differences are to be expected. FLMs work in a variety of organizations like banks, manufacturing organizations, fast food restaurants, schools, government agencies, and not-for-profit organizations. Their jobs may vary widely, depending on the goals and structure of the organization and their level within the organization. Certainly the personalities of FLMs and their employees and the kind of jobs to be done all influence the role of the FLM. The problems faced by FLMs, and the activities they perform, therefore, vary greatly.

While FLM jobs do differ there are some common elements that define a job as an FLM position. First, all FLMs have people working for them. FLMs are responsible for directing the work of others and accomplishing goals. They accomplish these goals by managing or supervising their employees to meet the performance goals set by higher-level managers.

FLMs work where the rubber meets the road: on the plant floor, in the secretarial pool, or in the customer service office.

First and foremost, FLMs are managers, and all managers are involved in meeting performance goals. However, this book will be devoted primarily to the FLM who serves as the important link between operating employees and middle management. The remainder of this section examines the environment inside the organization in which FLMs must function. It identifies the settings where FLMs work, the day-to-day activities that utilize much of their time, and some generalized skills necessary to cope with the internal environment. We begin by briefly describing various levels of management, then focus on FLM skills.

THE VARIOUS LEVELS OF MANAGEMENT

Most organizations function on at least three distinct but overlapping levels, each requiring a different managerial focus and emphasis. They include the *operations level*, the *technical level*, and the *strategic level*. Managers at each of these three levels must plan, organize, lead, and control.

Operations Level

Every organization, whether it produces a physical product or a service, has an operations function. In any organization the operations level focuses on effectively performing the function necessary to produce or do whatever the organization produces or does. A physical product, for instance, requires a flow of materials and management of the operations. Banks must see that checks are processed and financial transactions are recorded accurately and quickly. The operations function is at the core of every organization. The FLM's task at the operations level is to manage in a manner that results in the best allocation of resources that will produce the desired output.

Technical Level

As an organization increases in size, someone must coordinate the activities at the operations level as well as decide which products or services to offer. These problems are the focus of the technical level. A dissatisfied customer complains to the unit FLM. A retail FLM mediates disagreements between customers and salespeople. Production or maintenance schedules and amounts to be produced or equipment to be prepared must be planned for an automobile manufacturer or a residential facility.

At this level, the managerial task is really twofold: (1) managing the operations function and (2) serving as a liaison between those who produce the product or service and those who use the output. In other words, for the operations level to do its work, FLMs at the technical level must make sure they have the correct materials and see that output is sold or used.

Strategic Level

Every organization operates in a broad social environment. As a part of that environment, an organization also has a responsibility to other entities' environment. The strategic level must make sure the technical level operates within the bounds of society. Since the ultimate source of authority in any organization comes from society, the organization must provide goods and services in a socially acceptable manner. Thus, the strategic level determines the long-range objectives and direction for the organization—in other words, how the organization interacts with its environment. The organization also may seek to influence its environment through lobbying efforts, advertising efforts, or educational programs aimed at members of society.

Front-Line and Other Managers

Understanding the various levels of management can be helpful in determining the primary focus of FLMs' activities at different levels in an organization. For example, terms widely used in organizations include *top management*, *middle management*, and *first-level management* (led by FLMs).

Top management reflects a group of people responsible for establishing the organization's overall objectives and developing the policies to achieve those objectives. Titles typical of top management positions include chairman of the board, chief executive officer (CEO), president, senior vice president, and cabinet secretary.

Middle management includes all employees below the top-management level who manage other managers. These individuals are responsible for establishing and meeting specific goals in their particular departments or unit. Their goals, however, are not established in isolation. Instead, the objectives set by top management provide specific direction to middle managers regarding what they are expected to achieve. Ideally, if each middle manager met his or her goals, the entire organization would meet its objectives. Examples of job titles held by middle managers include division manager, district manager, vice president of finance, unit manager, commissioner, or division director.

FLMs, like top and middle managers, are also part of the organization's management team. Because FLMs oversee the work of operating employees they are often referred to as first-level or front-line managers.

The kinds of job titles likely to identify someone as an FLM include Shift FLM, Welding Foreman, and Receiving and Warehousing FLM, to name a few.

BASIC FLM SKILLS

Certain general skills are needed for effective managerial performance, regardless of the level of the manager in the hierarchy of the organization. However, the mix of skills differs depending on the level of the FLM and other managers in the organization. These basic skills—human (interpersonal), technical, and conceptual—are needed by all FLMs and managers. The application of each of the three types of skills depends not only on the level of management, but also the type of organization.

FLMs must accomplish much of their work through other people. For this, it is essential that the FLM possess and demonstrate *interpersonal skill*. A reflection of an FLM's leadership abilities, interpersonal skill is the ability to work with, communicate to, and understand others.

The importance of interpersonal skill is most obvious in those managerial jobs that involve extensive interactions with other employees. FLMs are particularly in need of interpersonal skill because they spend so much of their time interacting with other employees. FLMs must provide ongoing feedback to employees regarding interpersonal and performance problems. They have the responsibilities to motivate employees to change or improve performance. FLMs must also oversee the other activities involved in supervising individual and team performance.

Communication skills are an important component of interpersonal skill. They form the basis for sending and receiving messages on the job. Different types of communication skills are important for FLMs. Speaking and writing skills are of obvious importance. Listening is also an important skill. The ability to recognize differences among people aids effective communication, because the communicator can adapt the message to be more receptive to the receiver. Chapter 4 offers more discussion on communication.

Technical skill enables an FLM to apply specific knowledge, techniques, and resources to perform work. Technical skills have the greatest relevance for FLMs. This is true for two reasons. First, many FLMs perform technical work as well as managerial work. In contrast to other levels of management, the distinction between the individual contributor and first-line FLM is often blurred. Second, FLMs spend more time training and developing their employees than do other managers. This requires FLMs to have a greater technical knowledge of their employees' jobs than that needed by middle- and top-level managers.

For today's FLM, technical skills include the ability to prepare a budget, lay out a work schedule, and program and work with more technically sophisticated tools. Well-developed technical skills can facilitate an individual's rise to management. For example, many an FLM launched his or her career by being a competent member of their operations or work unit. In spite of the importance of technical skills, successful FLMs must recognize that being technically competent alone will not help them achieve their own, their team's, or their organization's success. The ultimate challenge for the FLM is always to get things done through others. This challenge requires that the FLM have strengths in interpersonal and conceptual skills along with technical skills.

Conceptual skill is the ability to see the relationships of parts of the organization to the whole and to one another. For an FLM, conceptual skills include recognizing how the department's work helps the organization achieve its goals and how the work of the various employees affects the performance of the department as a whole. FLMs with conceptual skills understand all activities and interests of the organization and how they interrelate.

All three skills are essential for effective performance. As noted earlier, the relative importance of the three skills to a specific FLM or manager depends on their level in the organization. Interpersonal skill is critical at the lower level of management. For instance, because they deal with the day-to-day interpersonal problems in a particular unit or team, FLMs need more interpersonal skills than higher level managers in the organization.

The importance of conceptual skills increases as managers move up in the organization. This is due to the type of problems they encounter and the decisions they make at higher levels. The higher a manager is in the hierarchy, the more involved he or she becomes in longer-term decisions that can influence many parts of the organization or the entire organization.

Generally speaking, the higher a manager rises in an organization, the more the problems he or she faces tend to be complex, ambiguous, and ill-defined. These problems require custom-made solutions or nonprogrammed decision making. In contrast, FLMs generally have more straightforward, familiar, and easily defined problems which lend themselves to more routine or programmed decision making. Ill-structured problems and custom-made solutions make greater conceptual demands on managers than do structured problems and programmed decision making. See Chapter 11 for more discussion on decisions and the different levels of decision making.

Breaking down skills into these three categories or levels is helpful. However, it is also somewhat artificial. FLMs must use a combination of skills to deal with different situations. In fact, all three types of skills will come into play in most situations. However, placing these skills into categories can be helpful in understanding behavior in organizations and learning how to become a more effective FLM. The FLM uses resources and carries out four FLM functions to achieve an objective. These functions are *planning, organizing, leading*, and *controlling*. Each function is a method of managing the various resources used by the FLM.

Resources Used by FLMs

FLMs use resources to accomplish their purposes, just as a carpenter uses resources to build a porch. An FLM's resources can be divided into four types: *human, financial, physical*, and *information*.

Human resources are the people needed to get the job done. An FLM's goals influence which employees an FLM chooses. For example, Tracy Fernandez, an FLM at a major chain restaurant has the goal of delivering quality food to her customers. Among the human resources she chooses are order clerks, cooks, delivery drivers, and other part-time employees. The types of human resources the Director of the Occupational Safety and Health Agency chooses will be much more numerous because the goals of that huge federal agency are much more varied than the goal of Fernandez's company.

The money that the FLM and the organization use to reach organizational goals is a *financial resource*. The financial resources of a business organization are profits and investments from stockholders. The financial resources of community agencies come from tax revenues, charitable contributions, and government grants. The financial resources of a particular department come from the budget developed by the FLM and approved by middle- and top-level management. See Chapter 8 for more discussion on budgets.

Physical resources are an organization's tangible goods and real estate, including materials, office space, production facilities, office equipment, and vehicles. Organizations use a variety of vendors to supply the physical resources needed to achieve organizational goals.

The data that the FLM and the organization use to get the job done are *information resources*. For example, to supply members of a safety unit with data from inspections and monitoring activities, many organizations rely on computers to store and process data on company history, and so forth.

To accomplish goals, the FLM performs four FLM functions related to the management of these various types of resources. As stated earlier, these functions are planning, organizing, leading, and controlling.

Planning

The planning function involves defining and setting goals, figuring out ways for achieving these goals, and developing a comprehensive hierarchy of plans to integrate and coordinate activities to reaching the goals (Chapter 8 provides a more in-depth discussion of the concept of planning). Setting goals keeps the work to be done in its proper perspective and helps organizational members keep their attention on what is most important. Planning is considered the central function of management, and it pervades everything an FLM does. In planning, an FLM looks to the future, saying, "Here is what we want to achieve, and here is how we are going to do it." Decision making is usually a component of planning, because choices have to be made in the process of finalizing plans.

For example, once Teresa McCullough took over the FLM's job at Marston Technologies, she and her manager, Stan Lawrence, set a goal of improving computer maintenance efficiency cost savings by $230,000 over a 12-month period. As the end of the eighth month approached, her unit was $127,000 short of reaching their goal. Adding to this shortfall was the realization that in spite of the unit's best efforts, mandatory certification training for several of her team members was behind schedule. Teresa and the rest of her team realized that they had an important decision to make. If they postponed the certification training for at least another month, they would have an excellent chance of achieving the computer maintenance cost savings objective for the year. Teresa made the decision to postpone certification training, leaving her team in position to spend the time they needed to achieve their cost savings. Team members were able to make up the training at a later date. In this case, Teresa and her team made the right decision. As you will see in our discussion in Chapter 11, decision making is also involved in the other functions of management.

Organizing

Organizing is the process of making sure the necessary human and physical resources are available to carry out a plan and achieve organizational goals (see Chapter 8 for a more detailed discussion of the organizing function). Organizing also involves determining what tasks are to be done, assigning activities, and dividing work into specific jobs and tasks. For example, Teresa McCullough began addressing the charge of the computer maintenance cost savings and certification training for her team by better organizing her team's computer maintenance projects and scheduling the necessary training.

Another major aspect of organizing is grouping activities into departments or some other logical subdivision, and specifying who reports to whom, as well as when decisions are to be made. The activities of an organization are often divided into departments, such as production and marketing, or territories, such as northern and southern. FLMs like Teresa often have the major responsibility for dividing work into manageable components and coordinating results to achieve objectives.

Leading

Leading is influencing others to achieve organizational objectives (Chapter 5 discusses the concept of leadership). Leading involves dozens of interpersonal processes: motivating, communicating, coaching, and showing employees how they can reach their goals. When FLMs motivate employees, direct the activities of others, select the most effective communication channel, or resolve conflicts among members, they're engaging in leading. Leadership is such an important part of management that managing is sometimes defined as accomplishing results through people.

As suggested above, leading or influencing people, requires many different actions by the FLM. A typical act of leadership for an FLM like Teresa is to praise a team member who has done an exceptional job. In this way, Teresa tries to motivate the employee to continue performing at such a high level (see Chapter 6 for more discussion on motivation). Teresa's discipline of a team member who has violated safety rules is also an example of leadership behavior.

Controlling

The final function FLMs perform is controlling (see Chapter 8 for a more in-depth discussion of the controlling function). Controlling is ensuring that performance conforms to plans. That is, after the goals are set, the plans formulated, the organizing arrangements determined, and the people hired, trained, and motivated, something may still go amiss. To make sure that things are going as they should, Teresa and other FLMs must monitor their organization's and unit's performance. Teresa must compare actual performance to the previously set goals. If there is a significant difference between actual and desired performance, Teresa must take corrective action.

A secondary aspect of controlling is determining whether the original plan needs revision, given the realities of the day. The controlling function sometimes causes an FLM to return to the planning function temporarily to fine-tune the original plan.

The large-scale use of computerized information has contributed to the complexity of the controlling process. Compared to the noncomputerized past, there is now much more information available to measure deviations from performance. The process of monitoring, comparing, and correcting is what comprises the controlling function.

Planning, organizing, leading and controlling are important FLM functions. FLMs like Teresa McCullough, who are concerned with being successful, must develop an understanding of these four functions.

WORKING THROUGH OTHERS

All FLMs' jobs have several common characteristics, and chief among them is working with and through operating employees to accomplish established work-unit goals. This function separates employees from FLMs. Consider Teresa McCullough. As an individual contributor (or direct report), one of her responsibilities was to maintain the boiler and other equipment in proper operating condition. When Teresa became an FLM, however, her function was supposed to change. Teresa is still responsible for some operational activities that her team performs. In many instances, however, she is not expected to actually do the operational work herself. She is expected to train other employees, provide them with direction, coordinate efforts, and give them the necessary resources and assistance so that *they* can maintain the equipment. In short, as an FLM, Teresa is supposed to achieve the maintenance goals through the efforts of other members of the team.

PROJECT MANAGEMENT

Many attempts have been made over the years to paint a realistic picture of what managers, in our case FLMs, do. Like the various skills presented earlier, this emphasis on skills is very much in tune with today's results-oriented organizations. While there is no unanimous agreement among those responsible for teaching and training FLMs, certain skills have surfaced as being more important than others. The FLM's role and skills in *project management* is one such example.

Most of us accept the notion of projects in our personal lives as the opportunities and problems encountered in our daily living. Projects are elements of change. Projects are conceptualized, designed, engineered, and produced (or constructed); something is created that did not previously exist. A strategy is executed to facilitate the support of an organization. Projects, therefore, support the ongoing activities of a going concern.

Project management provides for the creation and delivery of something while meeting costs and schedule objectives. The use of FLMs and the project teams they lead play a key role in preparing the organization to respond to the changing world of work. For example, FLMs are expected to use projects to capture opportunity in new technology and transfer existing technology in changing economic, environmental, political and social conditions, which leads to enhanced organizational performance and survival. To fulfill their project management role, FLMs must recognize that projects, like organizations, always are in motion as each proceeds along its life cycle. Projects go through a life cycle (planning, implementation, and close out) to completion, hopefully on time, within budget, and with the attainment of the performance objectives.

Successful project completion requires that the FLM use conceptual, technical, and interpersonal skills to determine if the project is really worth doing. This is the point at which the project is tied to the organization's strategic goals and objectives. A good analysis conducted at this point will provide more information and details on how to properly define and manage the project later. Some of the things that the FLM must do during this phase include:

1. Determine the technical and financial feasibility of the project.
2. Examine alternative ways of accomplishing the project objectives to include alternative projects.
3. Provide initial answers to the following questions: What will the project cost? When will the project be implemented? What will the project do? How will the project be integrated and coordinated with existing work and systems?
4. Identify the human and nonhuman resources that are required to support the project.
5. Select the initial project designs that will satisfy the project objectives.
6. Determine the initial project interfaces.
7. Establish a project team organization.
8. Verify the "strategic fit" of the project.

The FLM must also more clearly define the project. A clearly defined project states, in more detail, what it is we want to accomplish, when we want to accomplish it, how we shall accomplish it, and what accomplishing it will cost. The purpose of this phase is for the FLM to establish project costs, schedules, performance objectives, and resource requirements. This phase dictates that the FLM stop and take time to see whether this is what is really wanted before resources are committed to put the project into operation.

The FLM's role in project management will be most evident in the forthcoming discussions on planning, organizing, leading, and controlling. In the presentation of each of these topics it will become increasingly clear that the FLM must deal effectively with people to achieve successful results in general and in project management in particular.

To this point we have defined FLM, important FLM skills, functions, and project management. The remainder of this chapter will examine some of the major challenges and developments that are likely to affect FLMs like Teresa McCullough and the FLM process.

THE FLM's CHANGING ENVIRONMENT

Throughout the foreseeable future, FLMs will have to understand and deal with many complex environmental factors and trends. These factors and trends influence the FLM. To be effective in today's changing world of work, FLMs must be adaptable and maintain their perspective in the face of a rapidly changing environment. For instance, global competition, the knowledge and information explosion, and diversity represent not only some of the latest buzzwords, but also a harsh reality currently facing FLMs.

Twenty years ago issues like workforce diversity and globalization were not that important. There are many solutions being offered for dealing with these complex challenges. Yet the simplest but most profound solutions may be found in the words of Sam Walton, founder of Wal-Mart and richest person in the world when he died. When asked for the answer to successful organizations and management, Sam quickly replied, "People are the key."

Globalization

FLMs and other employees throughout an organization must perform at higher and higher levels because the world has been changing more rapidly than ever before. In the last 20 years, both domestic and global competition have increased dramatically. The rise of *global organizations*, organizations that operate and compete in more than one country, has and will continue to put severe pressure on many organizations to improve their performance and to identify better ways to use their resources.

Global challenges will continue to impact the FLM. Substantial investment has been made in U.S. firms by the British, Germans, Swiss, Canadians, Japanese, and others. Identifying the various cultural/value system and work ethic differences is beyond the scope of this book. However, the FLM must recognize that management practices differ culturally and structurally in these organizations compared to the U.S.-owned and operated companies. Today's FLMs will need to learn to operate in a one-world market made up of differing cultures and leadership styles, especially at the FLM level.

More than ever before, talented people will be needed to represent firms on a global basis. Clearly, there is increasing evidence that globalization will impact FLMs and their organizations. Today's FLMs who make no attempt to learn and adapt to changes in the global environment will find themselves reacting rather than innovating, and their organizations will often become uncompetitive and fail.

Information Availability and Technology

Another major environmental development is the second generation of the Information Age. The first generation was characterized by relatively straightforward, automated data processing. This second generation has moved to automated decision making, more technology-based telecommunications, and the information superhighway. Now commonplace, decision support systems, expert systems, and e-mail allow organizations to make real-time, on-line decisions backed by quantitative data and multiple input.

Many organizations have been completely revamped because of technological advances, computers, robotics, automation, changing markets, and other competitive influences that demand both internal and external adaptations. The great expansion of information technology—computers, e-mail, faxes, beepers, cellular phones, and voice mail—has profoundly changed the workplace. These devices have made it much easier for people to access information and to communicate with each other on the job. In many cases, FLMs no longer have to be the keepers of all information.

The computerization of tools and machines and the greater use of robots in manufacturing reduce the number of people needed in various jobs and, thus, in turn, the number of FLMs needed to manage those people. In other words, technology has affected management greatly, either by automating work formerly done by employees directed by FLMs or by giving employees direct access to information and people without having to go through an FLM. This change has freed FLMs to devote more time to other tasks, such as better planning, more coordination of work among teams, management of suppliers or vendors, and assisting their work groups or teams to improve processes.

Increases in information availability and technological change will require FLMs to have increased technical skills. Furthermore, these changes require more skilled and trained employees. Technology then increases the importance of the FLM's role in training and overcoming resistance to change as discussed in Chapter 12. Therefore, FLMs must keep up to date on the latest developments so that they can effectively train their people. Higher level skills and training require new approaches to motivation and leadership. Thus, FLMs like Teresa McCullough need more skill in the interpersonal area.

The Quality Revolution

Today's organizations operate quite differently than in decades past. For them the watchword is not "getting by," but "making things better," what has been referred to as the *quality revolution*. The best organizations are ones that strive to deliver better quality goods and services to customers at lower prices than ever before. Those that do so flourish, and those that do not tend to fade away.

There is increasing evidence that the delivery of quality products and services to customers has a direct impact on the success of organizations. The key, of course, is to realize that the people in the organization, not advertising slogans or statistical quality control, deliver quality goods and services. The challenge for FLMs and organizations across the world is to have their employees deliver quality products and—especially—services to each other (internal customers) and to customers and clients.

In the future, organizations will continue their efforts to improve quality and service through organizational practices like *total quality management* (TQM) (an organizational strategy of commitment to improving customer satisfaction by developing techniques to manage output quality carefully and achieving ISO 9000 certification) and *reengineering* (the fundamental rethinking and radical redesign of business processes to achieve dramatic improvements in performance). Because of the recent optimism toward these approaches, it is unlikely that they will become tomorrow's outdated fads.

New Organizational Forms

As noted earlier, technology has made it possible for fewer people to do more work than ever before. Unlike the gradual process of automation in the past, today's technology is occurring so rapidly that the very nature of work is changing as fast as we can keep up. With this, many jobs disappeared during the last two decades, leaving organizations (at least the most successful ones) smaller than before.

Downsizing. Indeed, during the 1980s and 1990s, organizations rapidly reduced the number of employees needed to operate effectively—a process known as *downsizing*. Typically, this process involved more than just laying off people in a move to save money. The process is directed at adjusting the number of employees needed to work in newly designed organizations and is therefore also known as *rightsizing*. Whatever you call it, the bottom line is clear: even during today's economic boom, many organizations still believe they need fewer people to operate today than in the past—sometimes, far fewer.

Outsourcing. Another way organizations are restructuring and doing more with less is by completely eliminating those parts that focus on non-core sectors of the business (i.e., tasks that are peripheral to the organization), and hiring outside firms to perform these functions instead—a practice known as *outsourcing*. Contracting with outsiders to do work previously done within the corporation, is not a new phenomenon, but it has been rapidly growing. In an effort to cut costs, organizations are farming out many varieties of work previously done by regular employees, resulting in layoffs and internal reorganization. By outsourcing secondary activities, an organization can focus on what it does best, its key capability—what is known as its *core competency*. For example, by outsourcing its payroll processing, a company may grow smaller and focus its resources on what it does best. Outsourcing, of course, creates layoffs and the associated problems, including union-management frictions, which all undoubtedly pose challenges for FLMs.

Mergers, the combining of two or more companies into one organization, continues to be epidemic, frequently resulting in large layoffs. Mergers tend to create issues in addition to those associated with layoffs. For example, who will be in charge, and what FLMs and other employees will be retained or laid off? Who, where and how will work be completed? The remaining FLMs, of course, must address all of these and other issues relative to their own operations if they are to assist the total organization effectively during and after the merger.

Virtual organization. As more and more organizations are outsourcing various organizational functions and pairing down to their core competencies, they might not be able to perform all the tasks required to complete a project. However, they can perform their own highly specialized part of it very well. If you put together several organizations whose competencies complement each other and have them work together on a special project, you have a very strong group of collaborators. This is the idea behind an organizational arrangement that is growing in popularity—the *virtual organization*. A virtual organization is a highly flexible, temporary organization formed by a group of companies that join forces to exploit a specific opportunity.

Although virtual organizations are not an everyday, common occurrence, experts expect them to grow in popularity in the years ahead. As one consultant put it, "It's not just a good idea; it's inevitable."

Work Schedules and Business Conditions

General working conditions are changing rapidly and will continue to evolve. Less than one-third of employed Americans over age 18 work the traditional Monday through Friday workweek. Even fewer Americans will be working the standard nine-to-five day because of the projected growth in jobs with evening, night, and weekend shifts. In order to attract and retain the most qualified employees, today's organizations must offer flexible work schedules, telecommuting, opportunities for temporary, part-time, or contract employees, and changes in job design.

Work schedules, like work rules, are a major condition of employee's acceptance of jobs. Work schedules refer to matters such as starting and stopping times, the number and length of work breaks, how work beyond the regularly scheduled day or week is administered, whether the work is done on company premises or at home, and whether the employee is full- or part-time. Like work rules, work schedules have gained an increasing influence on the satisfaction, and frequently the performance, of employees. The manner in which those work schedules are monitored, administered, and changed is important. From the standpoint of the FLM, work schedules are necessary to coordinate and control work. Further, a certain amount of uniformity is required (and expected) to meet employee expectations of equitable treatment. Work schedules are becoming more flexible, however, than has been traditionally assumed in many organizations.

Experimentation with different kinds of work schedules, such as the compressed workweek, flextime, permanent part-time work, peak-time work, job sharing, telecommuting, and temporary employment will increasingly be the rule, not the exception. The reasons for this experimentation will undoubtedly continue to be changing work attitudes and lifestyles, desire for more leisure time, attempts to minimize traffic problems, advances in computer technology, and attempts by management to increase both morale and productivity. Some, if not all, of the experimentation is also partly based on pragmatic attempts by FLMs and managers to cut costs.

In any case, today's FLM must be sensitive to the importance of changing work schedules in addressing employee needs and problems and the impact these changes may have on employee morale and performance. FLMs should conduct case-by-case analyses of the advantages and disadvantages of work schedule practices to evaluate their cost-effectiveness for their specific work units and organizations.

Telecommuting. Question: What current organizational activity simultaneously helps alleviate child-care problems, reduces traffic jams, and cuts air pollution and fuel consumption, while also saving millions of dollars on office space? The answer is *telecommuting*, or teleworking— the practice of using communications technology (i.e., computer, modem, the telephone, and/or fax machine) to enable work to be performed by employees from remote locations, such as the home or a nearby telecenter. Imagine the following example: An after-hour request from one of Marston Technologies' customers is made for some assistance on a computer problem. Everyone has gone home for the day. A call is made to the on-call computer technician who has a computer/modem at home for diagnosing and addressing customers' problems. The request is completed, the customer is happy, and no one had to make a trip back to the Marston office.

Telecommuting results in increased separation from the principal office, while, at the same time, it increases connection to the home. Telecommuting is perhaps one of the most profound examples of how technology impacts work, jobs, and FLMs.

Contingent workforce. Increasingly, organizations are employing more part-time employees. That is, instead of eliminating entire organizational functions and buying them back through outside service providers, organizations are eliminating individual jobs and hiring people to perform them on an as-needed basis. Such individuals comprise what has been referred to as a *contingent workforce.* This workforce is comprised of people hired temporarily, part-time, or as contract employees who work as needed for finite periods of time.

The temporary or contingent workforce has grown rapidly, paralleling the restructuring and layoff phenomena. The contingent workforce is of considerable size and includes specialists of all kinds, including nurses, accountants, lawyers, engineers, and computer and software experts. A growing number of middle managers and top executives are also part of this temporary workforce.

The "leasing" of employees by staffing service companies has become a rapidly growing industry because of the demand for temporary workers. Some analysts predict that in just a few years, half of all working Americans—some 60 million people—will be working on a part-time or freelance basis. Specifically, British consultant Charles Handy has described the organization of the future as being more like an apartment than a home for life, "an association of temporary residents gathered together for mutual convenience." Although others believe this prospect is far-fetched, it is clear that a growing number of people are seeking the freedom and variety of temporary employment rather than facing repeated layoffs from ever-downsizing corporations. They are opting for "permanent impermanence" in their jobs, so to speak.

How will the FLM motivate employees who consider themselves, at best, transient—that is, just working at the present organization until something better comes along? Numerous studies have indicated that lower productivity and increased accidents occur when employees are not fully committed to their jobs. Motivating employees who are not fully committed will be another FLM challenge.

Changes in job design. Changes in *job design* (the process of determining and organizing the specific tasks and responsibilities to be carried out by each member of the organization and/or teams) has and continues to drastically change the nature of work itself in many instances.

The widespread and growing use of self-managed teams (see Chapter 7) is an example of changes in job design. Organizations have moved toward the use of such teams to increase the flexibility of their workforces. They are redesigning work and jobs to allow employees with unique skills and backgrounds to tackle projects or problems together and to perform a wide variety of tasks, including dividing up the work, monitoring quality, ordering parts, interviewing applicants, and so on. The use of self-managed teams also frequently involves many organizational changes, including changes in technology, workflow, selection, training, and compensation.

As organizations continue to redesign jobs they will also reshape the relationship between FLMs and the people they are supposedly responsible for managing. You will find more and more FLMs being called coaches, advisors, sponsors, or facilitators. And there will be a continued blurring between the roles of FLMs and their employees. More and more decision making will be pushed down to the operating level, where workers will be given the freedom to make choices about schedules, procedures, and solving work-related problems. Organizations will also continue to put employees in charge of what they do. And in doing so, FLMs will have to learn how to give up control to employees who must learn how to take responsibility for their work and make appropriate decisions. Empowerment (putting employees in charge of what they do) will change leadership styles, power relationships, the way work is designed, and the way organizations are structured.

The job skills gap. The U.S. service sector has experienced much faster growth than the manufacturing sector over the past 40 years. Service, technical, and managerial positions that require college degrees will make up half of all manufacturing and service jobs in the coming years. Unfortunately, most available workers will be too unskilled to fill those jobs (i.e., *job skills gap*). Even now many companies complain that the supply of skilled labor is dwindling and that they must provide their employees with basic training to make up for the shortcomings of public education systems.

Although in the last decade the overall education level of Americans has increased in terms of schooling and even fundamental literacy, so also have the demands of the workplace. As a group, high school graduates are simply not keeping pace with the kinds of skills required in the new business world. The report card on college-educated workers is not particularly flattering either.

To deal with these problems, some businesses have developed agreements in which their companies join with public schools to form a compact that reserves jobs for high school graduates who meet academic and attendance requirements. A second strategy is in-house training for current or prospective employees through formal training and on-the-job training programs. Companies currently spend in excess of an estimated $60 billion a year on a wide variety of training programs. This is in addition to the more than $24 billion spent on training programs by the federal government each year. Nonetheless, the job skills gap, or shortage, is likely to remain a challenge for FLMs and their organizations in the United States.

Diversity in the Workforce

Workforce diversity refers to the wider variety of today's employees, who vary with respect to gender, age, culture, and ethnic background and who may have physical and/or mental disabilities. Whereas globalization focuses on differences between people from different countries, workforce diversity addresses differences among people within a given country. An important FLM challenge will be valuing the uniqueness of each employee while forming cohesive work groups and teams with people of different backgrounds and values. FLMs also must be prepared to deal with racial discrimination or sexual harassment, should either problem arise (see Chapter 3 for a discussion of both these concepts).

Workforce diversity has important implications for FLM practice. FLMs and their organizations will need to shift their philosophy from treating everyone alike to recognizing differences and responding to those differences in ways that will ensure employee retention and greater productivity while, at the same time, not discriminating. This shift includes, for instance, providing diversity training and revamping benefit programs to make them more "family-friendly." Some organizations are not only changing the range of benefit choices they offer, but also changing the basic structure of their benefits as they recognize that the "one-size fits all approach" to employee benefits does not work. Diversity, if positively managed, can increase creativity and innovation in organizations as well as improve decision making by providing different perspectives on problems. When diversity is not managed properly, there is potential for higher turnover, more difficult communication, and more interpersonal conflicts.

Changing Attitudes Toward Work

American workers are changing their attitudes toward work. Employees now demand better coordination between lifestyle needs, including family and leisure, and employment needs. Leisure pursuits have become more highly valued than work goals. Even previously loyal employees have become cynical of the corporate world. This cynicism has spawned a new interest in organized labor and collective bargaining, even among professionals.

American workers are more interested in jobs with meaningful work, which allow for self-fulfillment and work satisfaction. They want jobs that provide greater challenges and enable them to use more skills and knowledge. These changes in employee attitudes and values require that FLMs and their organizations use different organizational strategies than those used in the past.

Lifestyles and expectations about life circumstances are also changing.

Where people are willing to live and work is becoming a serious issue for a significant number of workers. People are prone to have decided preferences about where they want to live, whether in the city, the suburbs, or a rural setting, and in what region and climate. In addition, more and more people express concern about the appropriate balance of work and family and leisure and other aspects of their lives. They may not want the job interfering with taking a child to a Little League game or to a Girl Scout meeting or going to church. Thus they may be less willing to accept overtime assignments or to work long hours or weekends. However, fear of layoffs undoubtedly produces considerable acquiescence to management's wishes, but with resulting job dissatisfaction for many people.

These trends present both a significant challenge and a real opportunity for FLMs and their organizations. For example, one challenge for FLMs is that the diverse workforce contains those who have traditionally been discriminated against. Thus, diversity takes on ethical implications related to how FLMs and the rest of management can eliminate all forms of discrimination (age, sex, race, ethnic origin, religion, disability) and provide equal opportunity in all aspects of employment. Also stemming from the heightened sensitivity that results from the realization of a diverse workforce is a focus on problems such as sexual harassment, the glass ceiling effect, and work family issues. FLMs and organizations that formulate strategies that capitalize on employee diversity are more likely to survive and prosper.

MEETING TODAY'S CHALLENGES

It has often been said that the only thing that remains constant is change—and it's true! (See Chapter 12 for more discussion on change.) Today's FLMs will, more than ever before, need to be prepared for changing events that will have a significant effect on their lives. Some of the more recent changes and challenges have been highlighted throughout this chapter. The last section of this chapter takes a closer look at how some of these changes are affecting FLMs in organizations.

Globalization affects FLMs in many ways. A boundaryless world introduces new challenges for FLMs. These range from how FLMs view people from different countries to how they develop an understanding of these immigrating employees' cultures. A specific challenge for FLMs is recognizing differences that might exist and finding ways to make their interactions with all employees more effective.

Although downsizing, quality improvements, and changing forms of work are activities that are initiated at the top-management level of an organization, they do have an effect on FLMs. FLMs may be heavily involved in implementing the changes. They must be prepared to deal with the organizational issues these changes bring about. For example, when an organization downsizes an important challenge for FLMs is motivating a workforce that feels less secure in their jobs and less committed to their employers. FLMs must also ensure that their skills and those of their employees are kept up to date. Employees whose skills become obsolete are more likely to be candidates for downsizing. Those employees who keep their jobs will more than likely be doing the work of two or three people. This situation can create frustration, anxiety, and less motivation. For the FLM, this too can dramatically affect work-unit productivity.

An emphasis on quality focuses on the customer, seeks continual improvements, strives to improve the quality of work, seeks accurate measurement, and involves employees. Each FLM must clearly define what quality means to the jobs in his or her unit. This needs to be communicated to every staff member. Each individual must then exert the needed effort to move toward "perfection." FLMs and their employees must recognize that failing to do so could lead to unsatisfied customers taking their purchasing power to competitors. Should that happen, jobs in the unit might be in jeopardy.

Effective quality initiatives can generate a positive outcome for FLMs and employees. Everyone involved may now have input into how work is best done. A focus on quality provides opportunities for FLMs to build the participation of the people closest to the work. As such, quality can eliminate bottlenecks that have hampered work efforts in the past. Quality can help create more satisfying jobs—for both the FLM and his or her employees.

Few jobs today are unaffected by advances in computer technology. How specifically is it changing the FLM's job? One need only to look at how the typical office is set up to answer this question. Today's organizations have become integrated communications centers. By linking computers, telephones, fax machines, copiers, printers, and the like, FLMs can get more complete information more quickly than ever before. With that information, FLMs can better formulate plans, make faster decisions, more clearly define the jobs that workers need to perform, and monitor work activities on an "as-they-happen" basis. In essence, technology today has enhanced FLMs' ability to more effectively and efficiently perform their jobs.

Technology is also changing where an FLM's work is performed since they have immediate access to information that helps them in making decisions. Technological advances assist FLMs who have employees in remote locations, reducing the need for face-to-face interaction with these individuals. On the other hand, effectively communicating with individuals in remote locations (for example, teleworkers), as well as ensuring that performance objectives are being met, has become a major challenge for FLMs.

The implications of workforce diversity for FLMs are widespread. However, the most significant implication for FLMs is the requirements of sensitivity to the differences in each individual. That means they must shift their philosophy from treating everyone alike to recognizing, valuing, and responding to these differences in ways that will ensure employee retention and greater productivity.

Today's successful FLMs will be those who have learned to effectively respond to and manage change. FLMs will work in an environment in which change is taking place at an unprecedented rate. New competitors spring up overnight, and old ones disappear through mergers, acquisitions, or failure to keep up with the changing marketplace and customer demands. Downsized organizations mean fewer workers to complete the necessary work. Constant innovations in computer and telecommunications technologies are making communications instantaneous. These factors, combined with the globalization of product and financial markets, have created an environment of never ending change. As a result, many traditional management practices—created for a world that was far more stable and predictable—no longer apply.

New governmental and societal issues will continue to complicate the FLM's job in the future. Numerous environmental concerns will remain as serious long-term problems for FLMs and their organizations. Energy availability and costs will continue to be of great concern internationally and domestically. These types of issues and societal pressures have to become part of the FLMs' and organizations' planning and operations.

Federal legislation affects the FLM's. In addition, state and local governments have laws and regulations that impact business. The effect of such legislation can be quite costly, and FLMs and their organizations may be required to change their methods of operations in order to comply.

All indications are that these pressures will remain intense. With today's challenges, an FLM has to be more a lawyer, cop, teacher, accountant, political scientist, and psychologist than a manager. While this may be overstating the point, this reflects a realistic aspect of every FLM's contemporary role. FLMs must be more flexible in their styles, smarter in how they work, quicker in making decisions, more efficient in handling scarce resources, better at satisfying the customer, and more confident in enacting massive and revolutionary changes. As management writer Tom Peters pointed out in one of his best-selling books: "Today's FLMs must be able to thrive on change and uncertainty."

It is important to recognize that the workplace of today and tomorrow is indeed undergoing immense and permanent changes. Organizations are being challenged to change or be "reengineered" for greater speed, efficiency, and flexibility. Teams are pushing aside the individual as the primary building block of organizations. Command-and-control management is giving way to participative management and empowerment. Authoritative leaders are being replaced by charismatic and transformational leaders. Employees increasingly are being viewed as internal customers. All this creates a mandate for a new kind of FLM today.

FLMs will need a broader set of skills to achieve and maintain both their own, the department's, and the organization's success today. The areas in which they will need to develop expertise include strategic planning; budgeting; quality management, benchmarking, and best practices; and telecommunications and technology. Aside from honing these skills, FLMs can better prepare themselves for today's challenges by gaining a better understanding of the needs of their internal customers, recognizing the need for effective information systems for employees, building relationships with the best service providers, and aligning the FLM's unit and organization strategies and their processes.

Like other levels of management, today's FLM must be a true strategic partner in the organization. Each FLM must effectively respond to the ever changing world of work and the roles they are expected to play in that world. As the pace of change quickens, FLMs must become a tougher and more durable, albeit more flexible, interface between their organization and the lumpy road of a changing environment.

Chapter 2

Becoming a Front-Line Manager

INTRODUCTION

New FLMs often experience doubts as they start their first management jobs, due to the many challenges they face and the need to change their relationships with their co-workers. But if a person makes advance preparation and is willing to continually learn, the job can be fulfilling.

Today FLMs and their organizations must compete in changing domestic and global environments using diverse workforces. As a result, the practice of management is changing. Many of today's organizations are giving the employees who do the work more authority for planning and controlling what they do. In addition, these organizations are establishing teams and placing a high premium on teamwork. Of course, any group of people working on a job could be considered a team; after all, the individuals do work together in one way or another. But, in the past, these teams have not been very well coordinated. The emphasis has been on the performance of individuals rather than coordinated teamwork. As with many other teams everyone wants to shine more than his or her teammates. This results in lots of wasted energy and missed opportunities. It's a formula for ensuring that the team never really achieves its full potential.

Within the past two decades there has been an increased emphasis on helping the individuals on a team or work unit cooperate with one another, giving employees more authority to do their work ("empowering," in today's jargon), and handing over to them responsibility for many of the tasks formerly handled by FLMs. These tasks may include scheduling and organizing work, hiring new team members, and appraising each other's performance.

FLMs, now called "facilitators" or "team leaders," still have important tasks to perform, but they don't spend much time telling people what to do or watching to make sure they do it. So what do they do instead? The following comments reveal the new focus of FLMs:

"Some of the teams I coordinate really don't need me much. They're running their own operation. They let me know when they need something or have a problem they can't solve. I've been working on a task force to implement a new computer system. I'm getting pulled into decision making and planning tasks I never had time for before."

"I do a lot more coaching and training now. We are developing a multi-skilled team where people learn to do every job in the work unit. That means a lot of cross-training. Also, we are adding some new responsibilities into each employee's job. I play a big role in conducting training and working with others to plan, implement, and evaluate the training."

In the quest for increased performance and customer satisfaction, today's organizations are giving more of the everyday responsibility for scheduling work and solving problems to employees working in teams. In this chapter, we begin by discussing the transition from individual contributor to FLM. We then take a look at the pros and cons of being an FLM. The chapter then discusses how to make a smooth transition to the role of FLM. Next, the chapter offers some factors important to being a successful FLM. The chapter concludes with a discussion of a twenty-first-century perspective of the FLM.

FROM INDIVIDUAL CONTRIBUTOR TO FRONT-LINE MANAGER

Most new FLMs are promoted from the ranks of the front-line employees they are asked to manage as FLM. Management usually selects for FLM jobs employees with a good grasp of the technical skills needed to perform well in the department. The individual also might have more seniority than many of the other employees in the department. Good work records (and work habits) and leadership skills are also reasons for selecting an employee to be an FLM.

In reality, none of these criteria for promotion guarantees an individual knows how to manage. When computer specialist Jenny Jackson was promoted to departmental manager, she was unprepared for some aspects of managing a group of computer specialists. Instead of receiving any type of training in management, Jenny says, "I was just kind of dropped off the end of the plank." She was especially challenged by determining how to lead her former colleagues. Recalling an early effort at handling a computer specialist's poor performance, Jenny says, "She messed up, and I yelled at her. She started crying. I didn't expect that reaction, and my boss just looked at me and shook his head." Fortunately, over time Jenny learned how to better manage people, and she has since moved up to a middle level management position at the same company.

For those like Jenny who become FLMs, the shift from individual contributor to FLM is sometimes difficult, as it is a shift from doing work yourself to getting work done through others. The new FLM must suddenly be more adept at using his or her people skills and devote more time to planning ahead and keeping an eye on the department's activities. These and other changes are bound to lead to some anxiety. It is natural to wonder whether you are qualified or how you will handle the problems that surely will arise. The remainder of this section looks at what it takes to become an FLM and the challenges FLMs face in this new leadership role. The following comments from a recently promoted FLM capture the dilemma many new FLMs face when they're promoted from the ranks.

"It wasn't easy to make the move from being one of the unit specialists in the department to being the FLM. On Wednesday I had been one of them. Then, Thursday of the next week, I became their boss. Suddenly, people I had joked around with and socialized with for years were distancing themselves from me. I could see that they were apprehensive. They weren't sure how, or if, I could be trusted. I didn't think our relationship was going to be much different. Hey, we were friends. We went out together Fridays after work. But I'm management now. I still think I'm like them, part of the group. But they don't see me that way. Even when I join them for drinks, it's not like it used to be. They have their guard up now. It's been a hard adjustment for me. I've become a part of management and sometimes I'm even the target of blame or anger when they resent company policies."

Many new FLMs report feeling a sense of isolation, added responsibility, and a lack of control. They are no longer one of the gang, and they are not sure what is expected of them. They are responsible for the results of other people's work and not just their own.

Moving from one middle-management job to another or from a middle-management position to one in top management rarely creates the anxiety that comes when you move from being an individual contributor to an FLM. Because middle managers already have some experience with the challenges of being in a management position, they know what to expect.

The experience of many new FLMs helps us to understand what it's like to become an FLM. Even though most of these new FLMs had worked in their respective organizations for a number of years, they have simplistic expectations of their FLM roles. Each had originally been a star employee. But the requirements of an individual contributor are very different from the demands on an FLM—and few of these new FLMs understood that. Ironically, their previous successes as individual contributors may actually have made their transition to management harder. Because of their strong technical expertise and previous success, they had depended on their FLMs less than the average worker. When they became FLMs and suddenly had to deal with low-performing and unmotivated employees, they were unprepared.

New FLMs encounter a number of surprises. The major changes they face as they transform themselves from individual contributors to FLMs are listed below. The FLM

- becomes responsible for the output of other people, usually for the first time;
- acts as a leader rather than a "boss";
- stays informed on technical issues, but realizes that this is no longer the primary focus of the job, nor the primary determinant of success or failure;
- acquires many new and unfamiliar administrative duties, which may relate to personnel, procedural, and budgetary issues;
- deals with employees and their problems, but no longer as a co-worker;
- faces many new situations in which the action to be taken is unclear and requires a judgment call rather than reference to a rule book.

Moving from individual contributor to FLM thus requires a change in behavior and orientation and the development of a managerial point of view. With experience most new FLMs succeed in making this shift. They learn to get their sense of achievement through the accomplishments of their co-workers. They learn that while their employees may not always perform a specific task exactly as they might, jobs still get done and get done well. New FLMs learn that their new activities are quite different from, and even more important than, their old activities.

DOESN'T EVERYONE WANT TO BE AN FLM?

Working as an FLM can be challenging and exciting. As with anything worthwhile, however, certain trade-offs are necessary. Some of those who decide to enter management later reverse the decision and return to their previous jobs. They may say something like

- "There is just too much hassle involved."
- "I hated all the meetings. And I found the more you did for people who worked for you, the more they expected. I felt like I was coming in every day and

people were expecting me to meet their needs. I was a counselor, motivator, psychologist and financial master."

- "With technology changing rapidly, you can never slack off these days if you're on the technical side."

- "It's a rare person who can supervise, keep up on the technical side, *and* handle an FLM job, too."

- "You're a backstop, caught in the middle between upper management and the workforce."

- "I felt like I was being pulled in 15 different directions by my bosses and employees, and I had a hard time with all the complaining."

Although the issues discussed in this section are often matters of perception rather than reality, they present serious trade-offs for many FLMs. First, FLM positions are not easy. Even if an individual has been a superstar as an employee, this is no guarantee that the individual will succeed as an FLM. The fact that a person is capable of doing excellent work is a big plus, but there are many factors to consider.

Second, employees usually come to work, do their jobs, and then go home. FLMs, by contrast, often are on the job before regular working hours begin and still there after the employees have gone. So, it should be no surprise that FLMs work long hours. The job can literally be a 24-hour, seven-day-a-week job. That's not to be interpreted as being on the job every hour of every day. But when individuals accept the responsibility of managing others, they really never can "get away" from the job. Things happen, and they'll be expected to deal with them—no matter when they happen, or where they are. And the number of hours tends to increase as individuals climb the organization ladder.

Third, some FLMs think their pay is low in relation to that of their employees. In some instances, the difference in pay is insignificant. In fact, some beginning FLMs may make less than their most senior employees. In many organizations, a raise in base pay when an individual becomes an FLM does not translate into higher annual earnings. How so? Consider that, as an FLM, you are no longer eligible for overtime pay. Instead, in most organizations, FLMs get compensatory (comp) time (i.e., time off). As a front-line employee, your organization is legally required to pay you a premium rate (typically time and one-half) for overtime work. Most likely that will not be true when you move into an FLM position.

Fourth, in addition to their own concerns, FLMs are affected by the problems of others. Employees may bring to the job a variety of off-the-job problems. Perhaps one employee is going through a divorce and simply wants to talk. Another might ask for advice on financial problems. Employees can choose to worry only about their own problems, but FLMs cannot. They have some responsibility for the people working for them, who have different personalities, aspirations, and problems. For some FLMs, this can be too great a burden.

Fifth, FLMs are responsible not only for their own actions but for the actions of others as well. Whereas employees need only be concerned about meeting their individual objectives, FLMs must make sure that all members of the team are working together to achieve team or departmental goals. Daily, weekly, monthly, and even annual performance standards must be met. Some FLMs find it hard to maintain a positive attitude under such pressures.

Sixth, FLMs are sometimes not given enough control to get the job done. Often they are only permitted to recommend certain actions. For instance, an FLM thinks an employee is unable to do the work properly and should be fired. The FLM may have to request upper management approval before taking this action and may, in all likelihood, have the request tabled—which means the FLM will have to find a way to work with the employee and still get the job done.

Seventh, FLMs' work is fragmented; activities are often brief. Given FLMs' high activity level, they have little time to devote to any single activity. Interruptions, crises, and problems are the rule as the FLM is constantly juggling the needs of the organization (completion of tasks) and the needs of employees. The need to recognize these concepts and establish priorities is essential.

Eighth, FLMs, particularly those promoted from within, are no longer one of the front-line group. In many organizations the us-versus-them mentality develops. Newly promoted FLMs are no longer one of "them." Therefore, FLMs need to develop a professional rather than a personal relationship with employees.

Ninth, some FLMs do not enjoy making the tough decisions that go with the job. Disciplining an employee, especially a former co-worker, is uncomfortable, to say the least. Firing an employee can be very traumatic. The same can be said of demoting or laying off employees or giving an employee a negative or less than sterling performance appraisal.

Finally, the movement toward more employee participation, along with the growth of the human resources department, is perceived as an erosion of the FLM's authority. At the same time, it has been suggested that the majority of the FLM positions in U.S. corporations are redundant. These notions are threatening to many FLMs.

The possible trade-offs described above will deter some people from becoming FLMs. For others, however, they simply increase the challenge and excitement associated with the work.

Despite all the aspects of the job an FLM cannot control, the FLM is not excused from doing his or her best. The FLM will have to make sure not to become discouraged or cynical. With time, FLMs learn to recognize their limits, their opportunities, and which difficult situations they cannot change. Today's FLMs must believe that they can do the job and make a contribution to their organization's success.

Given the discussion in the previous paragraphs, it is important to think about why you want to be an FLM. Managing others can be rewarding, as evidenced by the discussion in the next section. It is important to understand exactly what your motivation is for becoming an FLM—and what trade-offs you're willing to make to become the best FLM you can be.

BEING AN FLM CAN BE SATISFYING

Being an FLM can be an immensely satisfying experience for you and those who work for you. By managing the efforts of others, you have more opportunities to make your ideas come to life. You can be a leader, a mentor, and a coach. You can be a person of vision and action, respected and rewarded for your contribution to your organization's success and the quality of work life.

There are a number of reasons why it is worthwhile for individual contributors to give up their comfortable, familiar jobs to become FLMs. One obvious reason is that FLMs get more rewards. Greater rewards come with greater contributions to the success of the organization. Some rewards are financial, some are perquisites (e.g., parking space), and some are psychological. Additionally, accomplishment itself is rewarding, particularly when others doubted.

Second, becoming an FLM opens the door to future promotions and opportunities to grow personally and professionally. Change can be uncertain and, at times, even uncomfortable, but employees are attracted to the ranks of management because they believe they are ready to learn something new, practice new skills, and solve bigger problems. Instead of just doing mechanical and technical tasks, FLMs perform the much more complex job of managing people. Each day they face new situations. For many FLMs, there is personal satisfaction in handling these situations successfully that is simply not available at the front-line employee level.

Third, many people enjoy the respect and influence normally accorded the FLM. In some instances, individuals are also thrilled by the prospect of being the boss. It is natural to want to have influence over others. FLMs can find great satisfaction in helping employees reach their full potential. The opportunity to make decisions and be held accountable for those decisions is satisfying. Increased involvement in decision making is a positive benefit to many FLMs.

Fourth, FLMs can make more of a difference as a supervisor than as an employee on the front line. People above and below them in the organization listen to their ideas. FLM experience provides experiences and learning that no textbook can provide. Generally, the higher a person moves in the organization, the more that individual can affect the success of the organization.

Fifth, FLMs have greater flexibility than their employees. Because they are usually paid a salary rather than wages based on hours worked, they are often allowed some flexibility in their working hours. That is because their job is to make sure that the tasks actually get done, as opposed to doing the tasks themselves.

Sixth, FLMs may enjoy the excitement of being involved in a wide range of technical activities. More than other managers, FLMs are knowledgeable about the job performed at the operating level. The FLM is able to share in the experiences of several employees, which adds variety and interest to the job. For example, during any given hour an FLM might interact with a manager, a specialist in the work unit, or an employee from another department each doing very different and sometimes specialized tasks. An FLM gains satisfaction from the opportunity to use a wide variety of skills and gains valuable experiences. FLMs are rarely bored.

Finally, the FLM has a special opportunity to help people. Employees have personal problems that can sometimes be solved by referring them to counseling. If these problems involve conflicts with the organization, no one is in a better position than the FLM to go to bat for the employees or to help them understand the organization's needs. The FLM is also able to train employees and help them prepare for advancement or additional responsibilities. An FLM can find great personal satisfaction in helping others reach their full potential. By constantly looking for the good in other people, an FLM will uncover personal strengths on which they can then build.

MAKING A SMOOTH TRANSITION TO FLM

New FLMs can begin enjoying the benefits of being an FLM and make a better transition to the job by getting started right. Their immediate challenge is to establish their credibility by demonstrating that they are the best person for the job. Why is personal credibility so important? Because the weight of the FLM title is not so great that the individual can simply command people to get things done. New FLMs need to work with everyone above, below, and beside them on the organizational ladder. New FLMs perceived as persons with little credibility will not be taken seriously, which means they will not be able to achieve their goals.

Personal credibility is easy to lose and hard to get back. It is determined by others and built on those values the individual learned as a child:

- Say what you mean, and mean what you say.
- Follow through and follow up.
- Don't let your teammates down.
- Be yourself.
- Deciding to play it safe by doing nothing, keeping a low profile, and generally avoiding conflict is almost always the wrong approach.
- You are more than a placeholder.
- Be smart, not just safe.
- You are not doing your job if you do not take a few risks.
- In the long run, your best security rests on your reputation for getting results.

When individuals move into FLM jobs, they shouldn't worry too much about establishing a management "style," which is a convenient way of describing how FLMs interact with people. A unique style will evolve as they get comfortable with the new role. They should concentrate instead on the substance of their job. What they choose to accomplish will affect their credibility. Selecting the right work to do, and finishing it on time and within budget, will show people that they are indeed competent to handle the new job. This is where new FLMs have to do some careful thinking and planning. They cannot afford to fail at their first management tasks, so they should choose them wisely.

An FLM may learn that one or more employees (possibly those he or she is now managing) had been candidates for the FLM's job and therefore may be jealous. One constructive approach that an FLM might take in addressing this problem is to acknowledge the other person's feelings, ask for the employee's support, and discuss his or her long-term goals. Jenny Jackson did this with one of the other computer specialists who had been considered for the job Jenny now held. The computer specialist said that his goal was to "move into management." Jenny said, "I told him, without making false promises, that I would do what I could to help him." Until this employee moved into a management job nine months later, he was one of the top performers among Jenny's employees. An important aspect of this approach is that the FLM is helping employees to meet or exceed their own goals. For example, as an FLM Jenny can help a potentially jealous employee improve his or her performance. Jenny shouldn't be surprised that employees regard her as a much better manager when she helps them make more money and achieve their career goals.

New FLMs must remember that their main responsibility is to see that all the work of their department gets done and gets done properly. FLMs must plan and organize the resources to accomplish the objectives of their department, and they must understand that they will be held accountable for the team's or department's results. The new FLM must be prepared to help others complete their assignments successfully. This means that they will have to:

- understand how their department contributes to the organization's goals;
- set and communicate the priorities that guide the work unit's day-to-day activities;
- develop and implement effective work plans that get the required work completed right the first time, on time and within budget;
- provide the necessary direction, feedback, and coaching to employees about their job performance.

Once on the job, the new FLM must be concerned with big-picture questions rather than focusing on an isolated bit of work. For example, What work do we have to accomplish? What work is in progress? What do we have to do to get ready for and complete the work? Who is doing what, and what will prevent them from finishing on time? What resources must we commit to solving the quality and service problems that employees and customers identified? Are we able to stay within budget? If not, why not? New FLMs must learn to make wise choices about where they direct employee efforts.

The new FLM needs to continue the learning process. It is very important that the new FLM learn as much as possible about the employees in the department or the work unit. Who are the quiet but productive employees, for example, and who are the unofficial leaders? To get to know employees, an FLM can talk to his or her own manager and read performance appraisals, but the most reliable sources of information are the employees themselves. Particularly in the early days on the job, an FLM should take the time to discuss goals with employees and observe their work habits.

Enthusiastic new FLMs are commonly trapped in the "I can do anything for everyone" mind set, so they say *yes* to too many people too soon. Their first few days as an FLM are filled with meetings, introductions, and other hazardous distractions. They have to say *no* to requests! If they don't, after a few days they will be overcommitted. The only way out of this dilemma is to work 24 hour days to catch up, explain to everyone why you are going to disappoint them, or pretend that nothing is wrong until your team members start complaining. Chronically overcommitted FLMs cannot be successful. Most of the management tasks they are doing are new, so it will logically take longer to get them done in the beginning. They must schedule themselves accordingly.

Instead of rushing into risky commitments indiscriminately, a new FLM like Jenny should pick a few near-term challenges which she knows she can quickly accomplish. If these challenges have a high profile and Jenny receives rave reviews, so much the better. But Jenny shouldn't jeopardize her relationship with her work team for any reason. These people are pivotal to Jenny's success. Jenny's first priority is to take care of them. She must establish her credibility with her work team with a few early successes, however modest.

When people like Jenny first become a new FLM it is more important to decide what should happen in the short-term (tomorrow and in the coming weeks) than to plan months ahead. Jenny should think carefully about what she needs to accomplish and then make lists of her short-term goals.

One of the more difficult tasks confronting new FLMs is the need to communicate with more people, more often. It is the FLM's job to know what is going on and to keep employees informed about what is going on so that everyone can work together smoothly. New FLMs must recognize that they will need to build and manage their information channels. While they are still new to the job, they should take the opportunity to ask employees:

- What are the goals of the department?
- How is the department evaluated?
- Who are the department's customers, both inside and outside the organization, and what do they say about us?
- How is the department doing?
- What prevents us from better serving our customers—both internal and external—in the ways they want us to?
- Do we have a common vision that we share for the department?
- Do we agree on what the department's priorities are?
- What are the department's short-, medium-, and long-term plans?

Some employees will be reluctant to share what they know because they are not willing to accept the responsibility that goes along with being an empowered employee. Other employees will give too much information because they want to impress the new FLM with their accomplishments or campaign for their favorite work assignments or projects. In either case, FLMs must be prepared to develop the information and communication flows necessary for working with their employees.

A further complication for new FLMs is that they will be blitzed with various communications in the form of memos, correspondence, and trade journals landing on their desks. What's really important? What information needs to be passed on to others? What other information aren't you receiving and needing to go out and get? Are employees getting the information they need to do their jobs? Are employees learning what they need to know? Are you getting an accurate understanding of what's going on in and between departments? It is important for FLMs not to get too many surprises. Few surprises are pleasant. If there are too many surprises then there may be unclear or incomplete communication, which means that the FLMs need to make sure that they are getting more of the right information.

Finally, the new FLM is now one of the partners important to the organization's success. The partnership is with the FLM's new boss and other upper-level managers. The partnership is with other FLMs, front-line employees, and even various vendors. In reality, the job of new FLMs is to work collaboratively with their partners so they can all work together for the success of the organization.

WHAT MAKES A SUCCESSFUL FLM?

A variety of characteristics and talents will determine whether or not an individual will be successful. The following are critically important to success as an FLM:

1. *Having a passion for the job.* Many individuals who have no passion to be FLMs are promoted into FLM merely because of their technical skills. Regardless of one's technical skill, the passion to be an FLM is necessary for success as an FLM. That passion encourages a person to develop all of the skills necessary to carry out the FLM responsibilities. Some people are happier using the technical skills of their profession or area of expertise. People who prefer this type of work to the functions of managing may be more content if they turn down an opportunity to become an FLM. In contrast, people who enjoy the challenge of making the plans and inspiring others to achieve the goals are more likely to be effective FLMs.

2. *Accepting the change in role.* Individuals who have been promoted to FLM must recognize that their roles have changed and that they are no longer members of the gang. They must remember that their role as FLM may require them to make unpopular decisions. FLMs are the connecting link between the other levels of management and the front-line employees and, as such, they must develop expertise in representing both groups.

3. *Being a good role model.* FLMs must always remember that employees look to them to be good role models by setting good examples. Front-line employees expect (and deserve) fair and equitable treatment from their FLMs. Unfortunately, too many FLMs play favorites and treat employees inconsistently. FLMs who play favorites or whose behavior is

inconsistent will lose the support and respect of their employees, and thus not be able to lead effectively. When FLMs make assignments and decisions based on who they like best, they will not necessarily make the assignments and decisions best suited to the organization. Effective FLMs are individuals who are consistent in their actions and practice what they preach. Lead by example. The FLM can set a good example by being on time and refraining from doing personal work on the job—the same behavior expected of employees.

4. *Having a positive attitude.* Another part of being a role model is that employees tend to reflect the attitudes of the people in charge. When the FLM's attitude toward work and the organization is positive, employees are more likely to be satisfied with and interested in their work. Managers and co-workers prefer working with and for someone who has a positive attitude.

5. *Delegating.* Most FLMs were promoted from front-line jobs and have been accustomed to doing the work themselves. As a result, an often difficult, and yet essential, skill that these FLMs must develop is the willingness to delegate work to others (i.e., to give their employees authority and responsibility to carry out activities). FLMs tend to have the excellent technical skills needed to perform job tasks, yet delegating those job tasks to others may be a challenge. They may resist giving an assignment to an employee who cannot do the job as well as they would. Nevertheless, FLMs cannot do the work of the whole department. Therefore, they must assign work to employees. Equally important, an FLM must give employees credit for their accomplishments. This, in turn, makes the FLM look good; the employees' successes show that the FLM is able to select and motivate as well as delegate effectively. (Chapter 8 discusses delegation in greater detail.)

6. *Using authority wisely.* A number of FLMs let their newly acquired authority go to their heads. It is sometimes difficult to remember that the use of authority alone does not get the support and cooperation required in working with today's front-line employees. Learning when *not* to use authority is often as important as learning when to use it.

7. *Communicating effectively.* Employees and other managers depend on the FLM to keep them informed of what is happening in the organization. Employees who receive clear guidance about what is expected of them will not only perform better but also will be more satisfied with their jobs. Good communication also includes making contact with employees each day and listening to what they have to say. (Chapter 4 takes an in-depth look at the communications skills that FLMs need to develop.)

8. *Leading a diverse work force.* FLMs will need to establish relationships and friendships with individuals outside their own culture, beyond work relationships. Even if they are not fluent in other languages, they will

need to understand enough of another language or two to feel comfortable around people who do not speak English. Additionally, it is important that today's FLMs be open-minded. They must be willing to break from the past, willing to do things that have never been done before, and willing to look at people and their viewpoints from a new perspective.

There are several other important things FLMs need to know if they are going to be successful in today's organizations. There are a number of personal issues they must address. First, FLMs must recognize that they are part of management. This means that they must support the organization and the wishes of management. Although FLMs might disagree with those wishes, as FLMs, they must be loyal to the organization. As a part of the management team, they must take actions that are best for the organization. This may include making decisions that are unpopular with employees. In such situations, an FLM must recognize that taking on an FLM job means he or she cannot always be "one of the gang."

Next, FLMs must develop a means of gaining respect from the employees they manage, as well as from their peers and boss. FLMs who are going to be effective must develop trust and build credibility. One means of doing this is to continually keep their knowledge, skills and competencies up-to-date. FLMs must continue their education, not only because it helps them, but also because it sets an example for their employees. It communicates that learning matters.

Finally, today's FLM must be sensitive to the needs of all his or her employees. FLMs must learn to tolerate and even celebrate employee differences. Success, in part, begins with the understanding of what being flexible means.

FLM: A TWENTY-FIRST-CENTURY PERSPECTIVE

The primary responsibility of today's FLMs is to effectively manage their organization's most important resource—it's people. It is the people upon whom any organization ultimately depends. Effective management of people starts with selecting the right people to fill job openings and then teaching those individuals to do the job. It continues with ongoing training and development, motivation, and leadership, preparing employees for promotion.

Thus, FLMs will have to constantly strive to become true masters at managing others with a growing professional perspective. They must be attentive to the importance of trends influencing human behavior and observe how these trends impact the management of people in an ever-changing and complex environment.

In all of this there is an imperative to take the professional perspective, which recognizes the need for constant self-improvement and self-renewal. No amount of formal or informal education can ever fulfill an FLM's personal program of self-improvement. Today's FLMs must recognize that they too can become obsolete unless they constantly take measures to update their own knowledge and skills through a program of continuous self-development.

Both newly appointed and experienced FLMs should begin each day by asking, "What can I do to sharpen my saw?" Stephen Covey suggests renewing the four dimensions of your nature—spiritual (value clarification and commitment, study and meditation), mental (reading, visualizing, planning, writing), social/emotional (service, empathy, synergy, intrinsic security), and physical (exercise, nutrition, stress management)—to improve your personal effectiveness (Covey, 1989).

FLMs who acquire the knowledge and master the ideas and skills presented in this book will make considerable progress in terms of personal development, but just acquiring the knowledge and mastering the ideas and skills is not enough. Today's twenty-first-century FLMs must constantly seek new ways to apply their knowledge and skills in the challenging, complex, and dynamic situations they will encounter.

In conclusion, too often the new FLM is forced to sink or swim. The newly hired FLM should consider the following:

Pitfalls to Avoid

- Trying to be "popular" instead of effective.
- Failing to ask for advice.
- Overlooking the role of supportive problem solver.
- Failing to keep employees informed.
- Micro-managing by overemphasizing policies, rules, and procedures.
- Acting like "the boss" rather than a coach.

Training Suggestions

- Network with other FLMs.
- Identify a potential mentor.
- Participate in FLM development workshops and seminars.
- Register for FLM courses at local colleges and universities.
- Subscribe to periodicals and FLM training journals and magazines.

Basic Success Strategies

- Admit mistakes rather than attempting to cover them up.
- Show consideration.
- Provide details to all members of the team.

- Exhibit confidence and belief in your team members.
- Provide ongoing feedback, praise and recognition.

The role of the FLM will be even more challenging in the twenty-first century. And clearly, the FLM will play a critical role in today's organizational success.

REFERENCE

Covey, S. R. 1989. *The seven habits of highly effective people: Restoring the character ethic*. New York: Simon & Schuster.

Chapter 3

Ethics and the Front-Line Manager

INTRODUCTION

Ethics are the rules, principles, standards, or beliefs that commonly define right and wrong. Ethics are involved in all facets of business from decision making to budgeting, from personnel issues to leadership. Today's FLMs must be able to see the ethical issues in the choices they face, make decisions within an ethical framework, and build and maintain an ethical work environment. FLMs must be particularly sensitive to ethical issues because of their key role as a bridge between upper management and operating employees. For most employees, their FLM is the only contact they have with middle- and top-management. As such, employees interpret the company's ethical standards through the actions and words of their FLMs. If FLMs take company supplies home, cheat on maintenance reports, or engage in other unethical practices, they set a tone for their work groups that is likely to undermine all the efforts by top management to create a corporate climate of high ethical standards. In a sense, therefore, FLMs must be even more ethical than their employees.

There are many stakeholders (i.e., organizational constituencies that include the organization itself, corporate boards, middle and top management, FLMs, operating employees, customers and clients, suppliers, competitors, the industry at large, the community, and the nation) with interests in ethical decision making. At one time or another, ethical decisions affect all of these constituencies, and ethical considerations may change based on the particular group of stakeholders affected. When an organization operates ethically, the people who manage that organization evaluate the organization's business practices in light of human values of morality. An ethical dilemma occurs when two or more values or goals (e.g., profit, growth, technological progress, desire to contribute to some basic good) conflict. The best solution to any conflict almost always involves a cost of some kind.

The difficulty is that ethical behavior often collides with the bottom line at least in the short-run. But things are changing. The word is getting out: ethical behavior is good business—it contributes to organizational success. A reputation for honesty and integrity attracts and holds customers, and it will ultimately show up in the bottom line. Organizations that have strong ethical values and consistently display them in all their activities derive other benefits: improved management control, increased productivity, avoidance of litigation, and an enhanced company image that attracts talent, improves morale, and earns the public's good will. For today's FLMs leading effectively therefore also means leading ethically and morally. While businesses expand over geographic and cultural boundaries, questions concerning the sense of right and wrong within an organization become more complex. It is the responsibility of FLMs to guide the design, implementation, and monitoring of the organization's moral environment and strategies. As organizations put increased pressure on FLMs and employees to cut costs and increase productivity, ethical dilemmas are almost certain to increase. By what they say and do, FLMs contribute toward setting their organization's ethical standards.

WHY THE INCREASED FOCUS ON BUSINESS ETHICS NOW?

There is a common belief that our society is currently suffering a moral crisis. Actions that were once thought reprehensible—cheating, misrepresenting, lying, covering mistakes—have become, in many people's eyes, common business practices. Products that can cause harm to their users still remain on the market. Sexual harassment and discrimination have gone unpunished. A major focus for business in recent years, therefore, has been to reassess its ethical behavior. The widely publicized breaches of ethical behavior by business leaders have been a major cause of the renewed interest in business ethics. Since the beginning of the 1980s, the American public has been bombarded with reports of major white-collar crime, which have rattled the foundations of the business community. Thousands of savings and loan associations overextended their borrowing capacities and went bankrupt while their executives profited personally from risky loan deals. Serious allegations were made that various Sears Auto Centers in California and New Jersey had sold customers unnecessary parts and services. Recent lawsuits revealed open racial discrimination at companies like Denny's and Texaco and sexual harassment at Mitsubishi Motors Corporation's U.S. unit in Normal, Illinois. Confidence in the ethics of the business community hit rock bottom.

In a less dramatic way, unethical behavior of lower level employees began to have an effect on the bottom line of many businesses in the same period. The loss of traditional family life meant that employees came to work without the ethical standards their parents may have had due to fewer opportunities to learn them at home. As companies downsized because of the downturn of the economy and began to compress management to reduce layers of bureaucracy between workers and bosses, every employee's productivity became critical to business survival. While the pilfering of goods from the workplace has long been a concern of businesses, more widespread stealing of time and productivity began to be felt in the late 1980s. To compete in the global economy, American businesses had to be more efficient. Workers who ran private businesses from their job site or did not contribute a full day's work caused a drain of resources that few businesses could tolerate.

A more sophisticated workforce also caused this renewed focus on ethical standards in the workplace. FLMs and other managers could not say one thing and do another without fostering employee mistrust. If FLMs were going to direct the workforce toward a higher ethical standard, they were going to have to improve their own behavior. FLMs' failures to deal candidly with employees during downsizing and buyouts increased employee mistrust and organizational disloyalty. Recognition of the need for fair treatment to create loyalty to the organization resulted. In some cases, the perception that top-level management took care of themselves but did not take care of their employees caused high employee turnover and the loss of skilled FLMs to competitors.

For some businesses, increased criminal enforcement of illegal activity caused a resurgence of interest in corporate ethics. Although many businesses might deny this, recent U.S. sentencing guidelines for federal criminals may have caused companies to implement much needed ethical standards. Judge William W. Wilkins, Jr., chairman of the U.S. Sentencing Commission, predicted that a corporation with a comprehensive program for ethical behavior including a code of conduct, an ombudsman, a hotline, and mandatory training seminars for FLMs would be treated more leniently should it face criminal charges based on an employee's wrongdoing. He recognized that despite an organization's best efforts all crimes cannot be prevented, and organizations that at least tried to prevent wrongdoing should benefit from their efforts.

INDIVIDUAL ETHICS

How would you rate your own standards of ethics? Are you always ethical? Are you ethical except in situations where you can't possibly be found out? Are you ethical except when you are under pressure from your boss or your peers? Are profits or your department's success more important than your personal values? Do your career goals sometimes take precedence over principle? Is it right to bend the rules to your company's advantage whenever you can? Should you always tell the truth? Now, consider a couple of specific cases: Is it wrong to use the company telephone for personal long-distance calls? Is it ethical to falsify safety reports? Is it ethical for a member of your team to offer a bribe to an OSHA inspector to ignore safety violations?

Anyone can be ethical when there is no pressure to act otherwise. Pressures to be unethical come from many sources—yourself, your boss, your peers, your employees, your organization—but FLMs today must be able to resist. Personal ambition and self-interest are probably the most common causes of unethical decisions and behaviors. People act in self-serving or unethical ways in order to improve their personal situation or reputation, to gain advancement, to increase income, or to avoid criticism or punishment.

Your peers can also put pressure on you to behave unethically. It is always difficult to turn down a request for help, especially from a colleague; yet if you are asked to support unethical behavior, abandoning your own standards serves neither of you. Unpleasant though it may be, you should decline. Say something like, "I appreciate the difficulty of the situation you face, I would like to be able to help you, but I cannot." At some point, FLMs face pressure from their employees to be unethical. People might ask you to conceal absences, to overlook infractions just this time, or to help them cover up a near-accident. As an FLM, you should never give in to such requests. Not only would it be unethical, but it would destroy the employees' respect for you and ruin your power as an FLM and leader. The difficult but right thing to do under these conditions is to get the group together and talk to them along these lines: "I understand that you're not asking me to do this of self-interest. But I will not tolerate dishonesty. We are going to abide by our code of conduct. We're going to do our job properly."

Pressure to be unethical can also come from your boss, usually stemming from his or her desire to look good to his or her bosses: "I don't care how you do it, but I want that safety award." Pressure from a boss is extremely difficult, particularly since it is often accompanied by a threat, either direct or implied, of some adverse action, such as a poor performance report or denial of a bonus. But the fact that the pressure comes from your boss is not an excuse to behave unethically. Don't deceive yourself into believing that you are doing something to make your department look better; recognize that your motivation is self-protection. Although it's difficult, you should refuse to compromise your values.

The culture of the organization is still another source of unethical conduct. Some organizations choose to engage in questionable practices. Other organizations are just as likely to stimulate unethical actions when they place too much emphasis on managerial aggressiveness or on organizational expansion, competitiveness, and profit.

COMMON RATIONALIZATIONS FOR QUESTIONABLE CONDUCT

Over the years, people have developed some common rationalizations to justify questionable conduct, such as when they ignore safety issues in order to increase financial returns. These rationalizations provide some insights into why FLMs might make poor ethical choices and feel comfortable doing so. Let's look at some of these rationalizations in greater detail. When you are faced with ethical choices, you are faced with a problem. Ethical concerns then become a part of your decision making. For instance, one alternative may generate a considerably higher financial return than the others, but it might be ethically questionable because it compromises employee safety. Some individuals will ignore the safety concerns to achieve the financial return and feel very comfortable in defending their actions through various rationalizations.

Since it helps the organization, the organization will condone it and protect me. This response represents loyalty gone berserk. Some FLMs come to believe that not only do the organization's interests override the laws and values of society, but also that the organization expects its employees to exhibit unqualified loyalty. FLMs who use this rationalization place the organization's good name in jeopardy. For example, this rationalization has motivated FLMs to justify labor mischarges, cost duplications, safety violations, and other abuses. While FLMs should be expected to exhibit loyalty in protecting the organization against competitors and detractors, they shouldn't put the organization above the law, common morality, or society itself.

It's in our best interest. The belief that unethical conduct is in a person's or an organization's best interest nearly always results from a narrow view of what those interests are. For instance, FLMs can come to believe that it's acceptable to bribe officials if the bribe results in a contract award or to falsify safety records if this improves their unit's performance record. In the long run, these actions are usually counter to the best interests of the company.

It's not really illegal or immoral. Where is the line between smart and shady? Between an ingenious decision and an immoral one? Because this line is often vague, people tend to rationalize their actions, reasoning that whatever isn't prohibited must be OK. This is especially true if there are rich rewards for attaining certain goals, but little evaluation of how those goals are achieved. The practice of accepting a gift from a vendor who was chosen to receive an out-source contract is one example of this behavior.

No one will find out. This final rationalization understands that the behavior is questionable, but assumes that it will never be uncovered. Philosophers ponder: *If a tree falls in a forest and no one hears it, did it make a noise?* Some FLMs answer the analogous question, *If an unethical act is committed and no one knows it, is it wrong?* in the negative. This rationalization is often stimulated by inadequate controls, strong pressures to perform, large rewards for good that ignore the means by which it is achieved, and the lack of punishment for wrongdoers who are caught.

There is little anyone can do to stop people from rationalizing about their questionable conduct, but companies can try to encourage ethical behavior. In the next section we present three different approaches that can be used to determine whether a decision is ethical.

DETERMINING WHETHER A DECISION IS ETHICAL

FLMs often experience an ethical dilemma when they confront a situation that requires them to choose between two courses of action, especially if each of them is likely to serve the opposing interest of different stakeholders. To make an appropriate decision, FLMs might weigh the competing claims or rights of the various groups. Sometimes, making a decision is easy because some obvious standard, value, or norm of behavior applies. In other cases, FLMs have trouble deciding what to do.

In many large companies, FLMs have a code of ethics to guide them as to what constitutes acceptable and unacceptable practices. A code of ethics is a formal document that states an organization's primary values and the ethical rules it expects employees to follow. For instance, a code of ethics might instruct employees to be law-abiding in all activities, truthful and accurate in what they say and write, and to recognize that high integrity sometimes requires the company to forego business opportunities. Codes of ethics do not however, provide enough guidance for the many difficult dilemmas FLMs face. Philosophers have debated for centuries about the specific criteria that should be used to determine whether decisions are ethical or unethical. The use of different criteria can result in different decisions. Three models of what determines whether a decision is ethical are the utilitarian, moral rights, and justice models. Each model offers a different and complementary way of determining whether a decision or behavior is ethical.

The Utilitarian Approach

The utilitarian approach suggests that FLMs should strive to provide the greatest degree of benefits for the largest number of people at the lowest cost. In other words, FLMs must weigh the costs against the benefits of their actions. In a manner of speaking, you do this whenever you make a decision, as you balance one alternative against another and choose the one that you believe will yield the best results for the lowest cost or least effort. The utilitarian view tends to dominate business decision making, because it's consistent with goals like efficiency, productivity, and high profits. By maximizing profits, for instance, FLMs can argue that they are securing the greatest good for the greatest number.

The Moral Rights Approach

The moral rights view of ethics is concerned with respecting and protecting the basic rights of individuals, such as the rights to privacy, free speech, and due process. Even if the decision accomplishes the greatest good for the greatest number of people, it is considered unethical if it denies individual rights. This position would protect employees who report unethical or illegal practices by their organization to the press or government agencies on the grounds of their right of free speech. As an FLM, you can use this approach to assess the implications of your decisions on individuals and not just groups of people. You should not make a decision that compromises individual rights.

The Justice Approach

The justice approach embodies democratic principles and protects the interests of those who might otherwise lack power. It requires FLMs to impose and enforce rules fairly and impartially so there is an equitable distribution of benefits and costs. Union members typically favor this view. It justifies paying people the same wage for a given job, regardless of performance differences, and it uses seniority as the criterion in making layoff decisions. The justice approach is based on two components:

1. the procedural justice component, which requires impartial administration of disciplinary actions;
2. the distributive justice component, which requires people to be judged only in terms of the performance criteria and not on such characteristics as race, gender, or religious preference.

For example, people who vary in job skill should be paid differently, but there should be no differences in pay based on race or gender. More will be said about these two components in our discussion of diversity later in this chapter.

COMBINING THE APPROACHES

It's difficult to apply a single approach consistently to all situations you encounter. All three approaches can be used as guidelines for helping you to sort out the ethics of a particular course of action. Each of these three models has advantages and disadvantages, however. The utilitarian view promotes efficiency and productivity, but it can ignore the rights of individuals, particularly those with minority representation in the organization. The moral rights view protects individuals from injury and is consistent with freedom and privacy, but it can create an overly legalistic work environment that hinders productivity and efficiency. The justice perspective protects the interests of the underrepresented and less powerful, but it can encourage a general sense of entitlement that reduces risk-taking, innovation, and productivity.

Although individuals in business have tended to focus on utilitarianism, times are changing. New trends toward individual rights and social justice mean that FLMs need ethical standards based on nonutilitarian criteria, which are more difficult to evaluate. Criteria such as individual rights and social justice are far more ambiguous than utilitarian criteria such as productivity and profits. You should, therefore, ask yourself what the consequences of your actions will be in terms of each approach. For example, suppose that an FLM, who has been working for a company for about six months, discovers that it is common practice to pour used solvents and cleaning solutions down a storm drain. The FLM isn't sure whether the practice is legal or ethical. In considering such a situation and what to do, the FLM can ask:

1. Does my decision fall within the accepted values or standards that typically apply in the organizational environment?
2. Am I willing to see the decision communicated to all stakeholders affected by it—for example, by having it reported on television?
3. Would the people with whom I have a significant personal relationship, such as family members, friends, or even supervisors in other organizations, approve of the decision?

Questions 4–14 should also be asked by FLMs when making important decisions with obvious ethical implications:

4. How did this problem occur in the first place?
5. Would you define the problem differently if you stood on the other side of the fence?

6. To whom and to what do you give your loyalty as a person and as a member of your organization?

7. What is your intention in making this decision?

8. What is the potential for your intentions to be misunderstood by others in the organization?

9. How do your intentions compare with the probable result?

10. Whom could your decision injure?

11. Can you discuss the problem with the affected parties before you make the decision?

12. Are you confident that your position will be as valid over a long period of time as it seems now?

13. Could you disclose your decision to your boss or your immediate family?

14. How would you feel if your decision was described, in detail, on the front page of your local newspaper? (Adapted from Nash, 1981, 8; Trevino, 1986; Shaw & Barry, 1995.)

One way to identify an unethical decision is to ask whether the FLM would prefer to disguise or hide it from other people because it would enable the company or a particular individual to gain at the expense of society or other stakeholders. Consider the following situation Mary faces in her role as an FLM.

MARY'S DILEMMA

Mary Francis supervises eight production specialists in a computer manufacturing company. Mary has a dilemma. She is being transferred to a new assignment with the company, and her boss has asked her to nominate one of her employees as her replacement. She has to decide whether to recommend Jose Fernandez, a Mexican American who was obviously the best-qualified employee, or John Thomas, who, though not as well qualified, would be better accepted by the other workers.

Jose is a very intelligent 27-year-old specialist who has just completed course work to earn his management degree. He has done an excellent job on every assignment Mary has given him. Jose has all the qualifications Mary feels a good FLM should have: he is punctual, diligent, mature, and intelligent. John, on the other hand, is a 28-year-old high school graduate with little other educational experience. He is a hard worker who is well liked and respected by the others including Jose. Like Jose, he has made it clear that he wants to move into management.

Mary also knows that her employees are prejudiced against Mexican Americans. Therefore, she thinks that if Jose is given the promotion, he will have difficulties, no matter what his qualifications. Mary must ask herself, "If Jose were white, would I have any hesitation about recommending him for the job?" The answer was clearly no. Jose is without doubt the better-qualified person. Mary also struggled with the question, "How will performance and employee attitudes be affected if Jose is given the job?" Mary knows that Jose will not be accepted as the new manager, and that morale and productivity will probably plunge for a time.

As Mary labors over the decision, she thinks about how unfair it would be to Jose if he were denied a deserved promotion based on his race. At the same time, Mary feels her primary responsibility should be to maintain the productivity of the unit. The existing prejudice is a fact of life that Mary cannot eliminate. Mary realizes that it would be very easy to rationalize either decision: she could recommend Jose on the basis of fairness or John on the basis of maintaining group moral.

Mary knows that the way she handles this promotion issue might substantially affect her future within the company. If her unit falls apart after her departure, it will hurt her reputation. More important, however, Mary believes that she will face even more difficult ethical decisions in her new job. If she stands by her principles in this case, she believes it will make those future ethical decisions easier.

At that moment, the phone rings. It is Mary's boss, Fred Fisher. "Mary," he said, "I need to see you. Can you come to my office in a few minutes?" As Mary hangs up the phone, she thinks, "I know Fred wants to talk about my replacement." Mary is concerned about her reputation within the company, but she must also be at peace with herself. Mary will personally benefit in the long run by keeping her actions consistent with her beliefs. Ethical issues like the one confronting Mary are a daily and increasingly important component of business.

Mary could use the three approaches (utilitarian, moral rights, justice) in deciding whom to promote. She could ask: Would the promotion of either Jose or John result in greater costs or benefits for the company?

If Mary promotes Jose, employee discrimination against him may cause productivity and profits to decline, while John could maintain productivity through being better accepted by his co-workers. Giving John the promotion would therefore be beneficial for the company in the short-term. On the other hand, if employees could accept Jose, he should be a better FLM and could improve productivity in the long term. Furthermore, if he is not promoted, he could leave the company, and the company would lose a valuable employee.

Would the promotion of either Jose or John deny any individuals of their rights? If Mary promotes John, it could deny Jose his basic right against discrimination, his right to be judged on his past performance, and his opportunity to receive a promotion.

Would the promotion of either Jose or John give people the justice they deserve? If Mary does not promote Jose, she will be acting unfairly. In order to promote justice within the organization, Mary must promote the best person for the job and not respond to pressures to discriminate. If she were to promote John instead, it would not only be unfair to Jose, but would send the wrong signal to all the employees at the company.

Given the answers to these questions, Mary should promote Jose. The company will have to provide Jose with the support he will need to maintain productivity, and management should clearly demonstrate its disapproval of discriminatory attitudes. When a company meets the ethical standards established by the federal government or by its industry or profession (e.g., doesn't discriminate against employees on the basis of race in a promotion decision), the organization is fulfilling its social obligation.

Various laws prohibit employers from putting employees at risk, polluting, or discriminating against certain groups, and this company is abiding by those laws. The story of Mary's decision is one example of encountering a dilemma with legal and social ramifications. Meeting social obligations doesn't always involve a question of legality. When a company packages its products in recycled paper or provides health care insurance for an employee's significant other, it is being socially responsive. How so? Although it may be responding to social pressures, it is providing something society desires without having to be told to do so by law!

CONTEMPORARY CORPORATE ETHICS

An organization has a value system that determines its ethical behavior. Individual and organizational wrongdoing during the 1980s and 1990s drew attention to the lack of ethical behavior in many organizations. Given the increased focus on ethics in recent years, it has become important for organizations to demonstrate their commitment to ethics and to being socially responsible. FLMs who wish to be a part of an ethical organization have to understand the organization's ethical character or culture. FLMs should be as aware of an employer's ethical character as they are of its economic health. For example, if an organization emphasizes short-term revenues over long-term results, it may be creating an unethical atmosphere. If it expects employees to leave their private ethics at home, thus encouraging unethical behavior or discouraging ethical behavior for financial reasons, it is promoting an unethical work environment. If an organization links its ethical behavior to a code of ethics but will not address the complexity of ethical dilemmas, then the code may merely be window dressing. Proactive organizations do more than adopt a document when they establish a code of ethics. They may establish board-level committees to monitor the ethical behavior of the organization or develop ethics training courses or other programs.

The treatment of employees can also indicate the ethical nature of an organization. If employees are not treated as well as customers or if performance-appraisal standards are unfair or arbitrary, the company may be unethical. Additionally, an absence of procedures for handling ethical issues, or the lack of a whistle-blowing mechanism, or even the lack of a basic communication avenue between employees and FLMs can indicate an organization that is ethically at risk.

Finally, an organization may be unethical if it fails to recognize its obligations to the public as well as to its shareholders. Ethical problems are not merely public relations issues, and legal decisions may not be ethical ones.

CORPORATIONS NEED TO DEMONSTRATE SOCIAL RESPONSIBILITY

What responsibility do FLMs have to provide benefits to their stakeholders and to adopt courses of action that enhance the well-being of society at large? Social responsibility is an obligation organizations have to society. It means going beyond legal responsibilities and profit-making. Social responsibility tries to align organizational long-term goals with what is good for society. An organization should recognize the impact of its actions on others and be able to predict how those actions would threaten or further its existence. Becoming a *moral actor* can be a fundamental issue of survival for the organization. Social responsibility therefore obligates FLMs to make decisions that nurture, protect, and promote the welfare and well-being of stakeholders and society as a whole.

We can understand social responsibility better if we compare it with two similar concepts: social obligation and social responsiveness. Social obligation is a business' most basic duty to society. A business has fulfilled its social obligation when it meets its economic and legal responsibilities and no more. It does the minimum that the law requires. In contrast to social obligation, social responsiveness adds a moral obligation to business responsibilities. It requires business to take actions that make society better and to refrain from actions that could make it worse. Societal norms guide this process.

WHY ORGANIZATIONS SHOULD BE SOCIALLY RESPONSIBLE

Several advantages may result from socially responsible behavior. First, workers and society benefit directly when organizations bear some of the costs of helping workers that would otherwise be borne by the government. Second, if all organizations in a society were socially responsible, the quality of life as a whole would be higher. Indeed, several management experts have argued that the way organizations behave toward their employees determines many of a society's values and the ethics of its citizens. It has been suggested that if all organizations adopted a caring approach and agreed to promote the interests of their employees, a climate of caring would pervade to greater society.

Experts point to Japan, Sweden, the Netherlands, and Switzerland as countries with very socially responsible organizations and where, as a result, crime and unemployment rates are relatively low, the literacy rate is relatively high, and socio-cultural values promote harmony between different groups of people. Finally, being socially responsible is the right thing to do. Evidence suggests that socially responsible FLMs and other managers are, in the long run, best for all organizational stakeholders. It appears that socially responsible organizations are also sought out by communities, which encourage these organizations to locate in their cities by offering them incentives such as property-tax reductions, new roads, and free utilities for their plants. Additionally, FLMs who promote a proactive approach to social responsibility are also sought out by organizations. There are many reasons to believe that, over time, strong support of social responsibility greatly benefits FLMs, their organizations, organizational stakeholders, and society at large.

HOW TO INSTITUTIONALIZE ETHICAL BEHAVIOR

How should FLMs and organizations decide which social issues are important and to what extent the organizations should trade profits for social gain. First, illegal behavior should not be tolerated, and FLMs, managers and operating employees should be alert to its occurrence and report it promptly. The term whistleblower is used to refer to a person who reports illegal or unethical behavior and takes a stand against unscrupulous FLMs and stakeholders who are pursuing their own ends. Laws now exist to protect the interest of whistleblowers, who risk their jobs and careers to reveal unethical behavior. In part, these laws were implemented because of the experiences of two engineers at Morton Thiokol who warned that the Challenger space shuttle's O-ring gaskets would be adversely affected by cold weather at launch. Their warnings were ignored by everyone involved in the headlong rush to launch the shuttle. As a result, seven astronauts died when the Challenger exploded shortly after its launch in January 1986. Although the actions of the engineers were applauded by the committee of inquiry, their subsequent careers suffered because managers at Morton Thiokol blamed them for damaging the company's reputation and harming its interests.

An organization must clarify that ethical considerations are valued by the organization. An organization's mission statement often details its goal of providing the highest quality product at the least cost and recognizes its commitment to all stakeholders. In addition, it needs to include a commitment to an ethical standard for all employee actions.

An organization must communicate its commitment to ethical values to all of its employees and external stakeholders. Codes of conduct or ethics should be adopted and distributed to all employees. Communication cannot be limited to the distribution of the code of ethics, however, because actions speak louder than words. Through their actions, FLMs should foster employee commitment to the organization's goal of ethical behavior in the same way that they foster employee commitment to its goal.

During the promotion and recruitment process, organizations can include in their criteria an interest in ethical decision making. Several methods can be used to evaluate employees, such as honesty tests, background checks, and an employee's willingness to sign commitment to the corporate code of ethics. Pizza Hut, Inc.'s top management looks for integrity when hiring and promoting employees in the organization. Integrity includes a personal allegiance to excellence, honesty, a sense of teamwork, and a balanced perspective on long-term goals and short-term profits. Early in a company's process, a psychological contract is formed between the employer and employee. Psychological contracts typically cover the expectations that the employer and the employee form about each other. The degree to which both parties satisfy these expectations affects the success of the relationship. It is important for FLMs to understand that if the two do not or cannot agree on their fundamental needs, then the relationship will suffer. Furthermore, because ethical behavior cannot be reduced to simple do's and don'ts, both parties' expectations will continually change, and thus there must be opportunity and structure to address evolving expectations.

Training employees to make an ethical analysis as part of their decision making is critical. Training can be formal, focused on the organization's goals and objectives, and on decision-making techniques. Training can also be achieved through the normal socialization that occurs during the orientation of a new employee. If the employer is operating ethically, then the role models whom the employee emulates will exhibit the proper ethical behavior. The system of rewards and punishments will confirm and reinforce ethical behavior.

MODELS FOR ETHICAL CONDUCT

Distributive Justice

The principle of distributive justice requires that FLMs not be arbitrary and use only relevant information to determine how to treat people. It demands a fair distribution of pay raises, promotions, job titles, interesting job assignments, office space, and other organizational resources among members of an organization. Fairness means that rewards should be based on the meaningful contributions that individuals have made to the organization, such as time, effort, education, skills, abilities, and performance levels, and not on irrelevant personal characteristics over which individuals have no control, such as gender, race, or age.

FLMs have an obligation to ensure their departments and organizations follow distributive justice principles. This does not mean that all members of a department or organization should be rewarded equally; rather it means that those employees who receive greater rewards than others should have made substantially higher or more significant contributions to the organization. In the scenario presented earlier in this chapter, Mary should clearly promote Jose, using these guidelines. In many countries, managers have not only an ethical obligation but also a legal obligation to strive to achieve distributive justice in their organizations, and they risk being sued by employees who feel that they are not being fairly treated.

Procedural Justice

The principle of procedural justice requires that FLMs clearly state and consistently administer the rules and established procedures of the organization and not bend the rules to serve their own interests or to show favoritism. This principle applies to procedures such as appraising an employee's performance, deciding who should receive a raise or a promotion, and deciding whom to lay off when an organization is forced to downsize. Procedural justice exists, for example, when FLMs

1. carefully appraise the job performance of employees reporting directly to them;
2. take into account any environmental obstacles to high performance beyond the employees' control, such as lack of supplies, machine breakdowns, or dwindling customer demand for a product;
3. ignore irrelevant personal characteristics such as an employee's age or ethnicity.

Like distributive justice, procedural justice is necessary not only to ensure ethical conduct but also to avoid costly lawsuits.

MANAGING A DIVERSE WORKFORCE

One of the most important trends to emerge in organizations over the last thirty years has been the increasing diversity of the workforce. Diversity means differences among people due to age, gender, race, ethnicity, religion, sexual orientation, socioeconomic background, and capabilities/disabilities. Diversity raises important issues of ethics and social responsibility for FLMs and organizations. If not handled well, diversity challenges bring an organization to its knees, especially in our increasingly global environment.

There are several reasons why diversity is valued, both in the popular press and by FLMs and their organizations. First, there is a strong ethical imperative that diverse people receive equal opportunities and be treated fairly and justly. In some countries, unfair treatment is also illegal. Second, when FLMs effectively manage diversity, they can improve organizational effectiveness. They not only improve morale by encouraging other FLMs to treat diverse members of an organization fairly, but also use diversity as an important resource that can give the organization a competitive advantage. Unfortunately, there is substantial evidence that diverse individuals continue to experience unfair treatment in the workplace as a result of biases, stereotypes, and overt discrimination. In one Philadelphia study, resumes of equally qualified male and female applicants for waiter positions were sent to high-priced restaurants, where potential earnings are high. Though equally qualified, the men were more than twice as likely as the women to be called for a job interview and more than five times as likely to receive a job offer. Another study reported that 97 percent of the top managers of the 1,500 largest companies in the United States are White men. The Federal Glass Ceiling Commission Report indicated that African Americans have the hardest time being promoted and climbing the corporate ladder. Asians are often stereotyped into technical jobs, and Hispanics are assumed to be less educated than other groups. In the rest of this section we examine workplace diversity in detail. Then we look at the steps the FLM can take to supervise diversity effectively. Effectively supervising diversity not only makes good business sense but is an ethical imperative in U.S. society.

DIVERSITY VERSUS AFFIRMATIVE ACTION

Sometimes managing diversity is confused with affirmative action or other laws favoring certain types of people. Actually, the two terms are quite different. Affirmative action emphasizes achieving equality of opportunity in the work setting by changing organizational demographics—age, gender, race, ethnic mixes, and the like. It is designed to benefit specific groups that have suffered past wrongs. Affirmative action is mandated by equal employment opportunity laws, and requires written reports containing plans and statistical goals for increasing the numbers of employees that belong to specific groups. It primarily affects hiring and promotion decisions, thus opening doors for some but leading to fears of reverse discrimination against others.

The goal of effectively managed diversity is to create a setting in which everyone feels valued and accepted, and differences are appreciated. It assumes that groups will retain their own characteristics and will shape the organization as well as be shaped by it, thus creating a common set of values. The proper management of diversity is designed to affect employee perceptions and attitudes, but it is resisted sometimes because of fear of change and discomfort with differences. In Canada, laws have been designed to encourage the supervision of diversity at the provincial level through employment equity legislation.

DIVERSITY MAKES GOOD BUSINESS SENSE

A diverse workforce can be a source of creativity and competitive advantage, helping an organization provide customers with better goods and services. Diverse employees provide a variety of view points and approaches to problems and opportunities that can improve FLMs' decision making. For example, suppose an FLM is trying to find some creative ideas for responding to a broad range of business problems. Which group do you think would be more likely to come up with the most creative ideas: a group of homogeneous employees with similar backgrounds and experiences or a diverse group of employees with different backgrounds and experiences? Most people would agree that the diverse group is likely to come up with a wider range of creative ideas. Although this example is simplistic, it underscores one way in which diversity can lead to a more dynamic company with more varied approaches to its business.

Just as the workforce is becoming increasingly diverse, so too are the customers who buy an organization's products and services. Diverse members of an organization are likely to be more attuned to the goods and services desired by diverse segments of the market. Major car companies, for example, are increasingly assigning women to their design teams to ensure that the needs and desires of the growing number of female car buyers are taken into account in new car design.

Effectively supervising a diverse workforce makes good business sense for another reason. More and more, FLMs and organizations concerned about diversity are insisting that their suppliers also support diversity. Managers at American Airlines, for example, recently announced that all the law firms they hire would need to submit quarterly reports indicating the extent to which diverse employees work on the airline's account. Similarly, managers at Chrysler, Aetna Life & Casualty, and General Motors all consider diversity information when they are deciding which law firms will represent them.

Managing diversity ought to be a top priority for FLMs in all organizations, large and small, public and private, for profit and not for profit.

Organizations need to ensure that FLMs and all levels of employees appreciate the value that diversity brings to an organization and have the ability to interact and work effectively with men and women who are physically challenged or who differ in age, race, gender, ethnicity, nationality, or sexual orientation. FLMs are often in a better position than middle and top managers when it comes to supervising a group of diverse employees. If they have just recently moved from being an individual contributor to an FLM, they have experienced the diversity issue first hand. The FLM's objective is to build a team of heterogeneous employees that functions at least as productively as homogeneous employees. Ideally, today's FLMs must be able to tap into the reservoir of a multitalented, diverse workforce that will make the organization more resourceful, more productive, more responsive to customers, and a more interesting place to work. The following sections describe how FLMs can increase diversity awareness and improve their skills in handling a diverse workforce.

INCREASING DIVERSITY AWARENESS

It is natural for you to view other people from your own perspective because your feelings, thoughts, attitudes, and experiences guide how you perceive and interact with others. The ability to appreciate diversity, however, requires you to become aware of the perspectives, attitudes, and experiences of others. Many organizations provide diversity awareness programs designed to help FLMs and employees to become aware of their own attitudes, biases, and stereotypes and to understand the differing perspectives of others. Diversity awareness programs often are designed to

- provide accurate information about diversity;
- uncover personal biases and stereotypes;
- assess personal beliefs, attitudes, and values;
- overturn inaccurate stereotypes and beliefs about different groups;
- develop an atmosphere in which people feel free to share their differing perspectives and learn about other points of view;
- improve understanding of others who are different.

DEVELOP SKILLS FOR WORKING WITH DIVERSE PEOPLE

Educating FLMs and their employees about why and how people differ in the ways they think, communicate, and approach work can help all members of the organization develop a healthy respect for diversity and at the same time facilitate mutual understanding. When American and Japanese managers interact, for example, the Americans often feel frustrated by what they view as indecisiveness in the Japanese, and the Japanese are often frustrated by what they perceive as hasty, short-sighted decision making by the Americans. If Japanese managers and American managers realize that their approaches to decision making are by-products of cultural differences and recognize the relative merits of each approach, they may be more likely to adopt a mutually satisfactory decision making style that incorporates the advantages of each approach and minimizes the disadvantages.

FLMs and their employees must learn to communicate effectively with one another if an organization is to take advantage of the skills and abilities of its diverse workforce. FLMs and employees may differ in their styles of communication, language fluency, and use of words. They may differ in the nonverbal signs they send through facial expression and body language, and in the way they perceive and interpret information. Educating them about different ways to communicate is often a good starting point.

FLMs and their employees must learn how to be open to different approaches and ways of doing things. This does not mean that they need to suppress their personal styles. Rather, it means that they must not feel threatened by other approaches and perspectives, and they must have the patience and flexibility needed to understand and appreciate diverse perspectives.

SUPERVISING EMPLOYEES WITH DISABILITIES

For decades, many organizations have made special efforts to provide employment opportunities for people with physical and mental disabilities. Many of these efforts were made voluntarily and from the conviction that it was the proper or ethical thing to do. However, as a result of a number of laws and government regulations beginning in 1973, people with disabilities were identified as a group that was to receive special consideration in employment and other areas. In 1990, the Americans with Disabilities Act (ADA) was passed. It is the most significant legislation giving legal protection to a group since the Civil Rights Act of 1964. All employers with 15 or more employees are required to comply with its provision. The ADA requires that employers make any necessary alterations to provide access to public spaces, public accommodations, and commercial facilities for people with disabilities. Many of the details of the ADA are technical and beyond the scope of this book. Nevertheless, FLMs should be familiar with major provisions of the act, and, more important, its implications for supervising employees with disabilities.

WHO IS A QUALIFIED DISABLED INDIVIDUAL?

The definition of a disabled person is very broad. By some estimates, about one in six Americans (or roughly about 45 million people) could be considered disabled under the statute's definitions. A number of categories of workers are not protected under its definitions of disability, however, such as those who have an infectious disease and whose job includes food handling, homosexuals, and people who currently use illegal drugs. The definition of disability otherwise covers most major impairments and diseases, including cancer, epilepsy, diabetes, and HIV-AIDS. In the definition of a qualified disabled individual, *reasonable* accommodation means altering the usual way of doing things so that an otherwise qualified disabled person can perform the essential duties of a job, but without creating an undue hardship for the employer. An undue hardship would be a significant expense or an unreasonable change in activities on the part of the employer to accommodate the disabled person.

Reasonable accommodation may take any number of forms. It typically means making buildings accessible by building ramps, removing barriers such as steps or curbs, and altering restroom facilities. Reasonable accommodations may mean that the arrangement of desks and widths of aisles have to be altered to allow people in wheelchairs access to job locations. It conceivably could include modifying work schedules, acquiring certain equipment or devices, providing readers or interpreters, and other types of adjustments. In some situations, job duties can be altered to accommodate people with disabilities. For example, in one company an employee who assembled small component units was also expected to place the completed units in a carton at the end of an assembly process. Several times a day the full carton had to be carried to the shipping area. In order for an employee in a wheelchair to perform the subassembly job, the FLM arranged for a shipping clerk to pick up completed component units at designated times each day. Thus, the FLM made a reasonable accommodation so that a physically impaired employee could handle the subassembly job. Another FLM added a flashing warning light to equipment that already contained a warning buzzer so that an employee with a hearing impairment could be employed safely.

In order to comply with other provisions of the ADA, many organizations have conducted training programs for FLMs who are responsible for making the necessary adjustments for disabled employees. In the employment process, an employer cannot require a pre–job offer medical examination, other than a drug test, to screen applicants, or make any type of preemployment inquiries about the nature of an applicant's disability. Most employers have reviewed their application forms to ensure that improper questions are not included. FLMs involved in the interview process must be very cautious in talking about the requirements of a job and not raise the possibility of an employee's disability or past medical record. An applicant may be given a medical examination only after receiving a job offer to determine whether he or she is physically capable of performing the essential functions of the job as defined in the job description.

CHANGING ATTITUDES OF FLMs AND EMPLOYEES TOWARD DISABILITIES

The ADA is aimed at changing perceptions as well as employer behavior. The law encourages FLMs and employees to recognize people's abilities rather than their disabilities. As much as anything else, attitudes play an important role in organizational efforts to accommodate people with disabilities. Many organizations have training programs to familiarize FLMs and employees with the needs of people with disabilities. These programs help workers to recognize that the ADA is the law and to believe in its goals. Training programs should allow an open discussion about different disabilities and give opportunities to air questions and feelings of discomfort. Like other diversity awareness training, employees should be aware that certain words may carry unintentionally negative messages. For example, the ADA uses the term *disability* rather than *handicapped* because this is the preference of most people with disabilities. Some training programs use simulated experiences in which nondisabled employees are required to experience certain types of mental, hearing, physical, or visual impairments. For example, they may sit in a wheelchair and try to maneuver through a work area. This type of training helps employees gain a better understanding of what it might be like to experience the difficulties of a disability. FLMs must also be willing to alter their leadership styles depending on a worker's particular type of disability. For example, employees who are mentally disabled may require somewhat close and direct supervision. However, a physically disabled employee who uses a wheelchair while working as a proofreader could be supervised with a more participative style.

Research has shown that individuals with disabilities can make excellent employees provided they are placed in jobs where their abilities can be utilized appropriately. As in so many other areas, the FLM is often the primary person to make this happen.

MANAGING A DIVERSE WORKFORCE: CONCLUSION

As an FLM, what can you do to manage a diverse workforce? Here are some suggestions.

- Recognize that problems caused by diversity issues should be handled as performance problems.
- Understand that solutions to diversity problems require more effective interpersonal communication skills for you and your employees.
- Adapt your supervising techniques to the needs of legally protected employees like disabled individuals.
- Educate yourself by studying diversity issues through books, videotapes, and educational programs. Better still, talk with employees who seem to be struggling with diversity. When you can put a personal story behind a situation, you are more likely to learn from it and teach it to others.
- Raise the profile of the diverse nature of your work team by talking about it candidly. Do this in the spirit of mutual respect for individuals and within the context of improving the performance of the overall organization. If you are uncomfortable facilitating a discussion like this, ask for help from your human resources management (HRM) department or an outside communications consultant.
- Participate in making sure that your organization is in compliance with the Americans with Disabilities Act of 1990. Checking your ethical policies and measuring your doorways, for example, can be a personally enlightening experience and will send a clear, positive message about your intentions.
- Always recognize that the best way to supervise or manage all employees in your team or department, protected or not, is to constantly apply the principles of good management as presented throughout this book.

SEXUAL HARASSMENT: WHAT EVERY FLM SHOULD KNOW

Few workplace topics have received more attention in recent years than sexual harassment. Unfortunately, sexual harassment on the job is a major problem, faced primarily by women. Needless to say, sexual harassment is legally and ethically wrong. It seriously damages both the people who are harassed and the reputation of the organization in which it occurs. It also can cost organizations large amounts of money. In 1995, for example, Chevron Corporation agreed to pay $2.2 million to settle a sexual harassment lawsuit filed by four women who worked at Chevron Information Technology Company in San Ramon, California. One woman involved in the suit said that she had received violent pornographic material through the company mail. Another, an electrical engineer, said that she had been asked to bring pornographic videos to Chevron workers at an Alaska drill site. Unfortunately, what happened at Chevron were not isolated incidents. The widely publicized federal sexual harassment suit filed in 1996 against Mitsubishi Motors Corporation's U.S. unit in Normal, Illinois served as a loud and clear warning to both foreign and U.S. companies that illegal sexual harassment practices would not be tolerated. In that case, female employees were offended by lewd pictures in bathrooms and continual teasing. The Equal Employment Opportunity Commission (EEOC) expressed particular dismay over widespread evidence suggesting that Mitsubishi's management was aware of the harassment, yet failed to act. In the case of U.S. Army, Astra, USA Inc. (Astra), a 17-year history of sexual harassment complaints against CEO Lars Bildman also went unanswered. FLMs have a legal and ethical obligation to ensure that they, their colleagues, and their employees never engage in sexual harassment, even unintentionally.

FORMS OF SEXUAL HARASSMENT

Since 1980 U.S. courts generally have used guidelines from the Equal Employment Opportunity Commission to define sexual harassment. There are two basic forms of sexual harassment. Quid pro quo sexual harassment occurs when a harasser asks or forces an employee to perform sexual favors to receive a promotion, raise, or other work-related opportunity, or to avoid negative consequences such as demotion or dismissal. This "Sleep with me, honey, or you're fired" form of harassment is the more extreme form and is easier to identify. Hostile work environment sexual harassment is more subtle. Hostile work environment sexual harassment occurs when employees are faced with an intimidating, hostile, or offensive work environment because of their gender. Lewd jokes, displays of pornography, displays or distribution of sexually-oriented objects, and sexually-oriented remarks about one's physical appearance are examples of hostile work environment sexual harassment. A hostile work environment interferes with employees' ability to perform their jobs effectively and has been deemed illegal by the courts.

Although women are the most frequent victims of sexual harassment (particularly when working in male-dominated occupations or in positions associated with stereotypical gender relationships such as a female secretary reporting to a male boss), men also can be victims of sexual harassment. Several male employees at Jenny Craig filed a lawsuit charging that they were subject to lewd and inappropriate comments from female co-workers and managers. It should also be noted that while most instances of sexual harassment involve unwelcome conduct by persons of the opposite sex, allegations of harassment against members of the same sex are increasing. In a recent case, a male oil-rig worker filed and won a sexual harassment case. FLMs who engage in hostile work environment harassment or allow others to do so risk costly lawsuits for their organizations.

ERADICATING SEXUAL HARASSMENT

FLMs have an ethical obligation to eradicate sexual harassment in their organizations. To ensure that you do not have a hostile or abusive environment, you must establish a clear and strong position against sexual harassment. There are many ways to accomplish this objective. Some steps that FLMs can take to deal with the problem are described below.

Clearly communicate the sexual harassment policy endorsed by top management. Senior leadership should adopt a policy against harassment that includes prohibitions against both quid pro quo and hostile work environment sexual harassment. It should contain

- requirements that all employees be treated with respect, giving examples of unacceptable behavior;
- a procedure for employees to use to report instances of harassment;
- a discussion of the disciplinary responses to harassment;
- a commitment to educate and train employees about sexual harassment.

FLMs must take complaints of sexual harassment seriously. They must also create an environment in which employees feel comfortable making complaints to an FLM, someone in HRM, or a higher level manager. If an employee describes behavior that could be harassment, the FLM should listen to the employee's concerns and assure the employee that he or she will follow up on it. The worst thing an FLM can do is to pass judgment immediately or imply that the employee should put up with the behavior without complaining. The FLM's initial talk with the employee serves as the very first step of the investigation. The FLM should learn all the details about what is bothering the employee. The employee should be asked if anyone else can corroborate the incidents or if anyone else may have experienced similar behavior. FLMs must then deal with complaints promptly. While there is no bright line measure for promptness, FLMs should at a minimum notify the HRM department as quickly as possible—that day or the next business day—so that the investigative process may begin. Unwarranted delay in investigating and otherwise responding to a complaint could cause the organization to be liable.

Once it has been determined that sexual harassment has taken place, take corrective actions as soon as possible. These actions can vary depending on the severity of the harassment. When harassment is extensive, prolonged over a period of time, of a quid pro quo nature, or severely objectionable in some other manner, corrective action may include firing the harasser. Explain to the employee that once an allegation of harassment is raised, the company has an obligation to investigate the allegation. If the company is made aware of the allegation and fails to investigate, it could be liable for not doing all it could to prevent harassment in the workplace. The FLM should therefore inform the employee of the need to notify the HRM department of the complaint. Even if the complaint is one that both the FLM and the employee feel confident is just a misunderstanding that could be handled within the FLM's department, HRM should be informed of the incident so that it can keep track of any repeat violations or recurring problems. The company must investigate in the most sensitive way possible, but complete confidentiality cannot be guaranteed. FLMs should stress that information about the allegations will be given only to those within the company with a need to know. FLMs should let the employee know that no one in the company—including the alleged harasser—will be allowed to retaliate or treat the employee badly because of the complaint. It should be explained that if the investigation shows that harassment has occurred, appropriate disciplinary action will be taken. The employee should be thanked for coming forward, because the company cannot fix problems if it does not know they exist.

Provide sexual harassment training to organizational members, including FLMs and other managers. The majority of Fortune 500 organizations currently provide this kind of training for their employees. Organizations like Corning, Digital Equipment, and the U.S. Navy are proactively addressing the sexual harassment problem. Digital Equipment Company offers a full-day training program that educates employees about the different forms of sexual harassment and makes extensive use of role playing. In the wake of the much publicized Tailhook scandal in which Navy and Marine Corps pilots sexually harassed naval aviators at a convention in Las Vegas, the Navy is trying to eradicate sexual harassment and improve its managing of diversity and its public image. Men and women who have committed sexual harassment offenses have been discharged. All members of the Navy, regardless of rank, are now educated about appropriate and inappropriate behavior. Eighteen courses are offered on issues surrounding sexual harassment, and all members of the Navy are required to participate in continuous training. Evidence that these initiatives were needed came solely from the Navy's toll-free sexual harassment advice line. During its first four months of operation, 500 calls were received.

Two recent rulings by the U.S. Supreme Court have made it even more imperative for employers to deter sexually harassing behavior by FLMs and other employees. The nation's highest court said that employers can be held liable for harassment even if sexually harassing FLMs don't carry out threatened job actions, or if employers don't have knowledge of harassing behavior. The court stated that employment policies and procedures to prevent harassment and provide avenues for victimized employees to report misconduct can improve an employer's ability to defend against claims.

SUMMARY

Business ethics is an important topic today. Business ethics is ethical behavior in the workplace that influences how a business functions, such as individual and corporate ethics. FLMs can apply ethical standards to help themselves decide on the proper way to behave toward organizational stakeholders.

Social responsibility refers to an organization's and an FLM's duty to make decisions that nurture, protect, enhance, and promote the welfare and well-being of stakeholders and society as a whole. Promoting ethical and socially responsible behavior is an FLM's major challenge. Organizations can institutionalize ethical behavior by establishing the value, communicating the value, and selecting and training employees with ethical behavior in mind. Three models available to FLMs to determine whether a decision is ethical are *utilitarian, justice*, and *moral rights*.

The issue of diversity (i.e., differences among people due to age, gender, race, ethnicity, religion, sexual orientation, socioeconomic background, and capabilities/disabilities) also poses ethical challenges for today's FLMs. In particular, generational values help decide where employees choose to work, how they approach the work, and how well they work together. Changes in the nature of the employee-employer relationship have come about in U.S. business, in part, because of the changing values of American workers.

Sexual harassment also poses an important challenge for today's FLMs and organizations. Steps that FLMs and organizations can take to eradicate sexual harassment include development and communication of a sexual harassment policy endorsed by top management (and reinforced by FLMs), use of fair complaint procedures, prompt corrective action when harassment occurs, and sexual training and education for organization members.

REFERENCES

Nash, L. L. 1981. Ethics without the sermon. *Harvard Business Review* (November–December), 8.

Shaw, W. H., & V. Barry. 1995. *Moral issues in business*, 6th ed. Belmont, CA: Wadsworth.

Trevino, L. K. 1986. Ethical decision making in organizations: A person-situation interactionist model. *Academy of Management Review* 11, 601–617.

Chapter 4

Communication: The Bridge to Organization Success

INTRODUCTION

Communication is not an easy word to define, nor is it an easy skill to master; however, it is essential for the functioning of every part of an organization. Although marketing, production, finance, personnel, and other departments may receive direction from corporate goals and objectives, communication links them together and facilitates organizational success.

The importance of effective communication for FLMs cannot be overemphasized for one specific reason: everything an FLM does involves communicating. Not some things, but everything! Planning, leading, organizing, and controlling all require communication. You cannot make a decision without information, and that information has to be communicated. Once a decision is made, it must be communicated to others, or no one will know about it. The best idea, the most creative suggestion, or the finest plan cannot take form without communication. Indeed, some experts estimate that FLMs spend approximately 85 percent of their time engaged in some form of communication.

The successful FLM, therefore, needs effective communication skills. We are not suggesting, of course, that good communication skills alone make a successful FLM. We can say, however, that ineffective communication skills can lead to a continuous stream of problems.

COMMUNICATION AND MANAGEMENT

Shelley Wilson and Jackson Francis were two FLMs in a large regional company. The company had suffered a major layoff in 1997, and top management had now decided to change from a departmental structure to one based on cross-functional teams. While the details of the proposed reorganization were being finalized, Wilson and Francis needed to keep their employees informed about the changes. Wilson and Francis each took a different approach to communicating this important news.

Wilson wrote a short memo that said: "As some of you may have already heard, our department will be undergoing a major change in structure within the next six months. Right now, the details haven't been worked out, so I don't have any more information than this to share with you. The effects of the change should be more clear next month, and I will keep you informed." Francis held a meeting with his direct reports in which he announced the change and described in general terms what would be happening and why. He then spent considerable time answering his employees' questions and listening to their concerns. When Wilson heard about Francis' meeting, she said to herself, "There he goes again, wasting everyone's time in unnecessary meetings when a simple memo would do."

Was Francis' meeting a waste of time? Not if the reactions of Wilson's and Francis' employees are taken into account. All of Wilson's employees feared another round of layoffs was coming, and their performance consequently suffered. Francis' employees, in contrast, felt the organization was concerned about them and were looking forward to learning more about the planned change. One of their first questions at the meeting concerned potential layoffs, and Francis truthfully assured them that no layoffs would occur. Knowing their jobs were secure, the employees spent the rest of the meeting discussing the pros and cons of the change, inadvertently providing Francis with useful points to bring up with his supervisor. Instead of being a waste of time, Francis' approach was highly effective and contributed to the successful implementation of the new structure. In contrast, Wilson's ineffective communication unnecessarily raised the stress levels of her employees and made them wary of the upcoming change.

In this chapter, we define communication and the communication process and describe ways to be an effective communicator. The latter part of the chapter discusses written and oral communication in detail and offers guidelines for developing these two very important skills.

WHAT IS COMMUNICATION?

Communication is the sharing of information between two or more individuals or groups to reach a common understanding. The most important part of this definition is that, to be successful, the information or ideas conveyed must be understood. To see what the definition means in practice, return to Wilson and Francis. Wilson and Francis shared information with their employees, but Francis' approach was much more effective than Wilson's for at least two reasons. First, the information Wilson shared was incomplete; Wilson never even communicated the nature of the organizational restructuring. Second, Wilson made no attempt to ensure that a common understanding was reached. Not surprisingly, therefore, her employees jumped to the wrong conclusion that there would be more layoffs. Francis made sure a common understanding was reached by providing an appropriate level of information, through a face-to-face meeting with his employees and by giving them the opportunity to ask questions. FLMs like Francis who are able to communicate with their employees so that a common understanding is reached are more effective than FLMs like Wilson who do not.

Good communication is often incorrectly defined by the communicator as "agreement" instead of "clarity of understanding." If someone disagrees with us, we may often assume the person just did not fully understand our position; but a person can clearly understand us and simply not agree. In fact, when an FLM concludes that a lack of communication must exist because a conflict between two employees has continued for a long time, a closer look often reveals that the two are communicating, they just don't agree.

THE COMMUNICATION PROCESS

The communication process consists of two phases. In the transmission phase, information is sent from one individual or group, the sender, to another individual or group, the receiver. During this phase the sender first decides what message to communicate and then decides what method to use to communicate that message. In our earlier example, Wilson and Francis both sent a message, but they chose different ways to send the message.

In the feedback phase a receiver responds to the message that has been sent. This response might include confirmation that the original message was clear or a request for additional information. For example, when Francis met with his employees, their responses to his message included questions about the proposed change. If the sender does not receive feedback regarding the message, it is possible that the message will be misinterpreted. In the case of Wilson, she chose to communicate about the organizational changes through a memo, which left little opportunity for her employees to give her feedback about the message and resulted in their misunderstanding the message. Francis, however, made sure that he received feedback from his employees and was able to correct misconceptions, thereby reaching a common understanding with them.

THE ROLE OF PERCEPTION IN COMMUNICATION

The way that people perceive others or a situation can influence both the way they communicate information, and the way they interpret information from others. Perception is inherently subjective and influenced by people's personalities, values, attitudes, moods, experience, and knowledge. Whenever two people attempt to communicate with each other, their subjective perceptions influence how messages are sent, received, and interpreted. Shelley Wilson perceived that her employees would understand the message about the restructuring if she communicated it in a short memo; this inaccurate perception about her employees led them to interpret her message incorrectly as an announcement of another round of layoffs.

In addition, perceptual biases can hamper effective communication. Biases about individuals or stereotypes about groups of people may result in FLMs communicating less effectively with some individuals and groups or failing to communicate key information for fear of others' reactions. For example, suppose an FLM stereotypes older workers as being fearful of change. When communicating about an upcoming change in the organization to John, an older worker, an FLM downplays the change in order to keep John from "worrying excessively." John, however, has no more fear of change than his co-workers but because of what he has been told, interprets his FLM's message to mean there will be little change, and thus he does not prepare for change. As a result, his performance suffers when the change does happen because he has failed to prepare. Clearly, the ineffective communication was due to the FLM's inaccurate assumptions about older workers. Instead of relying on stereotypes, effective FLMs try to perceive other people accurately by focusing on their actual behaviors, knowledge, skills, and abilities. Accurate perceptions contribute to effective communication.

NONVERBAL COMMUNICATION

In addition to what we actually say when we communicate, much of what people interpret from our messages is the result of our "nonverbal" communication. Nonverbal communication shares information by means of facial expressions, body language, and even style of dress. Suppose, for example, Jane Dixson, an FLM, is talking to her team about working together more effectively. She schedules a meeting with the team in her office. At the meeting she says, "Helping you work together effectively is the most important thing I do. I am committed to helping you work through this." While she is verbally expressing their importance, Jane is fumbling through papers. She then stops to answer the phone. Further, her voice shows little enthusiasm and she looks out the window while she is speaking to the team. The team hears Jane's words, "the most important thing I do," but the message they receive is that they really aren't that important after all.

FLMs need to pay close attention to nonverbal behaviors when communicating. They need to recognize that how they communicate is as important as what they communicate. Nonverbal messages can undermine contrary messages. A message can be given meaning only in a context, and cues or signals are important. You should change your own communication style if you discover that it is interpreted negatively or incorrectly. Table 4.1 presents common nonverbal behaviors exhibited by FLMs and how employees may interpret them negatively.

FLMs also can benefit from watching the nonverbal communication of others who are receiving their messages. If, for example, an FLM is speaking and most of her employees are staring at her with their arms crossed, this may signal that they are frustrated or upset by the message. Thus, by reading others' nonverbal communication, you can often find out their feelings and attitudes toward the communication and toward you.

COMMUNICATION MEDIA

To be effective communicators, FLMs (and other members of an organization) need to select an appropriate communication medium for each message they send. Should a change in procedures be communicated to direct reports in a memo sent through e-mail? Should a congratulatory message about a major accomplishment be communicated in a letter, in a phone call, or over lunch? Should a layoff announcement be made in a memo or at a general meeting? FLMs deal with these questions day in and day out.

Most of an FLM's communication time is spent one-on-one, face-to-face with employees and other members of the organization. Face-to-face communication provides opportunities for immediate feedback from recipients and is the richest information medium because the recipient hears the message and sees all of the nonverbal cues that you are communicating. It is the appropriate medium for delegating tasks, coaching, disciplining, instructing, sharing information, answering questions, checking progress toward objectives, and developing and maintaining interpersonal relations.

While communication that occurs face-to-face can be misinterpreted because of nonverbal cues, other forms of communication such as telephone, e-mail, or letters also have limitations. Overall, you may receive less feedback from the recipient using these forms of communication, which may result in a breakdown of communication. For example, in a telephone conversation, you can hear the enthusiasm or frustration in

Table 4.1
Common Nonverbal Cues from Supervisor to Employee

Nonverbal Communication	Signal Received	Reaction from Receiver
Supervisor looks away when talking to the employee.	Divided attention.	My supervisor is too busy to listen to my problem or simply does not care.
Supervisor fails to acknowledge greeting from fellow employee.	Unfriendliness.	The person is unapproachable.
Supervisor glares ominously (i.e., gives the evil eye).	Anger.	Reciprocal anger, fear, or avoidance, depending on who is sending the signal in the organization.
Supervisor rolls the eyes.	Not taking person seriously.	This person thinks he or she is smarter or better than I am.
Supervisor sighs deeply.	Disgust or displeasure.	My opinions do not count. I must be stupid or boring this person.
Supervisor uses heavy breathing (sometimes accompanied by hand waving).	Anger or heavy stress.	Avoid this person at all costs.
Supervisor does not maintain eye contact when communicating.	Suspicion or uncertainty.	What does this person have to hide?
Supervisor crosses arms and leans away.	Apathy and closed-mindedness.	This person already has made up his or her mind; my opinions are not important.
Supervisor peers over glasses.	Skepticism or distrust.	Her or she does not believe what I am saying.
Supervisor continues to read a report when employee is speaking.	Lack of interest.	My opinions are not important enough to get the supervisor's undivided attention.

Source: Stewart (1994), 56.

someone's voice, but you cannot tell whether they are paying attention. Further, in written communication, receivers may overinterpret or over-emphasize some of the words or phrases used by the sender.

Thus, an FLM should think carefully about what form to use for important communications to ensure that the information is provided efficiently and effectively. For example, if a message has a great potential for being misunderstood or is ambiguous, then a face to face interaction providing opportunities for immediate feedback enables FLMs to exchange information and ideas rapidly until a common understanding is reached. On the other hand, when the message is clear, well defined, and everyone involved has a similar understanding of the background of the issue, then written memos are appropriate.

HOW TECHNOLOGY AFFECTS COMMUNICATION

Exciting advances in information technology have dramatically increased the speed of communication. FLMs can now more easily communicate with their teams and can more quickly access information to make decisions. Further, it is possible to send and receive information from many different locations. In order for FLMs to be successful in today's workplaces, they need to keep up-to-date on advances in information technology.

In order for FLMs to be successful, they also should understand the latest advances in technology such as groupware (computer software that enables members of groups to share information with each other), Intranets (company-wide systems of computer networks), and the Internet (a global system of computer networks). But FLMs should not adopt these or other advances without first considering carefully whether the advance will truly be useful for their situation.

UNDERSTANDING COMMUNICATION NETWORKS

Communication in organizations tends to flow in certain patterns. The pathways along which information flows throughout an organization are called communication networks. The type of communication network that exists in a group depends on the nature of the group's tasks and the extent to which group members need to communicate with each other in order to achieve group goals.

FORMAL AND INFORMAL COMMUNICATION
NETWORKS WITHIN ORGANIZATIONS

An organization chart may seem to be a good summary of an organization's communication network, but often it is not. An organization chart summarizes formal reporting relationships in an organization and the formal pathways along which communication takes place. Communication occurs across departments, groups, and teams along these formal pathways. Often, however, communication of information flows around issues, goals, projects, and ideas instead of moving up and down the organizational hierarchy in an orderly fashion. An organization's communication network, therefore, includes not only the formal communication pathways summarized in an organizational chart, but also informal communication pathways along which a great deal of communication takes place.

THE GRAPEVINE

One informal organizational communication network along which information flows quickly, if not always accurately, is the grapevine. Every organization has its grapevine, and an amazing amount of information may be transmitted through the grapevine. Employees often know about major decisions such as changes in organizational structure or incentive packages before FLMs have been officially notified.

Unfortunately, information passed through the grapevine often gets exaggerated as it travels from employee to employee. This is particularly true when FLMs or organizations fail to distribute information openly. Given the absence of open and honest information from management, employees try to fill the vacuum by providing bits of information to each other, which may be based on speculation rather than facts, thus starting rumors.

The best prescription for dealing with a rumor is to expose its untruthfulness and to state the facts openly and honestly. If FLMs do not have all the necessary information available, they should frankly admit it and then try to gather the facts by consulting a higher-level manager, asking what information may be told, and when, and then reporting to employees. Otherwise, employees will make up their own, often incorrect, explanations. Further, if your employees trust you, they will be willing to let you know what they hear on the grapevine, thus giving you the opportunity to dispel rumors and provide accurate information. You can also use the grapevine as a way of taking the pulse of your organization. It can help you learn about the basic attitudes and thoughts of employees and whether they regard the company in a positive or negative light. This may help you better understand and address motivational issues of your work group.

BUILDING COMMUNICATION SKILLS

This section will discuss various kinds of barriers to effective communication in organizations and what FLMs can do to overcome them.

Some of these barriers have their origin in actions of senders and receivers. Others are based on differences in personal communication styles. FLMs can build their own communication skills to overcome these barriers. First we shall discuss FLMs as senders and receivers.

FLMs AS SENDERS

Organizational effectiveness depends on FLMs being able to send messages to people both inside and outside the organization. There are certain communication skills that help ensure that messages sent by FLMs are properly understood. Let's see what each skill entails.

Send clear and complete messages. FLMs need to learn how to send messages that are clear and complete. A message is clear when it is easy for the receiver to understand and interpret, and it is complete when it contains all the information that the sender and receiver need to reach a common understanding. In striving to send messages that are both clear and complete, FLMs must learn to anticipate how receivers will interpret messages and to adjust messages to eliminate sources of misunderstanding or confusion. Recall from the earlier scenario that Shelley Wilson's message to her direct reports about an upcoming restructuring was unclear, incomplete, and misinterpreted. Wilson did not anticipate that her employees would interpret the message as a warning of further layoffs, and therefore she did not adjust the message to eliminate this source of misunderstanding.

Encode messages in symbols the receiver understands. FLMs need to appreciate that when they encode messages, they should use symbols or language that the receiver understands. If, for example, the recipient does not speak English as a native language, the FLM should use simple terms and avoid using high level vocabulary. Further, when speaking with outside groups or individuals, the FLM should avoid jargon (e.g., technical or slang terms that only those in the workgroup understand) that will not be understood by others.

Select a medium appropriate for the message. As you have learned, FLMs can choose from a variety of communication media, including face-to-face discussions, letters, memos, newsletters, phone conversations, e-mail, voice mail, faxes, and video conferences. A primary concern in choosing an appropriate medium is the nature of the message. Jackson Francis' superior communication skills led him to exactly this conclusion in the opening scenario; Wilson probably never considered this option.

Select a medium that the receiver monitors or is able to understand. Another factor that FLMs need to take into account when selecting a communication medium is whether the medium is one that the receiver monitors. People differ in the amount of attention they pay to different communication media. FLMs should learn which employees like things in writing and which prefer face-to-face interactions and should then choose the most appropriate media for them.

Avoid filtering and information distortion. Filtering occurs when the sender withholds part of a message because he or she mistakenly thinks that the receiver does not need the information or will not want to receive it. In the earlier scenario, Wilson filtered the information she gave her employees. She told them nothing about the nature of the change or its implications for their job security. As a result of her mistake, they misinterpreted her message.

Information distortion occurs when the meaning of a message changes as the message passes through a series of senders and receivers. Some information distortion is accidental—due to faulty encoding and decoding or to lack of feedback. Other information distortion is deliberate. Senders may alter a message to make themselves or their groups look good and to receive special treatment.

FLMs themselves should avoid filtering and distorting information. They should also create an atmosphere of trust to minimize incentives to distort messages. Employees who trust their FLMs believe that they will not be blamed for things beyond their control and will be treated fairly. FLMs who trust their employees provide them with clear and complete information and do not hold things back.

Build a feedback mechanism into messages. Feedback is essential for effective communication. FLMs should build a feedback mechanism into the messages they send—either including a request for feedback or indicating when and how they will follow up on a message to make sure that it was understood. When FLMs send written messages, they can request that the receiver respond in a letter, memo, or fax; can schedule a meeting to discuss the issue; or can follow up with a phone call. By building feedback mechanisms such as these into their messages, FLMs ensure that they are heard and understood.

FLMs AS RECEIVERS

FLMs receive as many messages as they send. Thus, FLMs must possess or develop communication skills that allow them to be effective message receivers. In particular, they must pay attention, be good listeners, and be empathetic. These skills are examined in greater detail below.

Pay attention. Because of their multiple roles and tasks, FLMs often are overloaded and forced to think about several things at once. Torn in many different directions, they sometimes do not pay sufficient attention to the messages they receive. To be effective, however, FLMs should pay attention to all messages, regardless of their workload.

Listen and be empathic. Like most people, FLMs often like to hear themselves talk. Part of being a good communicator, however, is being a good listener. To listen effectively, FLMs should avoid interrupting and maintain eye contact when others are speaking. Once the sender is finished, the FLM should ask questions if necessary or summarize important points so that it is clear that the message is understood. Finally, FLMs should be empathetic and try to interpret a message from the sender's point of view, rather than from only their own point of view. This should increase the likelihood that they will interpret the message in the way it was intended. By displaying empathy, FLMs establish the groundwork for creating an atmosphere of trust and understanding which is important to effective communication.

COMMUNICATION STYLES

As you know from experience, different people tend to communicate differently, and their diverse approaches to saying the same thing may have different effects on their audiences. Some people tend to give more information than you need while others are vague. Further, some are loud and forceful in their communications while others are quiet and reflective. A successful FLM must understand all of these differences and how they can create barriers to effective communication.

PERSONAL COMMUNICATION STYLES

Kevin and Steven are two FLMs in the same company. Their employee, Frank, approaches them to discuss the possibility of receiving a salary increase. They both have supervised Frank during the past year and do not believe he deserves a raise. Kevin and Steven each go about communicating their feelings to Frank quite differently, however. Steven couldn't have been more direct. "I'll be blunt," he said, "a raise is out of the question." Kevin's approach was far more analytical: "Well, Frank, let's look at the big picture. I see here in your file that we just gave you a raise two months ago, and that you're not scheduled for another salary review for four months. Let me share with you some of the numbers and thoroughly explain why the company will have to stick with that schedule."

Although the message was the same in both cases, Kevin and Steven presented it quite differently. In other words, they differ with respect to their personal communication styles. FLMs will tend to prefer a specific style of communicating with all of their employees. Some may say whatever comes to mind and cut right to the bottom line. Others, may want to carefully discuss every issue before making a decision. Still others may focus on interpersonal relationships when communicating. Thus, it is important for FLMs to recognize their own personal style and to attempt to adapt this style to individual employees.

GROUP-BASED COMMUNICATION DIFFERENCES

Differences in backgrounds or cultures may also increase the likelihood that communication difficulties will occur in a group. Consider the following scenarios: An FLM from New Jersey is having a conversation with an FLM from Iowa. The Iowan FLM never seems to get a chance to talk. He keeps waiting for a pause to signal his turn to talk, but the New Jersey FLM never pauses long enough. The New Jersey FLM wonders why the Iowan FLM does not say much. He feels uncomfortable when he pauses and the Iowan FLM says nothing, so he starts talking again.

Karen compliments John on his presentation to upper management and asks John what he thought of her presentation. John launches into a lengthy critique of Karen's presentation and describes how he would have handled it differently. This is hardly the response Karen expected.

Sarah thinks of a new way to cut costs, which she shares with fellow members of her self-managed work team. Malik, another team member, thinks her idea is a good one and encourages the rest of the team to support it. Sarah is quietly pleased by Malik's support. The group then implements "Malik's" suggestion, and it is written up as such in the company newsletter, giving no credit to Sarah.

Each of the individuals in these scenarios has a comfortable, or characteristic way of speaking, called a "linguistic style," that is making communication difficult between them. The scenarios are based on the work of linguist Deborah Tannen (1990), who describes linguistic style as a person's characteristic way of speaking, which includes tone of voice, speed, volume, use of pauses, directness or indirectness, choice of words, credit-taking, and use of questions, jokes, and other types of speech. These linguistic style differences may occur because of cultural or regional differences between people. When people's linguistic styles differ and these differences are not taken into account and understood, ineffective communication is likely to occur.

REGIONAL DIFFERENCES

The first scenario illustrates regional differences in linguistic style. The Iowan FLM expects the pauses that signal turn-taking in conversations to be longer than the pauses made by his colleague in New Jersey. This difference causes communication problems. The Iowan thinks that his Eastern colleague never lets him get a word in edgewise, and the Easterner cannot figure out why his colleague from the Midwest does not get more actively involved in conversations.

CROSS-CULTURAL DIFFERENCES

It is important to recognize that communication is conducted in different ways around the world. For example, compare countries like the United States that place a high value on individualism with countries like Japan that emphasize collectivism. American FLMs rely heavily on memoranda, announcements, position papers, and other formal forms of communication to stake out their positions in an organization. Japanese FLMs, in contrast to American FLMs, will engage in extensive verbal consultation over an issue before making an announcement.

Today's FLMs must make themselves familiar with cross-cultural communication differences. Before FLMs and managers communicate with people from abroad, they should try to find out as much as they can about cultural differences and the aspects of communication styles that are specific to the country or culture in question.

GENDER-BASED DIFFERENCES

Referring back to the three scenarios that open this section, you may be wondering why John launched into a lengthy critique of Karen's presentation after she paid him a routine compliment, or why Malik got the credit for Sarah's idea in the self-managed work team. Research conducted by Tannen and other linguists has found that the linguistic styles of men and women differ in practically every culture or language. These differences which are described in this section are demonstrated for men and women in general, and are not indicative of all women or all men.

In the United States, many women tend to downplay differences between people, are not overly concerned about receiving credit for their own accomplishments, and want to make everyone feel that they are more or less on an equal footing, so that even poor performers or low-status individuals feel valued. Many men, in contrast, tend to emphasize their own superiority, take credit for accomplishments whenever possible, and are not reluctant to acknowledge differences in status. These differences in linguistic style led Karen to give John a routine compliment on his presentation even though she thought that he had not done a particularly good job. She asked him how her presentation was so that he could reciprocate, complimenting her and thereby putting them on an equal footing. John took Karen's compliment and question about her own presentation as an opportunity to confirm his superiority, never realizing that she was only expecting a routine compliment. Similarly, Malik's enthusiastic support for Sarah's cost-cutting idea and her apparent surrender of ownership of the idea after she described it led team members to assume incorrectly that the idea was Malik's.

MANAGING DIFFERENCES IN COMMUNICATION AND LINGUISTIC STYLES

FLMs should not expect to change people's communication or linguistic styles, nor should they try. Simply understand them. For example, FLMs should ensure that women have a chance to talk if they know that they are reluctant to speak up in meetings, not because they have nothing to contribute, but because of their linguistic style. FLMs should be extra careful to give credit where it is deserved.

DEVELOPING YOUR WRITING AND SPEAKING SKILLS

While understanding differences in communication styles is critical to success as an FLM, it is also important for FLMs to hone the fundamental skills of writing and speaking. The remainder of this chapter discusses the importance of writing and speaking and offers suggestions and guidelines for developing and using these two important skills.

THE WRITING PROCESS

FLMs can use written communication for various types of messages, including memos, letters, regulations, policies, newsworthy information, and announcements of changes in procedures or personnel. Written instructions can explain how to use equipment or how to process work orders or customer requests in a permanent form. Because the ability to communicate effectively plays an important part in an FLM's success on the job, more and more employers look for prospective FLMs who have skills in written communication.

WHAT IS GOOD WRITING?

Effective writing includes the appropriate content for the readers. It is concise, clear, coherent, well-organized, and free from errors. The information you provide should be accurate and relevant. Further, you should attempt to be concise—write as simply as possible using words and phrases familiar to the reader.

Effective writing is a process. The steps of the process include identifying your purpose and audience, gathering information, generating and organizing ideas, drafting, revising and proofreading. The remainder of this section shows you how to apply this process to ensure you communicate with others effectively.

GETTING STARTED: IDENTIFYING YOUR PURPOSE

The first stage in the writing process is to analyze the purpose of your document, or what you want to accomplish. The purpose of most FLMs' writing falls generally into one or more of the three categories: to give information about something, to propose a course of action, or to solve a problem. A report on injuries, for example, could have numerous purposes. Should the report simply compare and contrast injury information? Should it recommend a particular response to the injury information in a given situation? The purpose should determine what to include in the document.

ANALYZING YOUR READERS

Another important consideration in planning a writing project is the audience. A memo on a highly technical topic would be written one way for someone with technical expertise, but another way for a customer or individual with only limited knowledge of your particular job or procedures and terminology.

GETTING YOUR IDEAS TOGETHER

Once you have evaluated the purpose of the writing and the needs of the readers, you are ready for the next stage in the writing process: gathering information and organizing the ideas you want to present. This step may be easy. For a short letter, you may not need to do research, and you may have only a short list of topics to organize.

For much of the writing an FLM does, however, gathering information and organizing it may be a more complicated process. It may involve a great deal of thought, and perhaps some research as well. Let's look at some techniques you can use.

Gathering information. Before you begin to write the document, be sure you have all the information you need and that your information is accurate. You may want to check existing files or books on a topic, or interview people who are up-to-date on the issues.

Generating ideas. Once you have gathered the information you need, you're ready to decide exactly what to say. Try to break up the purpose into several subtopics. Suppose the purpose of your letter is to recommend to the building owner the value of a new computerized-maintenance management system (CMMS) to increase budgeting and preventive maintenance efforts by your unit. The statement of purpose for this letter could specify the different types of systems available and the major advantages and disadvantages of each.

Arranging ideas/Organization. Once you've decided what you want to say, it's important to consider how best to arrange your ideas so that the reader will find them easy to follow. You could arrange ideas in logical order or in a list according to their importance, beginning with the ideas that are most important to the reader. Before writing, you may want to begin with an outline of the document. Ultimately, most documents will include:

1. *Introduction*. Identifies the subject of the document and tells why it was written.
2. *Concise statement of the main ideas*. Summarizes main ideas, conclusions, or recommendations. This part of a document may be part of the statement of purpose or as long as a three-page executive summary.
3. *Development of the main ideas*. Includes further description of the main ideas, using explanations, examples, analyses, steps, reasons, and factual details. This part is often called the body of the document.
4. *Conclusion*. Brings the document to an effective close. The conclusion may restate the main idea in a fresh way, suggest further work, or summarize recommendations, but an effective conclusion avoids unnecessary repetition.

WRITING THE DOCUMENT

The next steps in writing involve drafting, revising, and finalizing the document. Using your outline, you will begin by filling in each section. Don't worry at this point about spelling and punctuation, or finding just the right word. Focus on getting your ideas out.

Second, you will revise the draft, polishing your style and ensuring your ideas are effectively and completely presented. At this point, read the document from the recipient's point of view, ensuring you have included all key information. Finally, after you have polished the style and organization of the document, you will be ready to put it in its final form. Consider questions of document design, such as the use of headings, white space, and other elements of the document's appearance. After the entire document is written, be sure to carefully proofread it for errors, preferably after you have been away from the document for a while.

This summary of tips for improving your writing skills can serve as an easy reference for you in writing documents in the future:

1. Analyze the purpose of the writing and the needs and expectations of the readers.
2. Organize your ideas so that readers will find them easy to follow.
3. Write the draft and then revise it to make the writing polished and correct.

4. Make the writing unified. All sentences should relate to the main idea, either directly or indirectly. Eliminate digressions and irrelevant detail.

5. Use summary sentences and transitions to make your writing coherent.

6. Write in short paragraphs that begin with clear topic sentences.

7. Be concise—make every word count.

8. Keep it simple—use simple vocabulary and short sentences.

9. Use jargon only when your readers understand it. Define technical terms when necessary.

10. Be precise—avoid ambiguous and unclear writing.

11. Proofread for grammar, punctuation, spelling, and typographical errors.

The next section presents techniques for giving, preparing, and evaluating speeches and highlights the importance of oral communication skills.

FLMS AS GOOD PUBLIC SPEAKERS

Effective oral presentation skills are also important to management success. FLMs who can impress others with their speech-making abilities are admired, and they frequently become the leaders in their organizations as well as in their communities. Today's FLM can become a successful public speaker by mastering the principles for preparing and making a speech or presentation.

PREPARING A SPEECH

In this section we shall discuss specific steps for preparing an effective oral presentation. These steps include knowing your audience, determining your purpose, choosing and limiting your topic, collecting and organizing information, preparing an outline, and finally, planning your speech.

Know your audience. If you understand your audience, you will be able to prepare a speech that will be of interest and benefit to them. For example, when making a formal speech to your superiors, you should make sure to address their concerns and interests, such as budgeting issues or personnel planning.

Determine your purpose. Ask yourself, why was I asked to give this speech? Is this talk for a special occasion, such as an annual management budget presentation? Should the speech be entertaining, persuasive, or informative? Your answers to these questions will help you identify your purpose and select appropriate materials.

Choose and limit your topic. If you have not already been assigned a topic, you must choose your topic carefully. You need to meet the needs and interests of the audience, fulfill the purpose of your talk, and be able to present the topic in the time allotted. You should be careful to limit your subject so that you don't lose the attention of the audience.

Collect your information. In order to prepare for your speech, talk to well-informed people and read reliable and up-to-date books and magazines on your topic. You also should recall personal experiences related to the topic to be able to personalize your presentation. Take accurate notes, distinguishing between facts and opinions.

Prepare a detailed outline and organize your information. Using the preliminary outline and the information collected, you should prepare a detailed outline from which to develop your speech. The main points in your preliminary outline should guide you in organizing your information. Considering your audience and the purpose of your talk, select the most important points to include in your final outline. You may discover that some topics need to be rearranged, or irrelevant topics need to be omitted. Your organization of information may reveal the need for audio and visual aids or other materials to help make your speech more interesting and understandable. These could include overhead transparencies, slides, hangouts, pictures, posters, and charts to help make your speech more interesting and understandable.

Write your speech. Use the outline as the basis for logically presenting your ideas.

Introduction. Introductory remarks should arouse audience interest in the speaker and the subject. Establish rapport with the audience by making comments that are appropriate for the occasion and that orient the audience to your speech. There are several possible approaches to introducing your speech. You might state the subject and purpose of the talk, tell a humorous story or anecdote, make an unusual or startling statement, quote from familiar or strongly worded material, use an illustration, or ask a question.

Body. One way to make a logical transition from the introduction to the discussion is to state the main points. In the body of the speech, you can review them again, supporting them with adequate explanations and illustrations, using transitions to move from point to point. Techniques for explaining and illustrating include:

1. citing examples
2. quoting recognized authorities
3. making comparisons
4. using descriptive language
5. relating a story
6. giving pertinent facts and figures
7. using audio and visual aids

Conclusion. Every presentation needs a conclusion. Give as much thought to concluding your presentation as you do to introducing it. Keep your conclusions brief by summarizing the main ideas, without being redundant. You might use any of these suggestions that seem appropriate:

1. Tell a story that emphasizes the purpose of the presentation or speech.
2. Request that a specific action be taken.
3. Stress the importance and timeliness of your subject.
4. Make a logical deduction from the information presented.
5. Ask the audience to adopt certain attitudes and beliefs.

Practice your speech. Rehearsing your speech a number of times in a room similar to the one in which you will give it should help you to speak spontaneously and within the time limit. You may want to tape yourself or ask someone to watch you and provide feedback.

GIVING YOUR PRESENTATION OR SPEECH

A well-written speech may fall flat if the delivery is poor. You can probably site many examples of times when you have had to sit through an excruciatingly boring speech. Perhaps the person spoke in monotone or rambled on for far too long. To avoid these pitfalls, consider the following suggestions:

Develop your own style. Don't try to imitate someone else. Being yourself will project who and what you are in the most effective way possible.

Maintain self-confidence. Your audience will be at ease and more receptive if you are confident and poised. Some nervousness is normal and good for you because it keeps you alert and sparks your delivery. Arrive a few minutes early to talk with the people who will introduce you, arrange the room and equipment, make sure the microphone is working, and give yourself an opportunity to relax.

Make a favorable first impression. Good grooming and proper dress cannot be overemphasized. The audience's first impression is based on your appearance, and a good appearance should improve self-confidence. An energetic talk, good posture, and pleasant facial expressions should cause your audience to respond favorably.

Avoid objectionable mannerisms. Some mannerisms or verbal expressions may distract the audience from concentrating on your speech. You should avoid mannerisms like twisting your hair, tapping your fingers on the podium, clicking a ball point pen, or shifting from one foot to the other. Avoid verbal expressions such as "ah," "anda," "you know," and

Table 4.2
Gesture Do's and Don'ts

Do's	Don'ts
• Use gestures to embrace the audience.	• Overuse gestures.
• Gesture naturally.	• Keep hands out of pockets.
• Relax hands by your side when not gesturing.	• Grasp/touch podium or lectern.
• Use both arms/hands.	• Lock hands/arms in front/back of you.
• Free your arms to gesture emphatically.	• Gesture with one hand/arm only.
• Keep your feet still to promote gestures.	• Avoid rhythmic gestures (looking mechanical).
• Observe yourself gesturing.	• Point excessively.

"like." Practicing your speech and asking others to watch you will help you identify and eliminate these distracting mannerisms or expressions.

Use appropriate gestures. Enhance your speech by using gestures that are natural and well timed. Gestures are important because they emphasize your main points, help your audience visualize your ideas, keep the audience interested in your comments, help relieve your nervousness, and help you to use nonverbal communication effectively as you speak. A list of gesture do's and don'ts is provided in Table 4.2.

Speak clearly. Project your voice by keeping your chin up so that each person in the audience can readily understand you. Proper enunciation is critical, especially if you are to be understood by a diverse audience.

Vary your speaking rate and pitch. Vary the pitch of your voice and rate of speaking, incorporating well-timed pauses so the audience will not be lulled to sleep.

Speak correctly. Speakers who use incorrect grammar may lose the respect of the audience. Many speakers are ineffective simply because of shoddy grammar or inappropriate slang.

Involve the audience. Maintaining good eye contact and reacting to body language helps you adapt your delivery for optimum audience involvement. Personal eye contact with individuals in all sections of the room gives your audience the feeling that you recognize them as individuals. If individuals look alert, are smiling, and are nodding their heads in approval, you can assume your talk interests them. If listeners are becoming restless or sleepy, however, you will realize that your talk is receiving a negative reaction and can try to alter your style.

SUMMARY

Good communication is necessary for an FLM and an organization to be successful. To be successful communicators, FLMs must understand that communication occurs in a cyclical process that entails two phases: transmission and feedback.

Communication by FLMs and organizations is impacted by information richness (i.e., the amount of information a communication medium can carry and the extent to which the medium enables the sender and receiver to reach a common understanding), and advances in technology, like the Internet, intranets, and groupware software continue to allow FLMs and their organizations to improve communication, performance, and customer service.

There are various barriers to effective communication in organizations. To overcome these barriers and effectively communicate with others, FLMs must possess or develop communication skills as senders and receivers of messages. For example, FLMs should send messages that are clear and complete, use words that the receiver understands, choose a medium appropriate for the message and monitored by the receiver, avoid filtering and information distortion, include a feedback mechanism in the message, provide accurate information to ensure that misleading rumors are not spread, pay attention, be a good listener, and be empathic. Understanding linguistic styles is also an essential communication skill for supervisors.

Finally, without good written and oral communication skills, supervisors cannot expect to build successful personal and business relationships. To do this, they should understand the writing process from beginning to end and the techniques for preparing, giving, and evaluating a speech.

REFERENCES

Stewart, T. A. 1994. Managing in a wired company. *Fortune* (July 11), 56.
Tannen, D. 1990. *You just don't understand: Women and men in conversation.* New York: Ballantine Books.

Chapter 5

Leading and Building Effective Teams

INTRODUCTION

It is almost assumed that today's progressive organization must employ teams in some capacity to achieve its objectives. The drive to use teams has come from many organizational pressures such as increased competition, downsizing, and the trend toward a flatter, more flexible organization. Much of the work that involves front-line managers (FLMs) in today's organizations takes place in groups or teams. As an FLM, a manager may serve as a team member on some teams and as a team leader or supervisor of other groups. As a part of these teams, the FLM must see that groups of employees work together to accomplish objectives.

This chapter addresses ways in which the FLM can work effectively as a leader and member of a team or other group. The structure and types of teams are presented followed by the benefits and challenges of working in a team.

Janet Franklin, production FLM at a company in the Southwest, has experience working with teams. "Teams have worked well in our company. We made the transition to teams about a year ago. I moved from supervisor to team leader. I once spent all of my time telling people what to do. Since we've gone to the team approach, occasionally they will come to me with this or that problem, and I will go out and see if I can help them, and they will go from there. On a normal day, I lay out the schedule for them, post it on the board, and they come and look at it, and that pretty much takes care of it. It's getting now so most of them can handle most maintenance problems, unless there is a major crisis with some equipment breaking down or whatever; then they want to let me know about it. I know that before we had teams—when I was just their boss instead of their team leader—people would be afraid to tell me anything because they were afraid somebody was going to get fired. Now we just sit down and discuss it, and everything comes out in the open, and they know nobody's going to get in trouble. I think a team strategy has been really positive for my organization. Even though the transition process was somewhat difficult in the beginning, I'm glad we made the change. The employees seem happier also."

WHAT IS A TEAM?

To guide the use of teams effectively, FLMs must understand what characteristics define a team. A team is a small number of people with complementary skills who are committed to a common purpose, set of performance goals, and an approach for which they hold themselves mutually accountable. Shared accountability and commitment to a common goal make the use of teams particularly appropriate when the co-ordination of the activities or skills of individuals is necessary. Tasks that do not require coordination are better left to individual contributors.

TYPES OF TEAMS

Once an FLM has determined that a team approach is conducive to the organization in question, the FLM must determine how to use teams. There are many types of teams that can be useful in a variety of organizational settings. An FLM must determine which team type most closely matches their organization's needs. There are a variety of choices, because teams can be structured differently and be used to meet different needs.

Problem-Solving Teams

If we look back 20 years or so, teams were just beginning to grow in popularity. At that time teams were typically composed of five to twelve hourly employees from the same department who met for a few hours each week to discuss ways of improving quality, efficiency, and the work environment. We call these problem-solving teams. In problem-solving teams, members share ideas or offer suggestions on how to improve work procedures and methods. These teams are rarely given the authority to unilaterally implement any of their suggested actions. One of the most popular applications of this type of team was quality circles, widely used in the 1980s.

Self-Managed Teams

While problem-solving teams were on the right track, they did not involve employees in work-related decisions and processes. A desire for greater employee participation led to experimentation with truly autonomous teams that could not only solve problems, but also implement solutions and take full responsibility for outcomes. These employee groups are self-managed teams and are also commonly referred to as self-directed work teams, autonomous work groups, high-commitment teams, or empowered employees.

Movement toward self-managed teams represented a complete change in organizational structure. The traditional hierarchy of managers, FLMs, and operating employees was replaced by these teams, which are entirely responsible for their own operations. The real change is that the first level of management has been eliminated and replaced by self-managing teams. The team members become individually and jointly accountable for performance and results. To build this accountability, team membership is a full-time, mandatory part of the job.

In this "FLM-free," more personally rewarding environment, employees are exposed to all of the team's operations and skills. This exposure forces employees to learn the work procedures in order to find more productive ways to work. While the benefits of using self-managed teams is evident, today's FLMs should realize that using self-managed teams does not eliminate the need for all managerial control. Instead self-managed teams should represent a balance between management and group control.

As in any team-based environment, simply imposing a team structure doesn't ensure an effective process. First, management must help employees develop the skills they will need to work together as a team. Implementation of teamwork training is perhaps the most important thing FLMs and organizations can do to increase the likelihood of success of self-managed teams. Additionally, FLMs and organizations would be wise to debunk some of the myths FLMs and other managers hold about self-managed teams and how they work. The following presents some common misconceptions and corresponding truths about self-managed teams:

- *"Self-managed teams do not need leaders."* Teams definitely need some type of leader to transfer traditional leadership responsibilities to team members. The role of the leader varies from team to team (e.g., coach, facilitator), but leaders are necessary in every team.

- *"Leaders lose power in the transition to teams."* In fact, leaders retain power but use it differently. Instead of exercising power within the group to control people, team leaders use their power to break down organizational barriers that can prevent team effectiveness.

- *"Newly formed teams are automatically self-managing."* Team development takes time. Describing new teams as self-managed may establish unrealistic expectations.

- *"Employees are eager to be empowered."* Although this may be true for many employees, it is not true for all. Some consultants estimate that 25 percent to 30 percent of working Americans—regardless of their position in the organization—don't want to be empowered. Team work must be learned, but also accepted.

- *"If you group employees in a team structure, they will function as a team, and the organization will reap the benefits of teamwork."* Unfortunately, it doesn't always work that way. Groups must go through a developmental process before they can function successfully in teams. (Adapted from Caudron, 1993)

Cross-Functional Teams

A team concept that has recently become popular is the cross-functional team. This is a team made up of employees from about the same hierarchical level, but from different work areas, who come together to accomplish a task. Cross-functional teams are an effective means for allowing people from different areas within an organization, or between organizations, to exchange information, develop new ideas, solve problems, and coordinate complex projects. An example of a commonly used cross-functional team is the task force. There are particular difficulties managing cross-functional teams. Later in this chapter, we shall discuss ways FLMs can help facilitate this type of team building.

Virtual Teams

With continuing developments in information technology, a new type of group has entered the workplace. This is the virtual team, whose members work together electronically via networked computers. In this new age of the Internet, intranets, and the World Wide Web, there is no doubt that more and more virtual teams will operate in all types of organizations.

Members of virtual teams typically do the same things as members of face-to-face teams, but the team members communicate in a different environment. They share information, make decisions, and complete tasks. Virtual teams are an everyday phenomenon at Texas Instruments where physical distance does not stop people from working together. On any given day you can find computer designers from all over the world working together—linked by computers—to pool ideas and create new products. Talented engineers in Bangalore, India, may work with other group members in Japan and Texas to develop a new chip. When the design is finished, it is sent via computer to Texas for fabrication and then goes back to Bangalore for any required "debugging." In describing the advantages of the team, a group vice president said, "Problems that used to take three years to solve now take a year."

Although using technology to make communication possible among a group of people separated by great distances has the advantage of focusing group interactions and decision making on facts and objective information rather than on emotional considerations, the absence of direct contact can also be a disadvantage to decision makers. The lack of rapport and social interaction among members of virtual teams may actually make it more challenging to work on these teams, possibly because it is more difficult to understand other team members' perspectives and biases. The high cost of supporting technology and training to bring virtual teams on-line can also be a drawback.

Response Teams

Some organizations have developed teams organized solely for the purpose of responding to specific situations in the organization. Emergency-response teams are designed to respond to emergency situations. These response teams often require mandatory participation by all employees in such efforts as incipient fire fighting, spill response, and bomb threat searches. Some organizations use a type of emergency-response team to address maintenance problems that may occur in the evenings and on weekends when the regular maintenance crew is not on duty. The members of these teams have the same responsibilities, backgrounds, and experience as regular team members although they primarily handle maintenance issues that occur outside regular hours.

In an effort to reduce workplace violence, some organizations have formed violence-response teams. These teams, composed of both hourly and managerial employees, conduct initial risk assessment surveys, develop action plans to respond to violent situations, and perform crisis intervention during violent or potentially violent encounters. There is every indication that more and more organizations will develop violence-response teams given the rise in violence at work. The Occupational Safety and Health Administration (OSHA) has developed voluntary guidelines that some organizations are following to prevent and deal with workforce violence. (See Chapter 10 for a more detailed discussion of these guidelines.)

It is evident that there are a variety of teams in place in organizations. Today's FLMs must understand the purposes of these teams and do what is necessary to develop successful teams in their particular work areas.

THE BENEFITS OF USING TEAMS

Twenty-five years ago, when companies like General Foods, Volvo, and Toyota introduced teams into their production processes, they made news because no one else was doing it. Today, it is just the opposite. Pick up almost any business magazine, and you will read that teams have become an essential part of the way business is being done in organizations like General Electric, AT&T, Motorola, Federal Express, Johnson & Johnson, and others. Even the world famous San Diego Zoo has restructured its native habitat zones around cross-departmental teams.

How do we explain the current popularity of teams? The evidence suggests that teams typically outperform individuals when the tasks require multiple skills, complex judgments, and a range of experience. As organizations have restructured themselves to compete more effectively and efficiently, they have turned to teams as a better way to utilize employee talents. Teams are more flexible and responsive to changing events than are traditional departments. Teams can be quickly assembled, deployed, refocused, or disbanded.

In addition, the use of teams can indirectly help with worker motivation and skill development. The team experience can be motivating to members in that participation can promote employee involvement in operating decisions. For instance, some assembly line workers at John Deere are part of sales teams that call on customers. These workers know the products better than any traditional salesperson, and by traveling and speaking with farmers, they develop marketing skills and a greater connection to the company.

Teams are just like any other tool, however. They can be very powerful if used correctly, and they can be useless or even detrimental if used inappropriately. There is no doubt that teams have the potential to improve performance dramatically. The success of team proponents such as Ford and General Electric cannot be disputed. Yet teams alone are not enough. Strong supervision and organizational vision, mission, and goals must guide the use of teams.

WHY SOME TEAMS FAIL

FLMs and organizations should understand that while advocates of the team approach to management paint a very optimistic picture, there is still a dark side to teams. While exact statistics are not available, teams can and often do fail.

If teams are to be effective, FLMs and other managers must make a concerted effort to avoid common management mistakes. Likewise, team members must be aware, be prepared for, and able to recognize common pitfalls as well. After all, working on a team is demanding. Not everyone may be ready to be a team member. Analysis of failed attempts at introducing teams into the workplace identify several obstacles to team success. These pitfalls, described below, can be avoided with a little work.

COMMON MANAGEMENT MISTAKES WITH TEAMS

When management is to blame for the failure of a team, it is usually because the leaders failed to create a supportive environment. For instance, reward plans that encourage individuals to compete with one another erode teamwork. Teams need a good, long-term organization life support system. Teams also cannot be used as a quick fix to any organizational problem—they require a sustained commitment over time. Some FLMs are unwilling to relinquish control to the team. In the past, good FLMs worked their way up from the plant floor by giving orders and having them followed, and they may find it difficult to change that approach.

One FLM, Todd Burton, has experienced the difficulty of implementing teams in the workplace. "We had a real struggle in the beginning of the transition to teams. The organization just wasn't set up for the team environment. We were still giving people bonuses based on the number of contacts they personally made. This certainly didn't encourage employees to give up their time to work with others on a team. Once we recognized the problem, some of us managing the teams approached upper management suggesting a system to reward the teams. They went along with it, and I think it has been very successful. Once the team members understood that management was in this for the duration and the team wasn't just a trial solution, they were more comfortable with this method of operation."

COMMON PROBLEMS FOR TEAM MEMBERS

FLMs must recognize that team members frequently experience common problems. Contrary to those who contend that teams fail because employees lack the motivation and creativity for real teamwork, teams frequently don't succeed because they take on too much too quickly and drive themselves too hard for fast results. Nurturing important group dynamics and developing strong team skills can get lost in the rush toward the goal.

Failure is part of the learning process with teams, as it is elsewhere in life. Comprehensive training in interpersonal skills can prevent many common teamwork problems as well, which may arise from conflicts in personalities, work styles, and approaches to communication. Teams fail when their members are unwilling to cooperate with each other and with other teams. In expectation that setbacks and small failures may occur, teams need to be counseled against quitting when they run into an un-anticipated obstacle.

As we have seen, merely requiring several people to work together does not necessarily make them into a team, much less a high-performing one. This section outlines symptoms of low-performing teams that indicate intervention may be necessary to keep them from failing. It also notes the common characteristics of high-performing teams.

SYMPTOMS OF LOW-PERFORMING TEAMS

Obviously, many problems can lead to low-performing teams. The absence of the basic conditions for a cohesive team—trust, complementary goals, and a clear mission—usually will result in low productivity. Various symptoms, outlined below, should help you to recognize low-performing teams:

- *Cautious or guarded communication.* Low performing teams may have members who ridicule or respond negatively to other team members. They may also say nothing or act guarded in what they do say.
- *Lack of disagreement.* Lack of disagreement among team members may reflect poor team interaction, indicating that members are unwilling to share their true feelings and ideas.
- *Use of personal criticism.* Personal criticism such as, "If you can't come up with a better idea than that, you better keep quiet," is a sign of unhealthy team member relations.
- *Ineffective meetings.* Low-performing teams often have ineffective meetings characterized by boredom, unenthusiastic participation, failure to reach decisions, and dominance by one or two people.
- *Unclear goals.* Low-performing teams often do not have a clear sense of the team mission or objectives.
- *Low commitment.* Without a clear sense of purpose, low-performing teams tend to have low commitment.
- *Destructive conflict within the team.* Low-performing teams are often characterized by a suspicious, combative environment and by conflict among team members.

CHARACTERISTICS OF HIGH-PERFORMING TEAMS

Remember, a team is a small number of people with complementary skills who are committed to a common purpose, set of performance goals, and approach for which they hold themselves mutually accountable. Specifically, high-performing teams have six characteristics. First, the very essence of a team is a *common commitment to a shared goal*. Without it, groups perform as individuals; with it, they become a powerful collective unit. Teams must, therefore, have a clear mission to which they are committed.

High-performing teams translate their common purpose into *specific performance goals*. In fact transforming broad directives into specific and measurable performance goals is the surest first step for a team trying to shape a purpose meaningful to its members.

It is important to create teams that are the *right size* made up of the *right mix* of individuals. Best-performing teams generally have between seven and fourteen members whose skills should complement each other. For example, a team usually needs people strong in technical expertise, as well as those skilled in problem solving, decision making, and interpersonal relationships.

High-performing teams agree on the system by which they will work together to accomplish their mission. They must adopt a *common approach*. Team members determine who will do particular jobs, how schedules will be set and followed, what skills need to be developed, what members will have to do to remain a part of the team, and how decisions will be made.

The most productive teams also develop a sense that, as team members, they must all hold themselves accountable for doing whatever is needed to help the team achieve its mission. Such *mutual accountability* cannot be coerced. Instead, it emerges from the commitment and trust that comes from working together toward a common purpose.

TEAMWORK

All teams need members who are motivated to work well with others to accomplish important tasks. Whether those tasks involve recommending things, making or doing things, or running things, teamwork is required. A commitment to teamwork is demonstrated by the willingness of every member to listen and respond constructively to views expressed by others, give others the benefit of the doubt, provide support, and recognize the interests and achievements of others. Teamwork can lead to greater

- goal commitment
- self-confidence
- sense of well-being
- motivation and enthusiasm
- job satisfaction
- problem-solving skills
- emotional support within team

- endurance and energy levels
- sharing of individual skills
- productivity
- quality and quantity of output
- loyalty to goals and objectives

BECOMING A TEAM LEADER

Besides having a good understanding of how to create a team, FLMs need to understand how to act as a team leader. They need to know and understand the team leader's role, the typical transition problems they will face as they move into the position of team leader, and the principles of an effective leader. Janet Franklin, FLM at a health care facility, expresses the difficulty of her transition: "It took some doing on my part, as well as on theirs. It was not an instant thing. It probably took nine months for me to let loose and let them do what they thought was best. And there are still guidelines. You just don't turn the ship over and say 'Here you are.' But on normal day-to-day activities, it's turned over to them. Most of the time now they can solve problems themselves."

THE FLM's ROLE AS A TEAM LEADER

The FLM is ultimately responsible for the functioning of the team, even though this responsibility obviously is shared by the team itself. In addition to removing organizational barriers for the team, the FLM must supply resources and support when needed.

An important job for FLMs is to ask questions to identify potential team problems. FLMs have the responsibility of helping the team diagnose problems. FLMs must also assess the degree to which they, as team leaders, feel comfortable working in teams. They must assess their own knowledge about team building and whether, in fact, they might be a major source of a team's difficulty. FLMs need to analyze the extent to which they themselves, their employees, and the organization itself are truly open to teams and team development.

THE TRANSITION TO TEAM LEADER

Like the transition from an individual contributor to an FLM, moving from being a traditional authoritative FLM to being a facilitating team leader is not easy. Why is it so difficult for some individuals to make the transition to team leader? There are at least four problems that can make the transition process less than smooth. First, many FLMs experience a perceived loss of power or status. One day you are the boss; the next day you are merely a facilitator, trying to make sure your team members have what they need to do their jobs—to a large extent, without you. You may not control, direct, or make all of the decisions anymore. FLM Todd Burton felt that his authority was threatened in the beginning, "At first, when we made the transition to teams, I felt like I was losing control of my own people. I wasn't making the decisions any longer—they were. Everything was decided as a group. The immediate loss of power and control took some getting used to."

The FLM whose job was once clear as supervisor is now undefined. The change to team leader can be difficult for many FLMs. When you move to a team leader role, companies can make the mistake of over-emphasizing what you are not, without clearly defining what you are. While the role of the team may be somewhat clearly defined, the role of the team leader is not. A team is created with a task to "make it happen." Without a good understanding of the role as team leader, the FLM can fail. Doug Belzer, an FLM in a small production firm, had difficulty defining his place in the new system. "I guess the most confusing thing about moving to teams was figuring out my role in all of it. I still had to guide the group—especially at first, but I wasn't supposed to *tell*. This was really an adjustment for me. I was no longer the problem-solver. The group did it together. That meant that I wasn't making all of the decisions, yet I was still responsible for them as group leader. I had to figure how to get the group to move in the right direction."

It's not uncommon for FLMs to experience job security concerns during the transition to team leader. Telling new team leaders that they are no longer in charge understandably undermines their sense of job security. After all, it is not unreasonable to ask, "Just how secure is the job of supervising or managing a self-managing team?" Team leaders may suspect that creating an effective team is essentially a means of working themselves out of a job.

The movement to teams often seems to be a positive, enriching, and empowering move for employees, yet defeating for the FLM. Some companies make the mistake of forgetting the FLM in the transition to teams, providing him or her with little or no attention, training, or clarification of the new role. The employee gains power and input while the FLM may seem to lose these things. One FLM, Yvonne Watts, expresses her initial frustration during the implementation of teams. "I have to admit that it was particularly difficult in the beginning. The employees received all of this training to be an effective team. I guess they just expected me to know what to do as a team leader. I had never done that before. I wasn't sure what to do. I finally found some information on teamwork and managing teams. I talked to my supervisor about sending me to a conference on managing teams. He admitted that management hadn't ever discussed the impact the move to teams might have on the front-line managers."

This type of treatment can obviously make FLMs annoyed and resistant to the use of teams. Organizations should instead create and implement a transition plan which includes FLMs. The plan should clarify their new team leadership duties, outline how their security will be ensured, and identify training they can expect to receive as they make the transition to team leaders.

THE PRINCIPLES OF AN EFFECTIVE TEAM LEADER

Not everyone is cut out to be an effective leader of self-managing teams. Not every leader is psychologically or philosophically prepared to stop "being a boss" and instead oversee a team that is empowered to work with a minimum of supervision.

A leader of a self-managing team should have a set of personal principles that supports the empowered nature of teams. What personal principles are consistent with building self-confidence, sharing authority, and ensuring the team has the tools and information it requires? Important team leader principles focus on the needs of the team. A team leader should put the team members first and trust that they will do their best. In order to help team members reach their potential, team leaders must enhance team members' capabilities through training and development. Team leaders must demonstrate that they believe in the team and value the team members. In order to do this, they must use delegation and let the team members make decisions and take action. The leaders should eliminate barriers that may hinder decision-making processes or team actions.

Perhaps the biggest difference between successful and unsuccessful team leaders is that those who are successful believe their primary responsibility is to make sure their teams have the means to get their jobs done. They give the team the support it needs.

HOW TEAM LEADERS CAN CREATE A TEAM OF SUCCESSFUL TEAM MEMBERS

In addition to understanding what affects their role as team leaders, FLMs must also understand how to

- develop team players
- build the team
- coach the members
- motivate team members

- reduce social loafing
- build trust
- help manage conflict
- communicate effectively

DEVELOPING TEAM PLAYERS

One substantial barrier to the success of teams in organizations is individual resistance. To perform well as team members, individuals must be able to communicate openly and honestly, to confront differences and resolve conflicts, and to make personal sacrifices for the good of the team.

Many people are not inherently team players. Some are loners by nature. Others want to be recognized for their individual achievements. These people have often worked in an organization that has historically nurtured individual accomplishments and created competitive work environments where only the strong survive. If these organizations adopt teams, what do they do about the selfish, "I've-got-to-look-out-for-me" employees that they have created?

The challenge for FLMs is less demanding in new organizations that use teams from the beginning. Saturn Corporation, for instance, is an American organization owned by General Motors. The company was designed around the use of teams. Everyone at Saturn was hired with the knowledge that they would be working in teams. The ability to be a good team player was a basic qualification required of all new employees.

The primary approaches used by FLMs and organizations to identify and develop individuals into team players are selecting good team members, training them, and rewarding them based on team—not only individual—performance.

Some people already possess the interpersonal skills to be effective team players. When hiring new employees who will work as team members, care should be taken to ensure that candidates can fulfill their team roles as well as the technical requirements of the job. Many job candidates, particularly those who have previously worked as an individual contributor, lack team skills. When faced with such candidates, FLMs can train them, use them elsewhere in the organizations, or refuse to hire them.

Most people can be trained to become team players. Training specialists conduct exercises that allow employees to experience the satisfaction that team-work can provide. Workshops can help employees improve their problem solving, communication, negotiation, conflict management, and coaching skills. At Bell Atlantic, for example, trainers focus on how a team goes through various stages before it finally works well together. Employees are reminded of the importance of patience—because it often takes a team longer to make a decision than an employee acting alone.

In established organizations that redesign jobs around teams, it should be expected that some employees will resist being team players and may be untrainable. Unfortunately, such people typically become casualties of the team approach and will lose their jobs or be transferred to a part of the organization without teams.

The reward system must be one that encourages cooperative rather than competitive efforts. Promotions, pay raises, and other forms of recognition should be given to individuals for how effective they are as collaborative team members. Recognition of team effectiveness does not mean individual contribution is ignored; rather, personal accomplishment is balanced with selfless contributions to the team. Trigon Blue Cross Blue Shield changed its system to reward individual and team achievements equally. Examples of behaviors that should be rewarded include training new colleagues, sharing information with teammates, helping to resolve team conflicts, and mastering new skills that the team needs but in which it is deficient. Additionally, teamwork provides the intrinsic reward of camaraderie. It is exciting and satisfying to be an integral part of a successful team. The opportunity to engage in personal development and to help teammates grow can be a very rewarding experience for employees.

TEAM BUILDING

Team building is a catch-all term for many different techniques aimed at improving the internal functioning of work groups. Some authorities have suggested that the primary purposes of team building are to set goals and priorities, to analyze or allocate the way work is performed, to examine the way a group is working and its processes, and to examine relations among the people doing the work. Trainers achieve these objectives by allowing team members to wrestle with simulated or real-life problems. The group analyzes its results to determine what group processes need improvement. Learning occurs by recognizing and addressing faulty group dynamics. With cross-cultural teams becoming commonplace in today's global economy, team building is more important than ever to help alleviate misunderstandings and improve communication.

Whether conducted by company trainers or outside consultants, team-building workshops are designed to promote greater cooperation, better communication, and less dysfunctional conflict. Learning tools such as interpersonal trust exercises, conflict-handling role-play sessions, and interactive games are commonly used to build teamwork skills. For example, Germany's Opel uses Lego blocks to teach its auto workers the type of teamwork necessary for just-in-time production. In the mountains of British Columbia, DowElanco employees try to overcome fear and build trust as they help each other negotiate a difficult treetop ropes course.

Team building is participative and data based. Whether the data are gathered by questionnaire, interview, nominal group meeting, or other creative methods, the goal is for team members to give good answers to such questions as, "How well are we doing in terms of task accomplishment?" "How satisfied am I as a group member?" and "How effectively does the group operate?" There are a variety of ways for such questions to be asked and answered in a collaborative and motivating manner.

USING EFFECTIVE COACHING SKILLS

Coaching is a big part of what team leaders do. Like coaching, team building involves assessing the team's skills and helping the team use them to the fullest. Employees tend to contribute more effectively when they are coached to make optimal use of all their strengths and resources.

What is required to coach employees? Experts agree that coaches must first know their people. As a coach you should assess each employee's skills so you can help team members use them to the fullest. Good coaches guide—not control—employees. If you tell them what to do, they will not develop the independence necessary to operate as a team. It is important that coaches provide the emotional support necessary for the team to work together. You should ensure that a supportive environment exists in which employees believe they have the freedom to make contributions and provide their input. Coaches provide specific feedback. You should explain what improvements are required and why from your point of view. Coaches let team members generate answers. You should ask questions that will lead your employees to find the answers for themselves. Finally, good coaches communicate high expectations for the team and its members. (See Chapter 7 for more discussion on coaching.)

MOTIVATING TEAMS TO ACHIEVE GOALS

When work is difficult, tedious, or requires a high level of commitment and energy, FLMs cannot assume that team members will always be motivated to work toward the achievement of organizational goals. Consider the case of a group of house painters who paint new homes for a construction company and are paid on an hourly basis. Why should they strive to complete painting jobs quickly and efficiently? Doing so will just make them feel more tired at the end of the day, and they will not receive any tangible benefits. It makes more sense for the painters to adopt a relaxed approach, working at a leisurely pace. This relaxed approach, however, impairs the construction company's ability to gain a competitive advantage because it raises costs and increases the time needed to complete a new home.

FLMs can motivate members of teams to achieve organizational goals by making sure that the members themselves benefit when the team performs well. If members of a self-managed team know that they will receive a percentage of any cost savings discovered and implemented by the team, they probably will strive to cut costs. If the house painters were paid based on the amount of surface area they actually painted, or if they were to receive a bonus for each house completed in a timely, efficient manner, it is likely that they would work more quickly.

FLMs often rely on some combination of individual and group-based incentives to motivate team members to work toward the achievement of organizational goals and a competitive advantage. When individual performance within a group can be assessed, pay is often determined by that individual performance or by both individual and group performance. When individual performance within a group cannot be accurately assessed, then group performance should determine pay levels. A major challenge for FLMs is to develop a fair pay system that will lead to both high individual motivation and high group or team performance.

REDUCING SOCIAL LOAFING IN TEAMS

We have been focused on the steps that FLMs can take to encourage high levels of team performance. FLMs, however, need to be aware of an important downside to teamwork: the potential for social loafing. Social loafing is the tendency of individuals to put forth less effort when they work in groups or teams than when they work alone. Have you ever worked on a group project in which one or two group members never seemed to be pulling their weight? If you have, you have witnessed social loafing.

Social loafing can occur in all kinds of groups and teams and in all kinds of organizations. It can result in lower group performance and may prevent a group from attaining its goals. Social loafing can be reduced or completely eliminated if the FLM will make individual contributions to a group identifiable, emphasize why each member's skills are important to the team's success, and form teams with no more members than are needed to accomplish team goals. Organizations can stop social loafing by keeping the team small and making sure they have challenging work tasks.

BUILDING TEAM TRUST

A crucial factor in developing an outstanding team is the team leader's ability to create a supportive climate in which the team can work together. The team leader should be supportive, maintaining each individual's sense of personal worth and importance. The relationship between a team leader and employees should be one of reciprocal support and joint commitment to success.

High performance teams are characterized by high mutual trust among members. But as you know from personal relationships, trust takes a long time to build, can be easily destroyed, and is hard to regain. Team leaders have a significant impact on a team's climate of trust. As a team leader, you should keep people informed, be candid, explain your decisions, act in a consistent manner, and fully disclose relevant information. To build trust, as the team leader you must evaluate team members objectively, demonstrate you are working for others' interests as well as your own, and give credit where it is due. Trust needs to be earned; it cannot be demanded. FLMs must take the time to build team members' trust—the foundation of a high-performance team.

FACILITATING COMMUNICATION IN THE TEAM ENVIRONMENT

The way the team leader communicates with the other team members will influence the success of the team. Successful teamwork requires open and positive communication among team members. In order to benefit from diverse viewpoints, all team members need to feel welcome to express their ideas constructively. In general, the team leader should build on a climate of trust and openness and encourage team members to collaborate. The team leader should acknowledge disagreement, not squelch it. Practically all groups and teams experience conflict either within the group or with other groups at some point. In Chapter 7 we discuss conflict in depth and explore ways to manage it effectively. As you will learn there, FLMs can help groups manage conflict and disagreements.

PROBLEMS UNIQUE TO LEADING TEAMS

To lead a team, a leader must have not only basic leadership characteristics, but also special team-building skills and the ability to meet challenges unique to the team structure. In this section we shall turn briefly to a few of those uniquely team-related challenges of being a leader.

New Team Member Entry Problems

Given the nature of group dynamics, team building is not a "one-time" task that you accomplish and put aside. Something is always happening that creates the need for further efforts to help improve teamwork and group effectiveness. Special difficulties are likely to occur when team members first get together in a new work group or when new members join an existing one. Problems often arise as a new member tries to understand what is expected of them while dealing with the anxiety and discomfort of a new social setting. New members, for example, may worry about the level of participation expected of them by the group, whether the group's goals mesh well with their own, individual level of control and influence, team member relationships, and group processes such as conflicts within the group.

Workforce Diversity and Teams

Managing diversity on teams is a balancing act. Diversity typically provides new approaches and fresh perspectives on issues, but differences can make it more difficult to unify team members and reach agreement. Diversity among group members obviously brings with it certain advantages such as multiple perspectives, greater openness of the group to new ideas, multiple interpretations, and increased creativity, flexibility and problem-solving. Unfortunately the advantages of a diverse group of individuals can sometimes be accompanied by the disadvantages of complexity, confusion, miscommunication, and difficulties in reaching agreement or taking action.

Diversity on work teams is most productive for problem-solving and decision-making tasks. Team members bring multiple perspectives to discussions, thus increasing the likelihood that the team will identify creative or unique solutions. The lack of a common perspective usually means diverse teams spend more time discussing issues, which decreases the chances that a poor decision will be made. As diverse groups work together more, two things tend to happen. The team tends to become less creative, offering fewer suggestions as team members become more familiar with perspectives of other team members. In turn, however, as members become more familiar with one another, it is likely that initial working conflicts will dissipate.

Inspiring Mature Teams

Just because a team is performing well at a given point in time is no assurance that it will continue to do so. Effective teams can become stagnant. Initial enthusiasm can give way to apathy and less openness to novel ideas and innovation. Team members believe they know what other team members are thinking. As a result, team members become reluctant to express their thoughts and less likely to challenge each other.

Another source of problems for mature teams is that success may not come as easily as the group matures. Early successes are often due partially to the easy tasks taken on during the early life of the team. Later, the team must confront more difficult issues at the point that it has developed entrenched processes and routines. Internal team processes no longer work smoothly. Communication bogs down. Conflicts increase because problems are less likely to have obvious solutions, and team performance can drop dramatically.

What can be done to reenergize mature teams? The solution involves preparation and encouragement. FLMs should prepare members to deal with the problems of maturity through discussions and training. It is important for team members to understand that all successful teams have to confront maturity issues. Providing team members with training or refresher courses in communication, conflict resolution, problem solving, and technical skills can serve to vitalize the team. Finally, team members can avoid a negative reaction to problems of maturity if the FLM simply encourages them to see these issues as part of the team's development—a constant learning experience in which they look for ways to improve, to confront member fears and frustrations, and to use conflict as a tool of growth.

SUMMARY

Many different types of teams are successfully and commonly used by today's organizations. Creating and developing teams involves four steps: prework, setting performance conditions, forming and building a team, and providing on-going assistance. While teams can be very productive and promote organizational success, there is also evidence that some teams fail due to problems, which include lack of cooperation among team members and with other teams, no support from management, and a failure of FLMs and other managers to relinquish control. To make sure that teams perform at the highest possible level, FLMs need to motivate members to work toward the achievement of organizational goals, reduce social loafing, effectively manage conflict, build trust within the team, and understand how to reenergize mature teams.

REFERENCE

Caudron, S. 1993. Are directed teams right for your company? *Personnel Journal* 81, 76–83.

Chapter 6

Motivating Today's Employees

INTRODUCTION

The world around us constantly presents examples of motivation. Rocky, the prize fighter, down for the count, sees his wife through bleary eyes and rises slowly from the mat, summoning the necessary energy to attack his opponent and win. During halftime, a group of lackluster football players is transformed by the coach into screaming, aggressive, highly motivated players who go on to win the big game. Gymnasts overcome painful injuries to win medals. How does this happen?

Many motivated employees have FLMs with good leadership qualities. It is not easy to be a motivating leader, as so much of motivation is psychological by nature. Although motivation cannot be seen directly, its presence or absence can be recognized by observing employee behavior. When an FLM observes an employee doing a task, the logical assumption is that the employee is motivated. If, on the other hand, an employee is frequently observed wasting time, it can be assumed that the employee is not motivated. When FLMs are effective leaders, the resulting motivated workforce is more likely to achieve organizational goals.

Many FLMs do not believe that motivation is part of their job. They think that once an employee is hired, it is the employee's responsibility to ensure that the job is done. Unfortunately, they envision their job as simply making corrections and adjustments when necessary. They erroneously believe that motivation is the responsibility of the individual employee. Today's organizations cannot be successful if they adopt this attitude. FLMs are the leaders whose primary responsibility is to get things done *through others*. In order to motivate effectively, FLMs must understand all aspects of the process and methods of motivation. They must readily recognize the negative consequences of unmotivated employees and how to avoid them.

WHAT *IS* MOTIVATION?

In recent weeks, team leader Jill Rappaport has noticed that whenever she enters the work area, several of her team members appear to be loafing or chatting. In Jill's opinion, they just don't seem to be working very hard. A quick review of the human resources records verified another suspicion: absenteeism and tardiness have increased in recent months. Jill is baffled. Just two months ago, everyone received an 8 percent pay raise. In addition, the facilities of her department were recently refurbished. What else could the employees possibly want? "Nobody wants to work like they did in the good old days. Half the problems we have around here are due to a lack of personal motivation. Workers just don't seem to care. What *can* I do?"

Jill's sentiments are often expressed by today's FLMs. Motivating employees is not a new problem. There are examples of motivation problems dating back to biblical times. In the early twentieth century, much of the pioneering work in the field of management was concerned with motivation. Motivation is the process of satisfying internal needs through actions and behavior. Motivation is derived from the root of the Latin word meaning "to move." It basically means to impel someone to act. The study of motivation examines why and how people behave as they do. It is concerned with the combination of mental and physical drives, and the environment that affects behavior.

FLMs such as Jill Rappaport must realize that people behave with a purpose or pattern based on motives. A motive is an internal factor that influences a person's actions. Motives may arise from physiological needs, such as the need for food, water, and air, or from psychological needs such as self-esteem, recognition, achievement, and status. For example, if an employee feels inferior to others and has a need for greater recognition and self-esteem, the employee might be motivated to satisfy this need by returning to school to secure additional training. Employees are individuals by nature, making the total concept of motivation extremely complicated.

The need satisfaction model is used to illustrate motivation from a simplified point of view. In this model, a motive or need serves as the basis for action. The person then takes an action, directly leading to satisfaction of the need. For example, thirst may lead an individual to go to the store and buy a soft drink. The need satisfaction model has obvious job implications: for example, the need for additional money may lead an employee to work overtime.

THE MOTIVATION PROCESS

In order to understand the motivation process, we need to consider various job-related factors. These include general factors, such as the organizational environment and the rewards or punishments provided for particular behaviors. It also includes factors that are unique to each employee: individual perceptions, the personal importance of different needs, personal traits, the ability to perform different types of work, and the amount of effort the employee is willing to expend.

The following provides a detailed explanation of the motivation process. The process begins with the identification of a need. Money, status, recognition, and promotion are typical job-related needs. For example, let's follow an employee who wants to be promoted. The same steps and rationale explored below would apply to many identified needs.

Once the employee wants a promotion, the satisfaction of that desire is subject to steps 2, 3 and 4. In step 2, the employee assesses the degree of importance attached to being promoted. Is the employee willing to make the necessary sacrifices to meet this goal? Is the promotion so important that the employee is willing to put aside other activities in favor of seeking it? For example, if promotion is based on superior performance, is the employee willing to commit the extra time and effort necessary to perform in a superior manner? If not, the process terminates at this stage. If the employee is willing to make the commitment, the process proceeds to the third step.

In step 3, pre-evaluation, the employee attempts to determine the availability of a promotion. The process is likely to terminate at this stage if no higher position is available. However, it is conceivable that the employee will continue with the evaluation although the promotion is not available, with the intention of securing a promotion in another organization. Assuming a promotion is available, the employee must consider any environmental constraints to securing it. The employee might ask, "Have I been here long enough? What does the job require? Do I have the necessary education? Do I have the necessary training and skills? Am I capable? Am I likely to get it? Is the boss's son or daughter standing in my way?" Again, a negative answer to one or more of these questions is likely to end the process.

If the responses to the questions raised in step 3 are encouraging, step 4 is initiated. In this step, the employee puts forth the effort necessary to cause the desired outcome. The employee makes a self-assessment to determine if he or she is meeting the employer's standards. In step 5, the employee evaluates the outcome, asking: "Did I get my reward?"

Step 6 analyzes the outcomes of step 5. Were the employee's efforts justified? If not, the long-term implications (step 7) could be serious; but if so, the long-term implications could be positive, giving the employee the self-confidence to tackle the process of satisfying new needs.

Just like the employee in our example, FLMs like Jill Rappaport must recognize that other employees may be motivated by a bonus or the opportunity for a pay increase and may be willing to work harder to get it. For today's FLM to be successful in motivating employees, it pays to understand the process of motivation.

METHODS COMMONLY USED TO MOTIVATE EMPLOYEES

Experts are saying that today's companies must concentrate on the three R's, recruiting, retraining, and retaining high-quality people. Motivation is involved in all of them, as companies try to appeal to employees' higher-level needs. As industry trends continue to shift toward self-managing teams, employees cannot be expected to turn into motivated self-managers overnight. They need to be given the proper tools through development and training programs.

When employees appear to be unmotivated, FLMs like Jill Rappaport will want to size up the situation, identify and understand what is happening, and formulate a response. The description of the motivation process, discussed in the previous section, should help FLMs identify and understand the problems they face. In this section, we describe methods that can be used to motivate employees.

Pay for Performance

Pay for performance is probably the first thing that comes to mind when most people think about motivating employees. Pay for performance refers to any compensation method that ties pay to the quantity or quality of work the person produces. Piecework pay plans are probably the most familiar: earnings are tied directly to the number of items the worker produces in the form of a "piece rate" for each unit he or she turns out. For example, an employee who gets 40 cents apiece for stamping out circuit boards would make $40 for stamping out 100 a day and $80 for stamping out 200. Sales commissions are another familiar example.

Piecework plans have a firm foundation in motivation theory. Behavior modification theories state that people will continue behavior that is rewarded, and pay for performance plans, of course, tie rewards directly to behavior.

Pay for performance plans of all types—including those that let employees share in profits by paying them with shares of company stock—are becoming more popular because they make sense. As Maggie Hughes, President of LifeUSA Holdings Inc. of Minneapolis puts it: "I find it amusing, frustrating, and often quite appalling how few business leaders recognize that people should share in the economic value they create. At LifeUSA, our employees have options on 2 million shares of company stock. It seems like common sense to us. So why is it still so uncommon in most companies?"

Variable Pay Plans and Gainsharing Plans

Variable pay plans put some portion of the employee's pay at risk, subject to the organization meeting its financial goals. In one such plan at the DuPont Company for example, employees could voluntarily place up to six percent of their base pay at risk. If they then met the department's earnings projections, they would get that six percent back plus an additional percentage, depending on how much the department exceeded its earnings projections.

Other companies have gainsharing plans. These are incentive plans that engage many or all employees in a common effort to achieve a company's productivity goals. Implementing a gainsharing plan requires several steps. The company establishes specific performance measures, such as the cost per unit produced, and a funding formula, such as "47 percent of savings go to employees." Management decides how to divide and distribute any cost savings between the employees and the company, and among employees themselves. If employees are then able to achieve the desired cost savings, they share in the resulting gains.

Merit Pay

When most employees do a good job, they expect to be rewarded with at least a merit raise at the end of the year. It is different from a bonus in that it provides a continuing pay increase, while a bonus is a one-time payment. Traditional merit raises are gradually being replaced by lump-sum increases that, like bonuses, are awarded in a single payment that does not become part of the employee's continuing pay.

To the extent that it is actually tied to performance, the prospect of a merit raise may focus the employee's attention on the link between performance and rewards. A year is a long time to wait for a reward, however, so relying too heavily on merit raises as rewards could be dangerous, as the reinforcement benefits of merit pay are somewhat suspect. The motivational basis for the merit plan can also be undermined by inadequate employee evaluations. You may have personally experienced the questionable nature of some performance appraisal systems, including the practice of some FLMs who take the easy way out and rate everyone's performance about the same, regardless of actual effort.

Spot Awards

As its name implies, a spot award is a financial award given to an employee literally "on the spot," as soon as superior performance is observed. Programs such as these have been around for some time. For example, in the early 1900s, Thomas J. Watson, Sr., the founder of IBM, reportedly wrote checks on the spot to employees doing an outstanding job.

These cash awards are used increasingly today. Federal Express's Bravo-Zulu voucher program is an example. This program was established to give FLMs the ability to provide immediate rewards to employees for outstanding performance above and beyond the normal requirements of the job. (Bravo-Zulu means "well done" in U.S. Navy semaphore signals.) Bravo-Zulu vouchers average about $50 and may be in the form of a check or some other type of reward, such as dinner vouchers or theater tickets. It is estimated that Federal Express managers present employees with these awards more than 150,000 times a year.

Other organizations use spot cash incentive awards as well. For example, Victor Kiam, president of Remington Products (who liked Remington shavers so much that "I bought the company"), maintains a $25,000 discretionary fund to give instant cash awards to workers doing an exceptional job. Kiam invites people to his office and awards them checks ranging from $200 to $500. Spot awards such as these have a sound basis in what we know about motivation. For example, to the extent that the rewards are both contingent on good performance and awarded immediately, they quickly provide the recognition most people desire.

Skill-Based Pay

You are probably aware of the fact that in most organizations pay is determined by the level of the job responsibilities. Thus, presidents generally make more than vice presidents, sales managers make more than assistant sales managers, and secretary IVs make more than secretary IIIs because higher-level jobs have more responsibilities.

Skill-based pay is different in that you are paid for the range, depth, and types of skills and knowledge you are capable of using, rather than for the level of responsibility you exercise in the job you currently hold. The difference is important: it is conceivable that in a company with a skill-based pay plan, a secretary III could be paid more per hour than a secretary IV, for instance, if it turns out that the person who happened to be the secretary III had more skills than did the person in the secretary IV job.

A skill-based plan was implemented at a General Mills manufacturing facility. General Mills was trying to boost the flexibility of its factory workforce by implementing a pay plan that would encourage employees to develop a wider range of skills in order to make it easier to find employees able to take over any vacant position in the plant as the plant's needs changed.

In this plan, the employees were paid based on their attained skill levels. For each type of job in the plant, workers could attain one of three levels of skill: limited ability (ability to perform simple tasks without direction), partial proficiency, and full competence (ability to analyze and solve problems associated with that job). After starting a job, employees were tested periodically to see whether they had earned certification at the next higher skill level. If so, they received higher pay even though they continued to hold the same job. This system allowed higher-skilled workers to receive higher pay than others doing the same job. Employees could then switch to other jobs in the plant, again starting at skill level one and working their way up if they so desired. In this way, employees could earn more pay for more skills, particularly as they became skilled at a variety of jobs and the company ended up with a more highly skilled and, therefore, more flexible workforce.

Skill-based pay makes sense in terms of what we know about motivation. People have a vision of who they can be, and they seek to fulfill their potential. The individual development emphasis of skill-based pay helps employees to do exactly that. Skill-based pay also appeals to an employee's sense of self-efficacy in that the reward is a formal and concrete recognition that the person can do a more challenging job and do it well.

Recognition

Most people like to feel appreciated. In one study, over two-thirds of respondents said they highly valued day-to-day recognition from their FLMs, peers, and team members. If you have ever spent a day cooking a meal for someone who gobbled it up without saying a word, or two weeks doing a report for a boss who did not even say, "Thanks," let alone, "Good job," you know the importance of having your work recognized and appreciated.

The motivating power of being recognized—and not necessarily just financially—for a job well done makes sense in terms of motivation theory. Immediate recognition can be a powerful reinforcer of good performance. Recognition also helps to satisfy people's need for a sense of achievement.

Many companies therefore formalize the common sense process of saying "Thank you for a job well done." For example, Xerox Corporation gives what it calls bell-ringer awards for good work: a bell is rung in the corridor while the person is formally recognized by his or her boss. At Busch Gardens in Tampa, Florida, the company reportedly gives a "pat on the back" award to employees who do an outstanding job, adding a notice of the award to the employee's file. At Metro Motors in Montclair, California, the name of the employee of the month goes up on the electronic billboard over the dealership. Bell Atlantic named cellular telephone sites after top employees.

FLMs must identify which kinds of behaviors they reward. "The things that get rewarded get done" is what one author calls "The Greatest Management Principle in the World" (LeBoeuf, 1991). With this in mind, the author describes ten types of behavior that should be recognized to motivate high performance. Organizations and individual FLMs should reward the following:

- solid solutions instead of quick fixes;
- risk taking instead of risk avoiding;
- applied creativity instead of mindless conformity;
- decisive action instead of paralysis by analysis;
- smart work instead of busywork;
- simplification instead of needless complication;
- quietly effective workers instead of self-promoting talkers;
- quality work instead of fast work;
- loyalty instead of turnover;
- working together instead of working against each other;
- lack of absenteeism and tardiness.

Job Redesign

FLMs have long been concerned about the unmotivating qualities of highly specialized, short-cycle, assembly-line jobs that are monotonous and boring. In an effort to respond to this problem, many employers set up programs to redesign those jobs. The term *job design* refers to the number and nature of activities in a job. The basic issue in job redesign is whether jobs should be more specialized or, at the other extreme, more "enriched" and less routine.

Empowering Employees

Empowering employees has become a popular approach to work organizations. It means giving employees the authority, tools, and information they need to do their jobs with greater autonomy, as well as the self-confidence required to perform their new duties effectively. Empowering is inherently a motivational approach. It boosts employees' feelings of self-efficacy and enables them to meet their potential, satisfying high-level needs for achievement, recognition, and self-actualization. Empowerment results in changes in employees' outlook: from feeling powerless to believing strongly in their own personal effectiveness. The result is that employees become willing to take more initiative and persevere in achieving their goals and their leader's vision even in the face of obstacles.

Today, organizations often empower their work teams. At Saturn Corporation, for example, empowered, self-managing work teams are responsible for a variety of duties. For each team, these duties include planning the team's work and schedule; designing and determining team member job assignments; resolving internal conflicts; selecting new members of the work unit; replacing any absentee members; working directly with suppliers, customers, and other partners maintaining and repairing the equipment it uses; seeking improvements in quality, cost, and the work environment; and performing within its budget.

Empowering does not just mean assigning broader job responsibilities. Teams also need the training, skills, and tools to allow them to do their jobs, such as knowing how to make consensus decisions. Firms like Saturn also make sure their FLMs actually let their people do their jobs as assigned.

Not all empowerment programs are as comprehensive as that at Saturn Corporation. At Scandinavian Air System (SAS) for instance, empowering the work force meant letting employees make more decisions by themselves. Ticket agents now have the authority to reticket a passenger or even move the passenger up a class, if they feel the situation warrants it. At one Marriott chain subsidiary, every hotel employee, from management to maintenance, is empowered to offer guests a free night's stay if, in the employee's opinion, the hotel has been lax in serving the guest. And at engine-maker Pratt & Whitney, salespeople can now authorize multimillion dollar repairs on the spot, instead of having to wait for approvals from up the line. In virtually all such cases, employees find empowerment exciting, while employers find it helps workers to enjoy using their potential to achieve new goals, thereby boosting motivation and employee commitment. The guidelines below can make FLMs more successful in empowering their employees:

- Make sure people understand their responsibilities.
- Give them authority equal to the responsibilities assigned to them.
- Set standards of excellence that will require employees to strive to do *all* work "right the first time."

- Provide them with training that will enable them to meet the standards.
- Give them information they need to do their job well.
- Trust them.
- Give them permission to fail.
- Treat them with dignity and respect.
- Provide them with feedback on their performance.
- Recognize them for their achievements.

Goal Setting

Have you ever set your sights on a goal—becoming an FLM or earning enough money for a trip abroad, for instance? What effect did setting the goal have on you? Setting specific goals with your employees can be one of the simplest yet most powerful ways of motivating them.

There are many ideas on how to set goals that motivate employees. Chapter 8 provides a more extensive description of goal setting for the purpose of planning. Here's a summary:

- *Be clear and specific.* Employees who are given specific goals usually perform better than those who are not.
- *Make goals measurable and verifiable.* Whenever possible, goals should be stated in quantitative terms and should include target dates or deadlines for accomplishment.
- *Make goals challenging but realistic.* Goals should be challenging but not so difficult that they appear impossible or unrealistic.
- *Set goals together.* If employees participate in setting their goals, they will usually perform better.

Lifelong Learning

Many employers today face a tremendous dilemma. On the one hand, in order to be competitive, a company needs highly committed employees who exercise self-discipline and basically do their jobs as if they owned the company. On the other hand, competitive pressures have forced many companies to downsize, which decreases employee motivation and commitment. They may question whether it pays for them to work their hearts out for the company.

Organizations are increasingly using lifelong learning to address both of these issues simultaneously. Lifelong learning provides extensive and career-long training, from basic remedial skills to advanced decision-making techniques. Implemented properly, lifelong learning programs can achieve three things. First, the training, development, and education provide employees with the decision-making and other knowledge, skills, and abilities they need to work competently in a demanding, team-based job. Second, the opportunity for lifelong learning is inherently motivational: it gives employees the ability to fulfill their potential, it boosts their sense of self-efficacy, and it helps them gain the sense of achievement that motivation theorists argue is so important. Third, lifelong learning can help alleviate the potential negative effects of downsizing by giving employees useful and marketable new skills.

One Honeywell manufacturing plant in Canada provides an example of a lifelong learning program, which it calls the Honeywell-Scarborough Learning for Life Initiative. It is "a concerted effort to upgrade skill and education levels so that employees can meet workplace challenges with confidence." This lifelong learning program has several components. It begins with basic adult education, in which the company, in partnership with the employees' union offers courses in English as a second language, basic literacy, numeracy, and computer literacy.

Next the factory has formed a partnership with a local community college. Through that partnership all factory employees—hourly, professional, and managerial—have the opportunity to earn college diplomas and certificates. Included is a 15-hour "skills for success" program designed to teach adults the study habits they need to succeed academically. All courses take place at the factory after work.

Finally, job training is provided for two hours every other week. These sessions focus on developing skills specifically important to the job, "such as the principles of just-in-time inventory systems, team effectiveness, interpersonal communication skills, conflict resolution, problem solving and dealing with a diverse work force."

It is never easy to evaluate the success of a program like this because not all employees choose to participate, and many other factors affect productivity and employee motivation. The evidence suggests, however, that lifelong learning programs improve commitment, skills, motivation, and possibly productivity too.

SPECIAL PROBLEMS IN MOTIVATING PARTICULAR GROUPS OF EMPLOYEES

FLMs today face specific challenges in motivating special groups of employees. In this concluding section we look at some of the unique problems FLMs face in trying to motivate contingent workers, groups of diverse and cross-cultural employees, low-skilled workers who perform repetitive tasks, and baby busters. We also address how to motivate yourself.

Contingent Workers

Chapter 1 noted that one of the more comprehensive changes taking place in organizations is the use of temporary or contingent employees. As downsizing has eliminated millions of "permanent" jobs, an increasing number of new openings are filled with part-time, contract, and other types of temporary workers. These contingent employees do not have the security or stability of permanent employees. They usually receive little or no health care coverage, pensions, or similar benefits. As such, they do not identify with the organization in the same way or display the same commitment as permanent employees.

What will motivate involuntarily temporary employees? An obvious answer is the opportunity for permanent status. In those cases where permanent employees are selected from a pool of temporaries, the temporaries will often work hard in hopes of becoming permanent. A less obvious answer is the opportunity for training. The ability of temporary employees to find new jobs is largely dependent on their skills. If employees see that their current jobs can help develop useful skills, then their motivation will increase.

From an equity standpoint, FLMs should also consider the motivation problems that result from mixing permanent and temporary workers who earn significantly different amounts. When temps work alongside permanent employees who earn more and get benefits for doing the same job, the performance of temps is likely to suffer. Separating such employees or converting all employees to a variable pay or skill-based pay plan might help lessen this problem.

Diversified Workforce

As evidenced by the changing demographics of the United States work force, there are many cultural groups represented. On any given day an FLM may have groups of employees who are Asians with ties to Japan, China, and Thailand; Spanish speakers from Mexico, El Salvador, Cuba, and Spain; and an array of Russian immigrants, Middle Eastern immigrants, and many other culturally diverse individuals. Each of these groups may present the FLM with unique motivation problems. Do the motivation strategies presented above work the same way for all of these culturally diverse individuals? The answer to this question is important for today's FLMs who wish to create an optimal motivational climate for their employees, whether it be in a domestic or a foreign-based organization.

As presented earlier, today's FLMs must realize that not everyone is motivated by money. Not everyone wants a challenging job. The needs of women, singles, immigrants, the physically disabled, senior citizens, and others may differ from those of a White American male with three dependents. Several examples can make this point clearer. Employees who are attending college or training classes typically place a high value on flexible work schedules. They may be attracted to organizations that offer flexible work hours, job sharing, or temporary assignments. Parents also have special needs. A father may prefer to work the midnight to 8:00 A.M. shift in order to spend time with his children after school when his wife is at work.

Assessing employees' needs, preferred rewards, work patterns, and sensitivities to workplace practices has become an important part of FLM responsibilities. If FLMs are going to maximize their employees' motivation, they must understand and respond to a variety of concerns. How? The key is flexibility. Be ready to design work schedules, compensation plans, benefits, physical work settings, and the like to reflect your employees' diverse needs. This might include offering child and elder care, flexible work hours, and job sharing for employees with family responsibilities. It also might include offering flexible leave policies for immigrants who occasionally want to make extensive return trips to their homelands, creating work teams for employees who come from countries with a strong collectivist orientation, or allowing employees who are taking courses to vary their work schedules from semester to semester or course to course.

Employees Doing Highly Repetitive Tasks

We next consider the motivation problems of employees who do standardized, repetitive jobs. For instance, working on an assembly line or transcribing court reports are jobs that workers often find boring and stressful. Motivating individuals in these jobs will be easier if they are selected carefully. People vary in their tolerance for ambiguity. Many people prefer jobs that have a minimal amount of discretion and variety. These people are obviously a better match for standardized jobs than individuals with strong needs for growth and autonomy. Standardized jobs should also be the first considered for automation, which would remove the problem.

Many standardized jobs, especially in the manufacturing sector, pay well. This makes it relatively easy to fill vacancies. While high pay can ease recruitment problems and reduce turnover, it does not necessarily create highly motivated workers.

Unfortunately, some jobs have little else to offer. This includes jobs that cannot realistically be redesigned. Some tasks, for instance, are far more efficiently done on assembly lines than in teams. This leaves limited options. An FLM may not be able to do much more than try to make a bad situation tolerable by being empathic and creating a pleasant work climate. This might include providing clean and attractive work surroundings, ample work breaks, and the opportunity to socialize with colleagues.

Baby Busters

Perhaps one of the more challenging questions confronting today's FLMs is how to create a motivational climate for the baby busters—those young employees just entering the workforce who fall between the ages of 20 and 30. Chrysler President Robert Lutz maintains that the secret to international competitive success may lie in how well the baby busters have been prepared by the nation's school systems.

Experts generally agree. In spite of a higher percentage of students enrolling in colleges over the past two decades, studies have shown that "vast numbers of them function dismally in math and science or are functionally illiterate" (Solomon, 1995). In addition, they are said to have a longer adolescence, with 75 percent of men from ages 18 to 24 living with their parents (Solomon, 1995). Consequently today's organizations must take the lead in training baby busters to develop needed skills until the education system improves.

The baby busters also have positive characteristics. They are generally idealistic and are concerned about quality-of-life issues. They also tend to value challenge and growth more than money or titles. Although it is difficult to generalize about any age group, the authors of the book *Twentysomething: Managing and Motivating Today's New Work Force* have done a good job in analyzing this group. In keeping with some of the findings on generational differences discussed in Chapter 1, the following presents some turn-ons and turn-offs while working with baby busters. These should be used as guidance by FLMs when considering how to motivate baby busters.

Turn-ons

- recognition
- praise
- time spent with immediate boss
- learning how what they're doing right now is making them more marketable
- opportunity to learn new things
- fun at work (structured play, harmless practical jokes, cartoons, light competition, surprises)
- small, unexpected rewards for jobs well done

Turn-offs

- hearing about the past (especially yours)
- inflexibility about time
- workaholism
- being watched and scrutinized
- feeling "disrespected"
- feeling pressure to "convert" to traditionalist behavior
- disparaging comments about their generation's tastes and styles (Adapted from Bradford & Raines, 1992, p. 38)

MOTIVATING YOURSELF

Throughout this chapter we have addressed practical ways FLMs can motivate employees. In concluding this chapter, this section suggests ways for FLMs to keep themselves motivated. As a current or future FLM, you may find that you concentrate so much on motivating your employees that you forget to motivate yourself. Zig Ziglar, chairman of his own training and development company, See You at the Top, offers some suggestions for motivating yourself:

- *Give yourself a pep talk.* If you expect your employees to believe in you, you have to believe in yourself.
- *Set goals.* Be specific about the goals you want to achieve. Create a "wild idea sheet" listing "everything you want to be, do, or have."
- *Think positive and have reasons to support your outlook.* It is important to be enthusiastic about what you are doing, but you also need to *know* what you are doing. Get the training you need to support a positive attitude.
- *If necessary get professional counseling* from the Human Resource Management Department. There may be times in your career when you need help. Do not be afraid to ask for it from someone who has the wisdom and necessary knowledge to assist you.
- *Control your environment.* Control as many elements of your environment as you can. Exercise and eat well. Listen to music with positive messages, especially in the morning.
- *Use positive words to convey your message.* Learn to phrase your communications in a positive manner. This will give you better results and make you feel good about yourself and your co-workers.
- *Leave every encounter on a positive note.* Try to end every challenging situation with another person on a good note. This may be difficult sometimes, but doing so will make you feel better and will make the other person feel good as well. The other person will remember you favorably for it.

SUMMARY

Motivation is a complex, yet important topic for the FLM to understand. Unfortunately, some FLMs do not believe that motivation is a part of their job, believing instead that motivation is the responsibility of the individual employee. Effective FLMs realize that they must understand that general patterns of individual behavior contribute to motivation.

Motivation is the process of satisfying internal needs through actions and behaviors. It involves a composite of mental and physical aspects combined with the environment and other factors that aid in explaining why people behave the way they do. The motivation process model suggests that a need or motive leads to action or behavior that, in turn, results in the satisfaction of the need.

A more comprehensive model of motivation involves the integration of additional factors believed to influence the process of motivation. Such factors as the environment, perception, degree of importance, personal traits, effort, ability to perform, and rewards and punishments are essential to the complete understanding of the motivation process.

There are a number of methods FLMs and organizations can use to motivate employees. The methods based on motivational approaches include pay for performance, spot awards, merit pay, recognition awards, job redesign, empowerment, goal-setting, positive reinforcement, and lifelong learning.

Different groups provide specific motivational challenges in today's organizations. FLMs must recognize the unique motivational problems they will face in working with contingent workers, a diversified workforce, employees doing highly repetitive tasks, and baby busters.

REFERENCES

Bradford, Lawrence J., & Claire Raines. 1992. *Twenty something: Managing and Motivating today's new work force.* New York: Master Media Ltd.

LeBoeuf, M. 1991. *The greatest management principle in the world.* New York: Putnam Publishing Group.

Solomon, C. M. 1995. Managing the baby busters. *Personnel Journal* 71(3), 85.

Chapter 7

Developing Effective Team Skills

INTRODUCTION

Working with and building teams has become an essential function for FLMs in today's workplace. It is critical that FLMs effectively prepare employees and provide them with the skills and tools necessary to work effectively as part of the work team. Without basic skills, employees fail to achieve the goals of the team. Further, if team members lack the ability to negotiate to successful conflict resolution, that team can become paralyzed and unable to meet work demands. Thus, it is the responsibility of FLMs to assess the capabilities of their employees, and provide the competencies necessary to allow the team to function at optimal levels.

A FRONT-LINE MANAGEMENT CHALLENGE

Jared Smalls manages 19 operating employees at Connelly Products. One of his responsibilities is to assist employees who are not able to read well enough to do their jobs. Illiteracy is costly and risky because employees who cannot read are more likely to make mistakes or cause injuries. Connelly's solution is to train employees in the reading skills they lack.

Jared's first step is to identify which employees need help. This can be challenging because people who lack basic skills are often embarrassed and try to hide their illiteracy. "There have been times I haven't realized an employee couldn't read or write," says Jared. "Then when I hand the person a work order and see their face go blank, I get the message." Employees' reading problems also show up when they make mistakes in following written orders. Jared says, "We use special chemicals in a number of our production processes. Workers introduced them at the wrong time during the production process, and we end up with quality problems and reproduction efforts."

The next step is the hardest for Jared: getting employees who need basic reading skills to participate in training programs. Connelly offers employees a literacy training program through the local technical community college. To persuade employees to enroll in this program, Jared points out what they are missing because of their inability to read well. He also explains that more education can lead to promotion. In addition, the training is offered during normal working hours, so that, in effect, employees are paid to learn.

Jared believes that the literacy training is well worth the time and effort required. "I end up with better employees," he explains. "If nothing else, the time loss is more than made up by cutting down on the extra management time that's needed by nonreaders."

Jared's case demonstrates one of the many ways FLMs provide tools to allow employees to do a better job, resulting in less need for detailed supervision. This chapter complements the previous discussion of the FLM's roles in that it discusses tools that can make the FLM's job easier and more effective: orientation, training, development, conflict management, and negotiation. Orientation, training, and development attempt to provide employees with the information they need to understand their work and to perform successfully in the organization. Teaching employees to manage conflicts and negotiate should help them deal more effectively with their co-workers to solve problems.

ORIENTING NEW EMPLOYEES

An often neglected part of training is the orientation of new employees to the company and its culture. The failure to provide a thorough orientation can be a very expensive mistake because it may lead to job dissatisfaction and turnover. The cost of hiring, orienting, and training a new person is far higher than most of us realize. For example, Merck & Company, the pharmaceutical giant, found that turnover costs 1.5 to 2.5 times the annual salary paid for a given job. With turnover rates among new hires as great as 50 percent during the first 12 months, such costs can be considerable.

NEW EMPLOYEE/TEAM MEMBER PROBLEMS

Do you remember your first day at a job? When you arrived, you may not have known where you would be working or where the restrooms were. You probably did not know your co-workers or how they spent their lunch hour. You might not have known the details of how to do your job or where to get the supplies you needed.

The uncertainty you felt is common to new employees in all kinds of organizations. New employees form lasting impressions of the organization—both good and bad—within their first 60 to 90 days on the job. For that reason, FLMs should assume that all employees need some form of orientation. Remember from our discussion in Chapter 5 that special problems may arise for new team members. Special difficulties are also likely to occur when new employees join an organization and try to understand what is expected of them while dealing with the anxiety and discomfort of a new social setting. They may feel like an "outsider" or fail to understand what the organization expects from them in order to "get ahead."

The first few weeks and months with an organization are usually the critical period during which an employee will or will not learn to become a high performer. A carefully designed and implemented orientation program can increase the likelihood that the new employee will become someone with a positive attitude who is willing to work hard for the organization.

Perhaps no organization accomplishes orientation quite as effectively as the military. As soon as new recruits arrive, they are confronted by the stereotypical "in your face" drill sergeant. The recruits know immediately who is in charge and that only absolute, unquestioning obedience is acceptable.

Do not misunderstand our example. We are not suggesting that other organizations should copy the military and demand unquestioning obedience from new employees. What we are saying is that the military immediately tells new recruits what is expected of them, and these expectations are consistent throughout their military careers. It is clear from the military example that the optimal time to establish expectations about appropriate behavior is at the beginning of the employee's tenure with the organization. Metropolitan Property and Casualty Insurance Company has taken this lesson to heart with its Focus from the Start Program. The program includes guidelines for FLMs and co-workers to follow when orienting new employees, mentors who are assigned to help new employees, an employee orientation workbook, a formal feedback process which encourages new employees to communicate with their FLMs, videos on the company and teamwork, and copies of the company's vision and values.

THE ORIENTATION PROGRAM

An effective orientation program attempts to accomplish two important tasks which are described in this section:

- informing employees of company policies and benefits, which is called *policy orientation*, and
- making employees aware of locations and procedures that affect their abilities to do their jobs, which is called *procedural orientation*.

These tasks may be accomplished by the FLM, along with the company's human resources department and other individuals in the work group. Once implemented, FLMs should consider orientation an ongoing process that requires follow-up with participants as well as monitoring and evaluation to ensure the program is successful.

POLICY ORIENTATION

New employees must become acquainted with the policies and practices of their departments and of the company as a whole. Orientation programs therefore usually cover absentee and vacation policies, holidays, disciplinary procedures, and how to fill out company forms. Employees will need to study the options for medical and other fringe benefits, stock purchase plans, and retirement and insurance plans. They will learn the policies on employee purchases and discounts and how to use the credit union. Some companies find that detailed information should not be presented for about a week, or until after new employees have had time to adjust to the job, the coworkers, and the work environment.

PROCEDURAL ORIENTATION

New employees must learn the locations of things that are pertinent to their working lives: parking spaces, employee entrances and exits, time clocks, lockers, restrooms, bulletin boards, the cafeteria, coffee and smoking areas, and work-related departments. It is a sad comment on an organization's orientation program when a new employee is found wandering the halls in search of the restroom or the cafeteria. This orientation should also cover company procedures, uniforms, safety equipment, rest breaks, and details of pay.

THE USE OF SPONSORS OR MENTORS

Some FLMs consider it good management practice for an established co-worker to sponsor a new employee, at least during the first few days. In this way, a new employee can establish immediate rapport with someone in the same department, which helps the newcomer to overcome feelings of shyness or strangeness. The sponsor should be available to answer questions and to introduce the new employee to others. In general, co-worker orientation helps to ease a new employee into an organization; but the FLM must be careful when choosing an individual for this responsibility. The sponsor should be a friendly and informative person who understands the goals of the orientation program and of the organization.

PLANNING AN EFFECTIVE ORIENTATION

An orientation checklist that FLMs can use to plan orientation efforts is presented below.

_____ A genuine, warm welcome from supervisors and coworkers (there should be room for fun and celebration)

_____ Preparation of co-workers (at least a telephone call in advance of introduction)

_____ Introduction to co-workers and other employees in the organization

_____ Overview of job setting including tour of facility

_____ Assigning a volunteer mentor

_____ Providing an employee manual/handbook—enough information without overload:

_____ Brief history of organization

_____ Organizational overview

_____ Other items included by personnel department

_____ List of specific job requirements:

_____ Job responsibilities

_____ New employee's position in organization

_____ Work values

_____ Work expectations of the employees

_____ Critical facilities (e.g., restroom, copy machine, parking, etc.)

_____ Working hours and breaks

_____ Pay and performance appraisal policies

The HRM department would have a different list covering employee classification and records, safety, work rules, benefits, and other personnel-related activities. There may be some duplication between the FLM's checklist and the HRM department's checklist, but that is fine if they are coordinated.

FLMs should make every effort to *avoid* these approaches to orientation:

- *An emphasis on paperwork.* After completing forms required by the HRM department and then being given a cursory welcome, the employee is directed to the FLM to begin working. The likely result: the employee will not feel like part of the company.
- *A sketchy overview of the basics.* After a quick, superficial orientation, the new employee is immediately put to work. The likely result: the sink or swim atmosphere will make the employee feel insecure.
- *"Mickey Mouse" assignments.* The new employee's first tasks are insignificant duties, supposedly intended to teach the job "from ground up." The likely result: the employee will feel bored.
- *Suffocation.* Giving too much information too fast is a well-intentioned but disastrous approach. The likely result: the new employee will feel overwhelmed.

We can learn from other companies' mistakes what works and what does not. For example, consider how the Marriott Corporation handles new employee orientation. At Marriott, all new recruits attend an 8-hour initial training session, the highlight of which is an elegant lunch, served by hotel veterans. To guide them through the next 90 days, each associate is assigned a mentor, known as a "buddy." Every member of the entering class attends refresher courses after the first and second months. Finally, once the new hires reach day 90, the hotel treats the whole class to a banquet.

As you can see, Marriott puts less emphasis on policies and procedures and more on emotion. Why? Because the company recognizes that excellent service is more than just a transaction. It is an experience that ought to satisfy the employee as well as the customer. As one observer noted, "You can't expect your employees to delight your customers unless you as an employer delight your employees."

EMPLOYEE TRAINING AND DEVELOPMENT

Although the terms *training* and *development* are often used together, they are not synonymous. Training typically focuses on providing employees with specific knowledge, skills, and abilities, or helping them correct deficiencies in their performance. For example, training may be needed to teach employees how to use new equipment or to help an employee who does not understand a particular work procedure.

Development, on the other hand, is an effort to provide employees with a broader range of knowledge and skills that they will need to perform effectively in other jobs in the future as well as in their current jobs. This chapter will primarily focus on training, but much of the material applies to development as well.

THE FLM's ROLE IN TRAINING AND DEVELOPMENT

In her annual performance appraisal, Karen Seven heard from her supervisor, "Your balance sheets are unacceptable. This cannot continue; it must improve." However, when asked, her supervisor could not identify the type of training that might benefit Karen and wasn't sure there was money in the budget to support her taking a course at the local college. Karen left feeling that she lacked the skills necessary to make improvements and her supervisor was unwilling or unable to provide her with help.

The FLM in Karen's story did not fulfill one of the most important aspects of his job: to identify both the skills Karen needed to develop and the training or development opportunities that would provide her with those skills. Ultimately, it is the FLM's responsibility to make sure that proper training is provided. This responsibility cannot be delegated.

DECIDING WHETHER TRAINING IS NEEDED

Before beginning training, its value must be considered. The training process raises a number of questions FLMs must answer:

• Is training the solution to the problem?
• Are the goals of training clear and realistic?
• Is the training a good investment?

IS TRAINING THE SOLUTION TO THE PROBLEM?

A fundamental objective of training is to eliminate or improve performance problems. Not all performance problems call for training, however. Performance deficits can have various causes, many of which are beyond the employees' control and would therefore not be affected by training. For example, unclear or conflicting requests by FLMs, morale problems, and poor-quality materials cannot be improved through training. Before choosing training as the solution, FLMs should carefully analyze the situation to determine whether training is appropriate.

ARE THE TRAINING GOALS CLEAR AND REALISTIC?

To be successful, a training program must have clearly stated and realistic goals that guide the program's content and determine the criteria by which its effectiveness will be judged. Unless the goals are clearly articulated before a training program is set up, the organization is likely to find itself training employees for the wrong reasons or toward the wrong ends. If the goals are not realistic, the training will not meet expectations. For example, FLMs cannot realistically expect one training session to convert employees into computer experts. Such an impossible expectation will guarantee failure because the goal is unattainable. FLMs however, can expect employees to understand the use of software in production processes and preventative maintenance.

IS THE TRAINING A GOOD INVESTMENT?

Training can be quite expensive. The total amount U.S. companies spent on training in 1998 was close to $60.7 billion, up from $58.6 billion in 1997. Thus, while training may be appropriate, it is not always cost-effective. Before beginning a training program, FLMs and organizations must weigh the cost of a problem against the cost of the training to eliminate it. It could be that the cure is more costly than the ailment—in which case alternatives to training should be considered.

DEVELOPING A SUCCESSFUL TRAINING PROGRAM

In formulating an employee training program, FLMs should seek answers to the following questions, some of which will have been answered when deciding whether or not to provide training:

- Who, if anyone, should be trained?
- What training do they need?
- What are the purposes of the training?
- What are the instructional objectives that need to be incorporated into the training program? (Instructional objectives are basically what the employer wants the employee to know or be able to do upon completion of the training.)
- What training and development programs best meet the instructional objectives?
- What are the anticipated benefits to be derived from the training?
- What will the program cost?
- When and where will the training take place?
- Who will conduct the training?
- How will the training effort by evaluated?

Training must be viewed as an ongoing development process, not a simple bandage for a short-term problem. Therefore, training must be relevant, informative, interesting, and applicable to the job, and it must actively involve the trainee in the process. As Confucius put it:

I hear and I forget.
I see and I remember.
I do and I understand.

TYPES OF TRAINING METHODS

Whether or not employees come to a job with previous experience, some kind of formal or informal job training is needed. Most training takes place on the job, due to the simplicity and, usually, the lower cost of on-the-job training methods. This training may involve rotating employees into different job assignments or giving them supervised assignments where they can practice specific job activities under the direction of a more experienced employee. On-the-job training can disrupt the workplace, however, and result in an increase in work errors as learning proceeds. Some skills are also too complex to learn on the job. In such cases, training should take place outside the work setting.

There are a number of off-the-job training methods that FLMs can make available to employees. The most popular are classroom lectures, videos, and simulation exercises. Classroom lectures are well suited for conveying specific information. They can be used effectively for developing technical skills that are not easily presented by other methods. Interpersonal and problem-solving skills may be best learned through simulation exercises such as case analyses, experiential exercises, role playing, and group interaction sessions. Complex computer models, such as those used by airlines in the training of pilots, are another kind of simulation exercise, which in this case is used to teach technical skills. Vestibule training, is also technical, in which employees learn their jobs on complicated equipment identical to what they will be using, but located away from the actual work floor.

FOCUS OF TRAINING PROGRAMS USED IN TODAY'S WORKPLACES

Joe Dean has recently hired a new employee, Jeff, on his team. Jane, one of his long-term employees, comes to him with a complaint. She says that Jeff is trying to take over her job. According to her, Jeff thinks he knows everything and all of the work her group has done previously is worthless. She says she will not work with him anymore and may just look for another job. Joe knows Jeff has many ideas about how to improve work processes in the department. Clearly, Joe has a problem on his hands. As the FLM, it is his responsibility to provide the team with skills they need to function more effectively.

With the increasing popularity of team-oriented work environments, these types of situations are all too common. Further, the demands for increased efficiency and creativity have led organizations to provide training to their workforce in order to meet the challenges of the competitive marketplace. In this section we shall discuss some of the more popular types of training in today's organizations.

Team Training

Team training can be divided into two basic areas: content tasks and group processes. Content tasks directly relate to the skills needed to perform a job to meet the team's work goals. For example, a team may learn how to budget and control costs. Group processes pertain to the way employees work. For example, training may cover how team members behave toward one another or how they resolve conflicts. Unlike traditional individual training, which covers only content skills, team training usually includes group processes.

Creativity Training

As a means of tapping their employees' innovative potential, many organizations have been turning to creativity training. According to *Training* magazine (1997), the number of organizations with 100 or more employees that offer creativity training doubled from 16 percent in 1986 to 32 percent in 1990. More recently, it has jumped to 48 percent.

Creativity training is based on the assumption that creativity can be learned. There are several approaches to teaching creativity, all of which attempt to help people solve problems in new ways. Brainstorming is one common approach, in which participants are given the opportunity to generate ideas, no matter how wild, without fear of judgment. Only after many ideas have been generated are they individually submitted to a rational review of their cost and feasibility. This approach satisfies both the imaginative and practical phases of the creative process.

Literacy Training

The term literacy is generally used to mean the mastery of basic skills, that is, the subjects normally taught in public schools—reading, writing, arithmetic—and their uses in problem solving. Literacy is critical in today's business environment. Unfortunately, as shown through the case of Jared Smalls in the beginning of this chapter, many employees do not meet employer requirements in these areas. For example, although most workplace materials require a tenth or eleventh grade reading level, about 20 percent of Americans between the ages of 21 and 25 cannot read at even an eighth grade level. In a recent survey of manufacturers, over half of the responding companies indicated serious worker deficiencies in such basic skills as math, reading, and problem solving (Koretz, 1996). In the face of these problems, fully half of the organizations that provide remedial education now offer classes in writing, arithmetic, and English as a second language.

Diversity Training

Ensuring that the diverse groups of people working in an organization can get along and cooperate is vital to organizational success. As presented in Chapter 3, diversity initiatives or programs are designed to educate employees about specific cultural and gender differences and how to respond to these differences in the workplace. Diversity training is particularly important when teams are used.

Crisis Training

Unfortunately, accidents, disasters, and violence are part of life. Events such as plane crashes, chemical spills, and workplace violence can wreak havoc on organizations. Yet many organizations are ill-prepared to deal with tragedies and their aftermaths. In addition to after-the-fact crisis management, crisis training can focus on prevention. For example, as presented in Chapter 10, organizations are becoming increasingly aware of the possibility of workplace violence, such as attacks by disgruntled former employees or violence against spouses. Prevention training often includes seminars on stress management, conflict resolution, and team building.

Customer Service Training

Organizations are increasingly recognizing the importance of satisfying customers. In addition to establishing philosophies, standards, and systems that support customer service, these companies often provide customer-service training to give employees the skills they need to meet and exceed customer expectations. This may include skills such as how to respond to an angry customer in a way that will diffuse their anger and promote good will.

COACHING TO SUPPORT TRAINING

After employees have received training, an FLM should take on the role of coach to help them maintain and use the skills they have acquired. *Coaching* supports training by guiding and instructing employees in how to do their jobs and use their training to satisfy performance goals. The concept comes from sports, where a coach constantly observes team members in action, identifies each player's strengths and weaknesses, and works to help them capitalize on their strengths and overcome weaknesses. The most respected coaches generally encourage their team members and take a personal interest in them.

In a business context, coaching involves similar activities. As a coach, an FLM engages in regular observation, teaching, and encouragement to help employees develop so that they can help the team succeed. Much of this coaching is done informally to back up the more formal training program. The following summarizes the process of coaching:

1. Observe the employee's performance.
2. Is the employee meeting expectations?
3. If yes, paise the employee and consider opportunities for further development. If no, describe the problem.
4. Decide with the employee how to correct the problem.
5. Observe the employee's performance.

The process of coaching is different from simply telling employees what to do. It emphasizes learning about the employees and then drawing on and developing their talents. Acting as a coach is especially appropriate for FLMs in organizations that encourage employees to participate in decision making and teamwork.

EVALUATION OF TRAINING

Training and development expert Donald Kirkpatrick (1983) has defined four areas that can be evaluated to measure the benefits of training:

- employees' reactions to the training program
- the material learned
- their application of that learning to their jobs
- the training's effect on business productivity

An FLM is often in the best position to determine whether training is working. The most basic way to evaluate training is to measure whether the training is resolving the problem. Are new employees learning to do their jobs? Is the defect rate falling? Do employees use the new software or equipment properly? Are customers now praising the service instead of complaining about it? Looking for answers to such questions is central to the control process, which will be discussed in Chapter 8.

Training represents a cost to the organization, and therefore it is worthwhile only when it leads to improved performance, as measured by increased quantity, quality, or both. Training that does not produce results should be changed or discontinued. In organizations that are selective in designing training programs to meet their goals, training programs are not a wasted expense but a valuable investment in the organization's human resources.

SELF- AND CAREER DEVELOPMENT

Whether or not an organization routinely offers development programs, it is essential that all employees take responsibility for working out their own development plans. These development plans should include both short-term and long-term "career development" goals. FLMs and organizations who support employees in both their short-term and long-term career development pursuits are likely to attract and retain a highly qualified workforce.

Below we list two sets of suggestions to help employees enhance their own development and increase their opportunities for advancement. The development suggestions focus on personal growth and direction, while the advancement suggestions focus on the steps employees can take to improve their promotability in the organization.

DEVELOPMENT

1. Create your own personal mission statement.
2. Take responsibility for your own direction and growth.
3. Make enhancement your priority, rather than advancement.
4. Talk to people in positions to which you aspire and get suggestions on how to proceed.
5. Set reasonable goals.
6. Make investment in yourself a priority.

ADVANCEMENT

1. Remember that performance in your function is important, but interpersonal performance is critical.
2. Set the right values and priorities.
3. Provide solutions, not problems.
4. Be a team player.
5. Be customer oriented.
6. Act as if what you're doing makes a difference.

Which of these suggestions are you already following? If you are not working on them, you need to begin now. As an FLM you also can share these lists with your employees to enhance their development activities.

BUDGETING FOR TRAINING

In order to meet the training and development needs of their employees, FLMs must take the time to develop a budget for training. The training budget should be part of the FLM's regular budgeting efforts. Taking the time to develop a training budget is as important as any of the other planning and budget activities.

To prepare such a training budget, the FLM and team have to do three things:

- Decide what training and development is important for their department and identify the costs.
- Determine what nontraining factors contribute to achieving their departmental goals.
- Demonstrate the costs and benefits of training investment in their budgets by showing value-added results.

Even with the use of sound budgeting, cost control, and cost/benefit analyses of training efforts, FLMs will still face calls for doing more with less. Keeping up the morale of members of a team or department, especially during times of cutbacks, can be exhausting, and facing the prospect of financial and personnel cuts is threatening and demoralizing to any FLM and team. However, by defining training needs or purposes clearly and developing a budget that is responsible to those needs, FLMs increase the likelihood that their budgets will be supported by middle and top management.

UNDERSTANDING CONFLICT

This section considers another important tool for the FLM toolkit: an understanding of conflict and methods for handling it, including how to stimulate positive, or functional, conflict. We identify types and sources of conflict, describe major conflict resolution approaches, and discuss workplace violence and aggression. The chapter concludes with an introduction to the related topics of negotiation and mediation.

Katherine James, a new FLM, approaches her mentor in the organization with a concern. She says her team is having difficulty getting along. During meetings, they argue about how to proceed with the work. There also seem to be some interpersonal problems between several team members that have resulted in their not speaking to one another unless absolutely necessary. Katherine thinks that her group should just "get along." Her idea of the perfect team is one where team members don't argue and these interpersonal situations don't occur.

What Katherine fails to recognize is that conflict, defined as a difference of opinion between two or more individuals or groups, is a natural, and sometimes necessary, part of working with others. These differences of opinion, if managed well, can lead to better workgroup decisions and actions because those decisions and actions have been thoroughly discussed (or debated). It also can, however, result in workgroups that are unproductive because of their inability to get along and their tendency to personalize disagreements.

FUNCTIONAL AND DYSFUNCTIONAL CONFLICT

Conflict can be *functional*, in that it can improve an individual's or group's performance, or *dysfunctional*, even destructive, with negative effects on the people or organizations involved. Functional conflict can bring about a greater awareness of problems, enhance the search for solutions, and motivate employees to change and adapt when advisable. Dysfunctional conflict, on the other hand, can create distorted perceptions, negative stereotyping, poor communication, decreased productivity, and can even result in sabotage.

Conflict can be viewed as a bell curve. A moderate level of healthy conflict can enhance achievement. Too much or too little conflict, on the other hand, can lead to negative and even destructive behaviors, especially if unreasonable pressures and tensions are present. One responsibility of an FLM is to decide how much functional conflict is needed to create, enhance, and sustain the productivity of employees and to make sure it does not degenerate into dysfunctional conflict.

In a recent study, Robert Baron (1991) examined the perceived positive and negative effects of conflict and the conditions under which those effects were likely to result.

Baron's study identified seven negative effects of conflict and three positive effects. On the negative side, conflict

- interferes with communication;
- leads to or intensifies grudges and feuds;
- interferes with cooperation and coordination;
- diverts energies from major tasks or goals;
- leads groups to stereotype each other;
- leads to an increase in politics (i.e., individual efforts to acquire power to advance their own efforts);
- reduces the organization's capacity to compete in the marketplace.

On the positive side, conflict

- brings important problems out into the open;
- encourages innovation, change, and consideration of new approaches and ideas;
- increases loyalty and performance within each of the groups in conflict.

SOURCES AND TYPES OF CONFLICT

Before FLMs can respond effectively to a particular conflict, they need to understand it. They need to ask, "Who is involved?" and "What is the source of the conflict?" FLMs are likely to respond differently to a conflict that results from a clash of opinions than to one stemming from frustration over limited resources. Conflict may occur between or within organizations, within departments, and even between an individual and the organization. However, the two most common types of conflict FLMs deal with are structural and interpersonal conflict.

In traditionally structured companies, employees are organized by functional areas and departments: marketing and sales, research and development (R&D), maintenance, production, finance, legal, and human resources. These groups have different goals, different cultures, and different approaches and resources, and conflicts can naturally be expected to arise between them. These structural conflicts occur because of cross-functional departmental differences over goals, time horizons, rewards, authority, line and staff activities, status, or resources.

When structural conflict arises between two groups of employees an FLM may be able to help minimize or resolve it. FLMs can provide opportunities for the two groups to communicate and get to know each others' viewpoints, ask them to collaborate to achieve a mutually desirable goal, or give each group training in the role of the other group.

Because FLMs do not establish an organization's structure, they have limited impact on the sources of structural conflict. If they are able to recognize that a conflict is structural, however, they will know not to take the issue personally and will be alerted to situations that require extra diplomacy. FLMs also may be better able to understand the other party's point of view and communicate it to their employees.

Interpersonal conflict occurs between two or more individuals. Interpersonal conflicts may arise from differing opinions, misunderstandings of a situation, or differences in value or beliefs. Sometimes two people just rub each other the wrong way.

FLMs may be involved in interpersonal conflicts with a manager, an employee, a peer, or even a customer. In addition, FLMs may have to manage conflicts between two or more of their employees. Solving and managing interpersonal conflict requires knowledge about the nature of the conflict and skills for dealing with it. Practice will help you to build those skills.

DIAGNOSING SOURCES OF CONFLICTS

A checklist can help employees and FLMs diagnose the sources and types of conflict. Key questions about conflict are listed below.

- Where is the conflict in the system? Is it at the leadership, individual, group/ team, intergroup, organizational, or organization-environment level?
- What is the nature of the conflict?
- Is the conflict "functional" or "dysfunctional" and for whom?
- How is the individual, team, or department that is experiencing the conflict related to other parts of the organization?
- How high up and how far down the organizational chart does the conflict extend?
- Which people experiencing the conflict are ready for change?
- Do we have an approved conflict resolution method for solving the problem?

Understanding the sources of conflict in and between organizations is a first step toward resolution. Effective conflict resolution techniques that can be used by FLMs and organizations as well as individuals and teams are discussed later in the chapter.

MANAGING CONFLICT AND ENCOURAGING RESOLUTION

The goal of conflict management is primarily to prevent negative or dysfunctional conflict from occurring while at the same time encouraging healthy conflict that stimulates individual and team innovation and performance. If dysfunctional conflict cannot be prevented, then the goal is to eliminate it, or at least minimize it. This section will provide the FLM with tools to encourage functional conflict and discourage dysfunctional conflict.

A major goal of FLMs is to channel potential conflict into a positive, functional framework, making it productive rather than destructive. Programmed conflict is conflict that allows the expression of all opinions in a structured setting, so that personal feelings are not involved. It encourages open dialogue and constructive debate among potentially conflicting parties.

Cosier and Schwank (1990) propose two programmed approaches for stimulating functional conflict. A "devil's advocate decision method" and a "dialectic decision method." Both approaches require the participants to submit proposals for debate and engage in structured role playing.

The devil's advocate decision program includes the following steps:

1. A proposed course of action is generated.
2. A devil's advocate (individual or group) is assigned to criticize the proposal.
3. The critique is presented to key decision makers and additional information is gathered.
4. The decision to adopt, modify, or discontinue the proposed course of action is taken and the decision is monitored.

The dialectic decision method includes the following steps:

1. A proposed course of action is generated.
2. Assumptions underlying the proposal are identified.
3. A conflicting counterproposal is generated based on different assumptions.
4. Advocates of each position present and debate the merits of their proposals before key decision makers.
5. The decision to adopt either position, or some other position, (e.g., a compromise) is taken.
6. The decision is monitored.

The primary difference in the two processes is the fact that, with the devil's advocate approach, one proposal is being critiqued while with the dialectic model two competing proposals are considered.

Royal Dutch Shell Group, General Electric, and Anheuser-Busch have built devil's advocates into their decision-making processes. For instance, when the policy committee at Anheuser-Busch considers a major move, such as getting into or out of a business or making a major capital expenditure, it often assigns teams to make the case for each side of the question. This process frequently results in decisions using alternatives that previously had not been considered.

While it is vital that FLMs encourage functional conflict, or disagreement with the "status quo," it can be a real challenge for FLMs to hear unwelcome news. The news may make their blood boil or their hopes collapse, but they can't show it. They have to learn to take bad news without flinching: no tirades, no tight-lipped sarcasm, no rolling eyes, no gritted teeth. FLMs should instead ask calm, even-tempered questions: "Can you tell me more about what happened? What do you think we ought to do?" A sincere "Thank you for bringing this to my attention" will increase the probability of similar communications in the future.

OTHER APPROACHES TO MANAGING CONFLICT

FLMs have a variety of approaches they can use to address conflict. They may have to intervene as the person to resolve conflict in the work group as well. Some of these are described below. FLMs can

- divide up the conflict by reducing a large conflict into smaller parts and working on each part separately;
- contain the conflict, by limiting discussion to the present problem, not the past; refrain from labeling the conflict as the "fault" of one party and describe the problem in objective terms;
- allow the griping to set the agenda for problem solving and cooperate to solve those problems;
- look for areas of "common ground" where both parties might agree.

FLMs should prepare for conflict resolution by understanding the reasons for the conflict. They should focus on behavior, which people can change, and not on personalities, which they cannot change. It also is important to determine what actions are causing the problem and how that action affects the FLM and others. For example, if you are receiving weekly reports late from another FLM, you can describe the problem and why it is difficult for you. You might say, "I haven't been getting the weekly production reports until late Friday afternoon. That means I have to give up precious family time to review them over the weekend, or else I embarrass myself by being unprepared at the Monday morning production team meetings."

After you have stated the problem, listen to how the other person responds and attempt to understand their point of view. If the other person does not acknowledge there is a problem, restate your concern until the other person understands it or until it is clear that you cannot make any progress on your own. Often a conflict exists simply because the other person has not understood your point of view or your situation. Or, you may not understand their point of view. When you have begun communicating about the problem, the two of you can work together to find a solution. Restate your solution to be sure that you both agree on what you are going to do next.

SUMMARY

Effective orientation of employees is an important FLM responsibility. The primary reason organizations have orientation programs is that the sooner employees know basic information related to doing their jobs, the sooner they become productive. Policy orientation informs employees of company policies and benefits and procedural orientation makes employees aware of locations and procedures that affect their abilities to do their jobs.

Training is a cyclical process involving at least four steps:

1. analyzing needs
2. designing and developing training materials
3. delivering training and development programs/assistance or counseling
4. evaluating results and follow-up

FLMs need to determine the skills employees need to do their jobs better. Factors such as failure to meet organizational objectives, operating employees, introduction of new machines and equipment, addition of new responsibilities to a position, and the like can help the FLM pinpoint training needs. Development of training objectives and a procedure for evaluating the effectiveness of training are essential.

To help employees maintain and use the knowledge, skills and abilities they have acquired, an FLM takes on the role of coach, guiding and instructing employees in how to do a job so that it satisfies performance goals. An FLM may also act as a mentor to an employee, providing guidance, advice, and encouragement through an ongoing one-on-one work relationship.

Conflict is an integral part of organizational life and occurs because of disagreements or incompatibilities between individuals, or within groups and entire organizations. Conflict can be functional or dysfunctional and even destructive. The strategies provided in this chapter will help the FLM maintain healthy conflict as well as resolve dysfunctional conflict.

REFERENCES

Baron, R. A. 1991. Positive effects of conflict: A cognitive perspective. *Employee Responsibilities and Rights Journal* 4(1), 25–35.

Cosier, R. A., & C. R. Schwank. 1990. Agreement and thinking alike: Ingredients for poor decisions. *Academy of Management Executive* (February), 72–73.

Kirkpatrick, D. L. 1983. Four steps to measuring training effectiveness. *Personnel Administrator* (November), 57–62.

Koretz, G. 1996. A crash course in the 3R's. *Business Week* (May 20), 26.

1997 industry report. 1997. *Training* (October), 55.

Chapter 8

Planning, Organizing, and Controlling

INTRODUCTION

Organization is the key to succeeding as an FLM. As an FLM, the responsibilities can be overwhelming if the FLM does not effectively plan, schedule, and delegate tasks appropriately. These processes lead to a more controlled environment which, in turn, leads to a less hectic workplace.

PLANNING

Planning is the process of establishing objectives and selecting courses of action, prior to taking action. Objectives are the specific desired results, such as the goal to "increase energy efficiency by 10 percent." Courses of action are the series of steps taken to reach an objective, such as "hire a new maintenance engineer to boost maintenance response time by 20 percent." At a minimum, plans should specify what steps will be taken, how the steps will be accomplished, and a deadline for completing the step.

In most organizations, an FLM must plan for the accomplishment of tasks in his or her own team or department. This planning may include developing goals and identifying the tasks, resources, and responsibilities necessary to accomplish these goals. Through planning, the goals, which become the basis of all other actions, are established. Goals influence who the department hires, what types of incentives are used, and the controls instituted. As James Lasko's experience shows, planning can create a more positive environment for the FLM and his or her employees.

This past December my manager told me to schedule a major repair for one of our production machines to be done the 3rd and 4th of January. To get this done, I worked late to inspect the equipment, update the checklist, and make an inventory of the parts and tool rooms, ordering additional items that might be needed. The very next morning I met with my maintenance team to prepare them for the job. Over the next few days I reviewed items needing repair. I wrote a schedule of tasks to be done and assigned each task to the employee who is most competent to complete the task. I knew that after the piece of equipment was shut down, I would find some unexpected defects and everything wouldn't go exactly as planned. I assigned my best person—Lucy—to be in charge of unexpected repairs and to help other team members when needed.

When the team returned from the Christmas holidays, I gave each employee a list of assigned repair tasks for the equipment repair project. On January 2nd, we had a final meeting to prepare for the shutdown. I worked some extra hours that weekend, but the equipment was up and running on Monday morning.

As can be seen from this case of a maintenance FLM for Johnson Products, planning is a critical part of an FLM's work. In order to do the project, James Lasko first identified what needed to be accomplished and the tasks involved. During December, James continued to plan the equipment repair while also making the daily plans for his maintenance team.

There are many advantages to being an effective planner. Planning makes life easier for the FLM and the employees. Planning creates expectations and strategies for accomplishing the work which leads to more effective outcomes. Good planning also leads to tangible rewards at the team and organization level (e.g., increased productivity) and personally (e.g., pay increases or promotions). Planning keeps FLMs from constantly fighting fires, allowing them to act rather than react.

Planning Skills

Planning is an activity that everyone does to some extent. There are skills which you can develop, however, to make you a more effective planner. Understanding the basics of planning can make the task much easier. First, there are many different types of plans. Plans differ in terms of format (how they are expressed), horizon (the span of time they cover), and time span (how often they will be used). Let's take a look at each of these differences.

Formats

Plans are defined by their content. The content of the plan dictates the format to some extent. Some plans are developed to accomplish a task or a goal. This type of plan is a *descriptive plan*. A descriptive plan is what comes to mind when most people say they have a "plan of action."

This type of plan includes a written account of what is to be achieved and how.

Budgets are plans stated in numerical or financial terms. This type of plan typically expresses anticipated results and expenses in dollar terms for a specific time period, such as budgeting $8,000 this year for travel. Budgets may also be calculated in nondollar terms, including employee hours, capacity utilization, or units of production. Budgets may cover daily, weekly, monthly, quarterly, semiannual, or annual periods.

Budgets not only enter into the planning process but are considered control devices as well. The creation of a budget identifies what activities are important and how resources should be allocated to each activity. A budget becomes a control mechanism when it provides standards against which resource consumption can be measured and compared.

Plans which identify the activities to be done, the priorities of those activities, and the individual responsible for each is a *schedule*. The effective FLM continually considers how much work the department or team needs to accomplish in a given period and how the deadlines can be met. Scheduling is basically the process of formulating detailed lists of activities that must be accomplished to attain an objective, determining which activities have priority over others, and deciding who will do what tasks and when. This detailed listing is an integral part of a department's plan.

Plan Horizons

Plans also differ in the spans of time they cover. Some plans are developed to address a short-term need. Other plans target longer time frames. *Strategic* and *long-term plans* are often used by top management. A strategic plan specifies the long-term business goals of the organization and the major steps it must take to reach them. It usually includes a mission statement that answers fundamental questions about the business. FLMs will have little effect on the strategic plan, but they should know what it is and be able to communicate it to their employees.

Middle managers typically focus on developing shorter-term *tactical plans* with an intermediate term of one to five years. Tactical plans show how top management's plans are to be carried out at the departmental level. They are subsets of the long-term or strategic plan, addressing many of the same issues within the context of a competitive marketplace. Typical questions asked when preparing a tactical plan are: "What changes are going to occur among our customers, suppliers, and competitors, and how must we change to prepare for this new environment? What skills will our personnel need to compete effectively, and what must we do now so that they will be ready?"

First-line FLMs focus on *shorter-term operational plans*. These day-to-day or week-to-week plans are concerned with specific, current issues, such as levels of staffing, project scheduling, vendor reliability, and customer satisfaction, among others. Operational plans might show, for instance, exactly which employees are to be assigned to which tasks or projects or exactly how many repairs will be made on a given day. Operational plans are focused on the moment.

Frequency of Plan Use

Plans may be used only once, or repeatedly. *Single-use plans* are aimed at achieving a specific goal that, once reached, is not likely to recur in the future. One type of single-use plans is a *program*. A program is designed to carry out a one-time event or activity. It usually includes the steps involved, a schedule for their execution, a budget, and a list of affected personnel and their duties. A program may involve the expansion of a facility or the installation of major new technology. Deciding to undertake a program is the responsibility of top management. In well-managed organizations, FLMs who are affected by the program will be asked to contribute information to help develop it and will be involved in its execution in their areas of responsibility. A common example of a program is a management development program, designed to raise FLMs' levels of technical skills, conceptual skills, or interpersonal skills. Increasing the skill levels of FLMs is not an end in itself, as the purpose of the program is to produce competent FLMs who are equipped to help achieve organizational success over the long run. Once management skills have been raised to a desired level, the program is de-emphasized.

Another type of single-use plan is a *project*. A project is a one-time activity with a well-defined set of results. Other characteristics of a project include a definite start and finish, a time frame for completion, uniqueness, involvement of people on a temporary basis, a limited set of resources (people, money, and time), and a sequence of activities and phases. A project does not have to be part of a larger program, but may be a separate, self-contained set of activities.

In contrast to single-use programs, *standing plans* are plans made to be used repeatedly, as the need arises. For example, when an FLM has an employee who increasingly fails to show up for work, the problem can be handled more efficiently and consistently if a disciplinary procedure has been established in advance. There are three major categories of standing plans: policies, procedures, and rules.

Policies usually set broad guidelines for the organization. Policies may be written guidelines (e.g., each employee accrues eight hours of sick leave each month) or unwritten practice (e.g., we do whatever it takes to satisfy customers, we promote from within wherever possible). They cover a range of subjects, from how to deal with customer complaints, to the company dress code, to personnel issues, such as vacations, compensation, and promotions. Policies define the limits within which FLMs can make decisions and reduce ambiguity. Policies help FLMs make decisions, but they are not firm rules.

Procedures, as the name implies, specify what to do in a specific situation. For example, a procedure might state, "Before refunding the customer's purchase price, the salesperson should carefully inspect the garment and then obtain approval from the floor manager for the refund." Procedures are more specific than policies. Like policies, they provide consistency. By defining the steps to take and the order in which to take them, procedures provide a standardized way of responding to repetitive problems.

FLMs follow procedures set by higher levels of management. They also create their own standardized procedures for their employees to follow as conditions change and new, recurring problems surface. FLMs should make sure employees know company procedures and that they follow them. It is also important, however, to avoid clinging to ineffectual procedures when there are more efficient ways to do a task.

A *rule* is a highly specific, non-negotiable guide to action. They are formulated to avoid problems that would occur without them. Rules often have to do with issues of health and safety, interaction among employees, and attendance. Some examples of rules are "Always wear a hard hat on the job site," "No smoking on the plant floor," and "Except for emergencies, all absences must be approved by your FLM." Failing to follow rules usually involves a penalty, perhaps even dismissal. It is important to keep rules up-to-date and to enforce them impartially and consistently so that employees will take them seriously. FLMs frequently use rules when they confront a recurring problem because they are simple to follow and ensure consistency.

Why Plans Fail

Now that we have a better understanding of plans and planning, let's take a look at why plans fail. Some plans fail because *they are unrealistic*. The quickest way to doom a plan to failure from the start is to set unrealistic goals or expected outcomes. This ensures failure. Unrealistic goals are often due to outside pressure to succeed. If you tend to make unrealistic plans, stop committing yourself before you understand what is realistic.

Some plans fail because *they do not take the team into account*. It is difficult to make a successful plan without input from the people who will carry it out. To make success more likely, each person must be willing to participate and take responsibility for the work, have the capability and possess the skills and time to participate, and be willing to make plan success a priority.

Failure to provide performance expectations and feedback can lead to failure of the plan. Desired outcomes must be specified in measurable terms, setting the standards against which performance will be assessed and ultimately improved. Employees should frequently and frankly communicate about their progress in meeting performance objectives, and FLMs should give them frequent feedback.

Characteristics of Good Plans

Good plans are *realistic* plans. Carefully consider whether the desired outcome is actually an attainable goal. If the success of a delivery service hinges on getting the average order delivered within 35 minutes of the customer's phone call, and the driver's best average has been 42 minutes, the objective may be unrealistic. Simply wanting a change is not enough to make it happen.

If plans require people with special skills or knowledge to carry out the required tasks, training may be needed. It is important to *match the skill requirements* to the available staff. If the skills aren't readily available from the staff, training should be implemented.

A plan that *states specific means to an end* is a workable plan. If the FLM does not define the desired outcome and the method to achieve that outcome, the plan may not be seen as attainable. Specificity is a key to successful planning. This leaves less responsibility for the parties carrying out the plan.

Successful plans are specific, but they are also *flexible*. Every plan should have a "plan B" just in case the first option goes off track. Some roadblocks to plan success can be seen as detours when the FLM demonstrates flexibility with the plan. The prudent FLM watches carefully for signs of how well the target plan is working and then adjusts accordingly.

Finally, the strategy for successful plan achievement is a strategy that involves *communication*. Communication up and down in the organization's hierarchy must be a priority. If the delivery drivers are to be held accountable for new levels of performance, they must understand the plan to achieve those standards. Senior management also cannot be expected to allocate money to buy the drivers' phones if they do not understand or accept the plan.

Defining the Objectives

FLMs must communicate their precise expectations to their employees if they expect to obtain optimal results. FLMs should begin by defining their objectives. Objectives can range from the tasks the FLM intends to accomplish on a certain day to the level of production the department or team should achieve for the year. Good objectives

- state a clear purpose ("to increase productivity by 10 percent");
- are measurable ("assemble 50 additional television sets");
- specify a time frame within which they will be achieved ("every eight-hour shift");
- specify the resources needed ("by operating an additional assembly line for sub-assemblies");
- specify the quality of the output ("without increasing the rate of rejects above 2 percent");
- are challenging but also attainable ("handle employee grievances within 24 hours");
- are stated in writing to increase commitment and understanding.

The more specific an objective is, the more likely it is to be accomplished. By quantifying how much will be done, when it will be finished, and who will do it using which resources, the plan leaves less possibility of misunderstanding or error. The following suggests a format for writing clear, workable objectives:

What's the action? (verb)	What's the result? (noun)	When's it due? (time frame)	Who will check? (monitor)	What's the purpose? (reason/ purpose)

FLMs should determine, before beginning the project, what will determine progress. This means that indications of progress and deadlines for those expected indications should be included in the objective.

Writing an Action Plan

The process of writing objectives down forces you to think through the steps you will have to take in order to accomplish the objectives. This is more than a mental exercise: by breaking down large tasks into simple actions, the tasks seem easier. If the objectives are precisely stated and quantified, they will provide clear direction to the people actually doing the work. Clear objectives lead to clear work plans, also called activity plans or action plans. Objectives state what must be done; action plans explain how it will be done, specifying all the work details. While an objective is typically no longer than a paragraph, an action plan can be many pages in length.

The best way to write an action plan is to imagine doing the work, step-by-step, and then write down the key details. The following checklist describes an action planning process for a moderately complex project.

- List everything that must be done to accomplish the objective.
- List the tasks to be done in the order they should be finished.
- Identify, by name, who will do which tasks.
- List the resources that will be necessary for the completion of each task.
- Note the time needed for each task, including the estimated delivery time needed for materials not already on hand.
- Consider the constraints that might upset the plan and note the steps that can be taken to avoid them.
- Write the plan on a chart that reflects the passage of time, such as an event calendar or a Gantt chart that shows the beginning and ending points of every activity.
- Identify the control points that will mark the progress of activity.
- Develop a back-up plan just in case you cannot finish the action plan, or in case you finish the plan early.
- Update the plan periodically to reflect feedback and the most current data.
- Refer to the plan frequently. Make it a dynamic part of your operations. It is actually easier to write a plan than to follow it!

A plan with clear, measurable objectives supported by well-defined actions is ready to be communicated to the people who will implement.

Management by Objectives

Management by objective (MBO) is a process in which FLMs and employees identify common goals, specify ways employees will contribute to the accomplishment of those goals, and agree to use the measured results to evaluate the employees' performance. Here is how an MBO program works. Imagine you are the FLM of the data processing (DP) department. You must meet with your employees to discuss and set the department's goals, which are changing because so many microcomputers are being purchased for use throughout the company, as well as in your department.

It is reasonable to assume that the role of the DP department will change because many routine reports will soon be generated without DP staff involvement. In essence, your department is becoming less of a batch processing operation and more of a microcomputer support resource. What will your new goals look like? They will probably identify new customer service needs that will require the technical support people to acquire new skills, for example. Communicating the new goals of the department to your employees will probably require several lengthy discussions.

Next, you and your employees must write out the new objectives to help the department fulfill its new role as a support resource for microcomputer users. The current objectives that relate to batch processing assignments probably need to be updated or scrapped. Any necessary new technical training programs should be specified. Together, you and your employees should decide upon the following:

- what the employees will do
- how soon these tasks will be done
- what resources, approaches, or training will be used
- how the employees' performances will be measured
- when to meet next so the plan can be evaluated

A great advantage of the MBO process is that it gives employees low on the corporate ladder access to the decision-making process. This has two distinct benefits. First, it gives employees some control over their individual work plans. Employees' involvement increases their commitment to the objectives and enhances the likelihood that the objectives will be accomplished. Second, the organization receives the benefits of the employees' input, which may be more insightful about how to reach the new objectives than the ideas of management and may offer new suggestions for improving productivity that FLMs might not have considered. The MBO process may also result in a higher morale among the workforce.

There are four main ingredients common to MBO programs:

- *goal specificity*—specific statements of expected accomplishments
- *participative decision making*—the FLM and employee choose the goals and agree on how they will be achieved and evaluated
- *explicit time limits*—each objective has a concise time period in which it is to be completed
- *performance feedback*—continuous feedback on progress toward goals

Time Management

Time management is a tool anyone can use to schedule time and plan activities effectively. There are so many interruptions in the work day that there is little, if any, time to do much planning or scheduling. Efficient time management requires that you know what things you need to accomplish and you use the self-discipline necessary to keep your attention focused on accomplishing them. Unfortunately, there are no hard and fast rules for managing time that will work in every case; however, there are several time-management techniques that can make you a better time manager. At a minimum, you should learn to take the following steps:

1. Identify your objectives.
2. Prioritize your objectives.
3. Make a "To Do" list of the activities that must accomplished.
4. Set priorities for "To Do" list tasks.
5. Schedule your day.
6. Try to keep to the schedule throughout the day.

Time management is not something that generally comes easily. It takes a dedicated effort to be a good time manager. It requires learning how to set priorities and keep a schedule. Good time managers also know how to minimize disruptions. There are a number of "time wasters," such as interruptions or phone calls that steal a person's time.

FLMs attend many meetings, which can also waste time if the meeting doesn't have a purpose (see Chapter 5). Efficiently run meetings are time effective. When your presence is requested at a meeting, ask for an agenda and find out why you need to attend. Send a substitute if possible. Try to practice effective time management to maximize your personal productivity. Attempting to work faster or harder is not the answer; learn to work "smarter" instead.

James Lasko works "smart." He ends each day by reviewing the day's accomplishments and identifying work that remains unfinished. He makes a prioritized list of the work to be done the next day, with tentative schedule and job assignments. When he arrives at work the next morning, he only needs to make adjustments to include any new events, such as an emergency repair or an absent employee, and he is ready to put everyone to work without wasting time.

Scheduling Your Employees

Often there is some confusion between the scheduling and planning functions. Part of the problem is that two functions are frequently consolidated, particularly on smaller jobs. You should remember that the FLM's *plan* lists all of the resources and requirements needed while the *schedule* is a list of necessary activities, their order of accomplishment, who is to do each, and the time needed to complete each activity.

Scheduling requires the evaluation of three basic components: the work, the resources, and the customer. First, the FLM must identify and prioritize the work, including the backlog, pending jobs, and emergencies. Second, the FLM must know which workers and contractors are available when, and the skills, experience, and preferences of each. The availability of nonhuman resources is also essential.

Finally, the FLM can only schedule effectively by taking into account the convenience of the customer. For example, maintenance scheduling in hospitals must wait until it is convenient for the patients and staff, who could be in the operating room. It may mean that work should be scheduled for nights and weekends. Repairs to the HVAC system should be scheduled during the cool of an evening or during the colder months. Student support areas at universities should be scheduled for times when students are away, such as holidays or summers. The point is clear: every organization has its special maintenance requirements, and they are generally based on the organization's plan for serving customers at the customer's convenience.

To be effective in planning and scheduling work, the FLM must be proactive. That means that work should be scheduled before employees arrive at work, and the materials needed for work should be identified and allocated to each task or project. In addition, the FLM should be sensitive to the need for providing all employees with advance knowledge of the daily plans. Like other parts of the planning process, good scheduling allows the FLM to maximize the department's efforts.

A proactive scheduling program has many advantages. It is efficient: travel, time, special tool usage, and so forth can be optimized. It provides a good customer service, in that the production department runs better and the customer knows exactly when a maintenance service will be undertaken. It allows the FLM to build in training opportunities for team members to develop the experience they need. It also builds morale, by providing a constant level of work for all employees.

A reactive program, on the other hand, is driven by equipment failures and rife with deferred plans. It ensures large overtime charges, long lists of backlogs, aesthetic problems, reduced control over plans and budgets, and worst of all, customer dissatisfaction. This situation is easily spotted and does not bode well for the FLM, as customers and team members alike will react negatively to it. For effective scheduling, an FLM

- reviews all tasks not yet performed and any incomplete jobs;
- puts the jobs in priority order;
- lists all of the people available to complete the jobs, with their available hours, skills, and preferences;
- looks for opportunities to increase efficiency, such as making multiple assignments based on job location (e.g., two jobs in the same general area) or tools, materials, or skill set needed to perform jobs;

- designates assignments to each team member using a schedule, placing high priority jobs first;
- updates the schedule as new information comes in and jobs get completed;
- shuffles resources as needed, such as adding people or contractors or approving overtime to assist in large efforts, such as a repair that is falling behind schedule;
- keeps a list of back-up jobs so those employees can jump to another job if they finish one quickly or get stuck by a lack of parts or tools;
- communicates with customers about job schedules and pending disruptions.

There are many techniques used to make the scheduling process more effective. Many organizations expect FLMs to use certain scheduling techniques to assist them. Two of the most widely used techniques are the Gantt chart and the PERT chart. These scheduling techniques are methods of putting all of the information down on paper. Any effective scheduling technique requires the scheduler to be specific, be detailed and document every step.

ORGANIZING

The process of assigning people and allocating resources to accomplish the objectives set forth in the planning process requires organizational skills. Organizing is a step beyond planning and scheduling. Organizing is the process of making the plans and schedules happen. An organization consists of people whose specialized tasks are coordinated to contribute to the entity's goals. During the planning process FLMs decide what they are going to do; organizing is part of deciding how to do it, along with scheduling and budgeting. Organizing means figuring out how to make the action plan happen within the organization's formal and informal organizations. The skills and capabilities of people must be accurately assessed, and the FLM must establish a flow of work. Plans must be translated into job duties and job responsibilities.

Every organization has a formal structure that prescribes relationships among people and resources in order to facilitate the accomplishment of the organization's work. It is important for you to know how your organization is organized and understand why it is organized the way it is.

An organization chart shows the formal structure of an organization. It identifies key managerial positions and, by means of connecting lines, shows who is accountable to whom and who is in charge of what areas or departments. The informal organization is not shown on the chart. The organization chart also shows the chain of command or the line of authority between the top of the organization and the lowest positions in the chart. The chain of command represents the path a directive or suggestion should take in traveling from the president to operating employees at the bottom of the organization chart or from the operating employees to the top.

Each position on the organization chart has either a line (operating) or a staff relationship with the other positions. Line positions are directly involved in doing the moneymaking work of the organization. They accomplish the primary purpose of the organization. Staff positions provide operating departments with advice and assistance in specialized areas like personnel, finance, and research. The staff employees support the FLMs and operating employees at every level of the organization. This structure essentially serves the organization's two types of customers: the operating employees serve the "real" customers outside the organization, while the staff employees serve the internal customers, who happen to be the operating employees.

Centralization versus Decentralization

When businesses design their optimal organization structure, they usually find that parts of the company are centralized and other parts decentralized. A computer manufacturer, for example, may have a centralized manufacturing facility with a decentralized network of service providers spread throughout the country. This structure reflects the organization's objectives. Centralization and decentralization refer to the manner in which degrees of authority are spread throughout the organization. In a centralized organization, upper management makes most of the important decisions.

Decentralization describes a physical relationship, but it also describes a management style. The degree of decentralization in an organization can be quickly ascertained by asking one question, "Which decisions are made by whom?" If the first-line FLMs are allowed to make decisions involving large sums of money or affecting many employees, the organization is highly decentralized. On the other hand, if even senior managers must check with headquarters for approval on routine matters, the organization is highly centralized.

Authority is the legitimate or rightful power to lead others, the right to order and to act. It is the power by which an FLM or other manager can require employees to do or not to do a certain thing that the FLM deems necessary to achieve objectives. Management authority is not granted to an individual but rather to the position the individual holds at the time.

Authority is a continuum, with decentralized and centralized authority at each end. With the exception of very small companies, which tend to be centralized, most organizations lie somewhere between the two extremes, but can be classified overall. The key to success in today's world of work seems to be having the right balance between the two extremes.

Understanding the Informal Organization

The informal organization surrounds the formal organization. It is a complex and dynamic network of interpersonal relationships between organization members. These relationships cannot easily be diagramed like the formal organization, yet they are just as important to the smooth operation of any group of people. By their nature, they are different for every company and are continually changing. An FLM's success depends on the recognition and use of the informal organization. The informal organization and its communication channels provide more than just news; they are also important conduits for sharing experiences, fostering innovation and cooperation, generating support for new ideas, reaching consensus, collecting data for planning purposes, and directly or indirectly influencing people, groups, and events.

FLMs must realize that they cannot eliminate an informal organization and they can never completely control it. Even if it were possible to do so, it might not be desirable. Acknowledging the existence of the informal organization is the FLM's first step toward understanding it. An FLM can create an environment that nurtures the informal organization in such a way that it contributes significantly to the realization of the organization's formal objectives. Managing and using the informal organization requires an appreciation of its nature and its benefits. The FLM must learn to live with its vagueness, its spirit, and its strength. Like it or not, FLMs are a part of the informal organization by virtue of being members of the business. Successful FLMs learn to use their personal power to become active and effective participants in the informal organization.

To influence the informal organization to play a positive role, FLMs should group employees so that those most likely to work harmoniously together are teamed on the same assignments. FLMs should also avoid activities that would unnecessarily disrupt any informal groups whose interests and behavior patterns support the department's overall objectives. Conversely, if an informal group is influencing employees in a negative direction, causing a serious threat to the department's functioning, the FLM may have to reorganize by redistributing work assignments or adjusting work schedules, for example. One way to organize employees and to empower them is by delegating, which we shall discuss next.

Delegating

As noted in Chapter 6, today's successful FLMs need to empower their employees by giving them greater participation in decisions that affect them and by expanding their responsibility for results. One way to empower people is to delegate authority to them. Many FLMs find that this is difficult because they are afraid to give up control. "I like to do things myself," says one FLM, "because then I know it is done, and I know it is done right." Another FLM voiced a similar comment: "I have to learn to trust others. Sometimes I am afraid to delegate the more important projects because I like to stay hands on." Unfortunately there are many reasons why FLMs do not delegate.

FLMs who do not want to delegate will focus on all the reasons why they should not while FLMs who want to delegate will find ways to do so without adverse results. This section will show that properly planned delegation can actually increase FLMs' effectiveness and allow them to retain some control. Delegation is frequently depicted as a four-step process:

Allocation of duties. Duties are tasks and activities that need to be done. These duties are allocated to an employee or team.

Delegation of authority. Once duties have been assigned, the corresponding authority over those duties can be granted. The essence of the delegation process is empowering employees to act for you. It is passing to the employee the formal rights to act on your behalf. Be sure you have given the employee enough authority to get the materials, the equipment, and the support from others necessary to get the job done.

Assignment of responsibility. When authority is delegated, you must assign responsibility. That is, when you give someone "rights," you must also assign to that person a corresponding "obligation" to perform.

Creation of accountability. To complete the delegation process, you must hold the employees accountable for properly carrying out their duties. So while responsibility means an employee is obliged to carry out assigned duties, accountability means that the individual has to perform that assignment in a satisfactory manner. Employees are responsible for the completion of tasks assigned to them and are accountable to you for the satisfactory performance of that work.

The FLM's Role in Delegation

There are many FLMs who use delegation as a tool for developing employees through coaching and feedback. FLMs should recognize that they have an important role in providing employees with "stretch assignments," or more challenging opportunities to increase their skills. Delegation can be used to expand an employee's capabilities from a dependent, low-level performer to an independent, highly competent performer. This process takes time and effort by both the FLM and the employee. Delegation not only enhances employees' self-esteem but also increases their value to the team and organization. Delegation will only work, however, when the FLM is willing to delegate and the employee is willing to take on the responsibility and to develop appropriate skills.

One way FLMs increase their effectiveness through delegating is by careful planning, studying the tasks that need to be done and making appropriate matches between the work assignments and the employees. For each work assignment, the FLM should consider the nature of the responsibility and the readiness of the employee to assume it. The FLM can therefore avoid hovering, smothering, and generally "over-managing" the work of an employee who does not need much super-vision, and can avoid "under-managing" an employee who is not ready to be left alone to complete a task through a hands-off, sink or swim policy. After making an assignment, FLMs must mentally prepare to let go of any emotional investment they have in the responsibility for the task.

When FLMs delegate, they must understand that delegation is not the same as participation. In participative decision-making there is a sharing of authority. With delegation, employees and teams make decisions on their own. That is why delegation is such a vital component of empowering employees! Anyone who follows the suggestions below can be an effective delegator.

- Allow the employees to participate in determining what is delegated, how much authority is needed to get the job done, and the standards by which they will be judged, to increase employee motivation, satisfaction, and accountability for performance.
- Give a detailed assignment by providing clear information on what is being delegated, the results you expect, and any time or performance expectations.
- Specify the employees' range of discretion, including the amount and extent of their authority and their degree of responsibility.
- Inform others that the delegation has occurred, specifying the tasks, the amount of authority and employees involved.
- Establish feedback controls to monitor the employees' progress (i.e., specific time of completion of tasks, dates, when the employee will report back on how well they are doing, and any major problems that have surfaced).

Delegation allows FLMs to accomplish more than they could alone, due to the limitations of their own time and abilities. By letting go of tasks that can be and should be done more efficiently by others, FLMs put everyone's talents to better use. Table 8.1 describes FLM actions which lead to effective and ineffective delegation.

MANAGING FROM A DISTANCE

In planning for and organizing work in today's organization, FLMs must also learn how to manage effectively from a distance. This is be-

Table 8.1
Effective Delegation versus Ineffective Delegation

Effective Delegation	Ineffective Delegation
• Encourage the free flow of information.	• Hoard information.
• Focus on results.	• Emphasize methods.
• Set firm deadlines.	• Fail to set deadlines.
• Provide all necessary resources.	• Fail to provide necessary resources.
• Give advice without interfering.	• Fail to get input or point out pitfalls.
• Build control into the delegation process.	• Relinquish all control.
• Give credit for accomplishments.	• Fail to provide credit to employees.
• Back up employees in legitimate disputes.	• Fail to provide necessary support.

cause more and more employees work in scattered sites rather than one central location. Remember from our discussion in Chapter 1 on telecommuting that no longer do FLMs have to be at the office or job site to manage teams or individuals. Today's adept FLMs can and should be able to accomplish their charge from a distance.

How can an FLM operating at a distance ensure high performance? It all begins with developing and instilling trust and cooperation between the members of the team. FLMs can develop both of these elements by recognizing that a commitment to teamwork, planning, and good constant communication are important. Delegation can also be used. The following is a list of guidelines that can help FLMs become effective in supervising from a distance:

- Provide opportunities for face-to-face interaction among team members on a regular basis.
- Plan team meetings in as such a way that there is ample time for team members to get to know and learn from one another.
- Be responsive to the needs of team members working offsite.
- Bend over backwards to provide all necessary resources, materials, and supplies and remove obstacles for the team.
- Ensure that work schedules and job assignments are not prejudicial to team members, so that off-site work is scheduled equitably.
- Go offsite with team members as needed to understand the work environment, and spot check each employee's work on a regular basis.

- Communicate work priorities and timetables at team meetings and in writing when necessary.
- Give clear directions and instructions, set clear standards and expectations, and measure results against them.
- Give frequent performance feedback.
- When appropriate, send team members offsite to work in pairs.
- Trust your team members—do not assume that if they are out of sight they will goof off.

CONTROLLING

Once a plan is established and the FLM has organized a system for accomplishing the plan, everything should seemingly lead to success. Unfortunately, when working with humans who make errors, machines that break down, and changing customer demands, plans can fail—even when the FLM has organized their execution. To avoid plan failure and quickly identify and respond to potential failures, the wise FLM will put control processes into place. Control processes assist in the monitoring of resources and serve as guidelines for use of resources and completion of plans.

USING BUDGETS IN PLANNING

Almost every FLM gets involved in planning the budget. You probably already know something about budgets, even if you do not think of a budget as a plan. There is one thing you should remember about budgets: a budget is not an independent goal but a tool to help you improve procedures and deliver more value and service to customers.

A budget is a type of comprehensive, numerical plan for the allocation of resources to achieve team, departmental, or organizational goals and objectives. To put it somewhat differently, a budget is a statement of expected results expressed in numerical terms. It may be financially oriented, as in revenues, expenses, cash, and capital budgets, or it may be nonfinancial but still numerical, covering direct-labor hours, materials, equipment, number of programs and services, trainee output, and so on.

A budget is also a form of managerial control. It is a means of ensuring that results conform to plans by providing a basis for measuring performance. Budgets are used to identify deviations and shortfalls and to remedy those deficiencies or to adjust expectations. The purpose of a budget, therefore, is to make it possible for managers at different levels of the organization to determine what resources should be expended, by whom, and for what (planning), and what resources are being expended, where, by whom, and for what (control). Budgets help FLMs perform better and help improve the company's overall operation. Here's how. Budgets

- focus FLMs' attention and effort on results;
- compel FLMs to contribute to the attainment of organizational objectives, such as profitability, growth, efficiency, and resource development;
- facilitate measuring performance by comparing results with goals and objectives;
- provide a basis for assessing the appropriateness of the organizational structure, goals, and objectives;
- enhance interdepartmental coordination, effectiveness, and teamwork;
- encourage the use of historical reports and records in the planning process;
- help identify areas where cost controls and hard-dollar savings can be realized.

THE BUDGET PROCESS

Within their own departments, FLMs are the budget officers. They must prepare the department's budget, present and defend it to their managers, and manage its operation throughout the year. All of the departmental budgets provide input into the overall corporate budget.

Developing a budget is a complex process. Two factors make this complex process much simpler: sufficient time, and clear areas of responsibility and authority. There should be various deadlines throughout, and FLMs must be sure to allow enough time for review and discussion at each step along the way.

Seen from the perspective of the organization as a whole, a healthy and effective budgeting process needs five ingredients:

- a clearly defined organizational structure, with explicit functions, and lines of authority and communication;
- a comprehensive and well-understood budget planning process, with a budget calendar, and procedures and guidance for budget preparation, internal controls, and review and analysis;
- a fully developed accounting system, including standard costing, break-even analysis, and profit-contribution accounting;
- fixed responsibility for the comprehensive budget program;
- FLMs who are knowledgeable about financial planning and the budgeting process.

In designing a budget, FLMs should be sure that the process is clearly defined, preferably in writing, identifying exactly who does what, and should make sure all team members understand it. Usually FLMs prepare the budget with help from their managers and contributions from their employees. Budget preparation must be based on continuous scrutiny of the department's initiatives, operating methods, organization structure, and facilities. It must always be based on departmental plans, and it must be applied within a framework of corporate and department or team goals and objectives.

After preparing the department's expense budget, the FLM usually submits it to the managers at the next higher level for review and approval of accuracy, completeness, and adherence to organizational policy. FLMs may also, depending on their needs, create budgets for employee work hours, revenue forecast, or capital expenditures like machinery and equipment. These budgets set specific standards for FLMs and their department or team to achieve.

Preparing the budget is one challenge; getting their managers' and top management's approval is another. FLMs, like all other managers in organizations, compete with one another for their share of limited organizational resources. They must be able to justify their requirements clearly and convincingly or fail to receive the funds they need. The FLM is the only one who has the stature and knowledge to present the department budget to the decision maker authoritatively and persuasively, and win approval.

After a budget has been approved and adopted, it becomes a management tool. FLMs must continuously monitor their budgets throughout the year and ensure those policies and rules are followed. They must also be alert to the need for budget adjustments and reprogramming as conditions change and impact budget allocations. In other words, FLMs should be flexible during budget allocations and use the numbers established during the budgeting process as guidelines for what's reasonable. For example, the FLM may find that the work unit has almost used up its overtime budget. When a new work request comes in that will require more overtime, the FLM must decide whether to spend extra money on labor to take care of the request or stick to the budget regardless of the request. In some organizations, keeping to the budget becomes so important that the latter choice is preferable and provides little budget allocation for the FLM. This should not happen. Budget numbers are not objectives—they provide guidance for achieving objectives at a reasonable cost.

These are the key steps an FLM can take to assist in effective budgeting:

• Develop or review the organization's long-range strategy.
• Determine and set your department's objectives and means of attaining them.
• Establish budget procedures and a schedule.
• Gather cost information.

- Prepare the department's draft budget.
- Share your goals and cost estimates with your boss.
- Revise the draft budget into a proposed budget for review by management.
- Be prepared to negotiate for your budget items.
- Monitor your budget, noting areas of savings and unanticipated expenses.
- Take corrective actions when the budget is not being met.
- Keep your boss informed of your progress.

Budget problems exist in many departments. All too often, people within and outside the department play budget games. There are also numerous pitfalls for the unwary FLM. FLMs should take responsibility for their own budgets. Although they should use the expertise of their managers for advice and assistance, they should never rely on others to prepare their budgets.

FLMs have found countless ways to mislead or deceive decision makers into believing that the FLMs are performing well. One favorite approach is to underestimate sales and overestimate costs. These techniques skew the budget and make the process a useless exercise. FLMs may pad the budget or hide extra funds within it due to the budget folklore: "They'll cut it, so inflate it," or "Conceal it for contingencies." These practices occur when FLMs believe they will be rewarded or punished for either spending their total budget allocations or returning funds at the end of a budget period.

SUMMARY

Planning establishes the goals which should be the basis of all the other management functions—organizing, leading, and controlling. The people hired, the incentives used, and the controls instituted all relate to what FLMs want to achieve and to the plans and goals they set. Plans differ in terms of format, horizon, and frequency of use.

FLMs focus on short-term operational plans. Some plans are programs established to lay out in an orderly fashion all the steps in a major one-time project, each in its proper sequence. Programs and projects are single-use plans that are aimed at achieving a single goal. Policies, procedures, and rules are standing plans made to be used repeatedly, as the need arises.

The plans fail most often because they are unrealistic, they do not take the team into account, they lack meaningful checkpoints, and/or they fail to provide performance feedback. Successful plans are specific, but they also are flexible, reflect reality, and reflect the knowledge, skills, abilities, and experiences of the individuals implementing the plans. Successful plans are the result of precisely stated and quantified objectives that provide clear direction to the people actually doing the work. Clear objectives lead to clear work plans or action plans.

Once a plan is established, the FLM must ensure that the plan is followed. Without implementation, the plan is nothing more than an idea about how work should be accomplished. Plan implementation requires that the FLM use organizing and controlling functions. Organizing is the key to carrying out the plan or schedule. Organizing requires the FLM use available resources in performing required tasks. Often, the FLM chooses to delegate tasks to those whom the FLM manages as the most efficient means of accomplishing those tasks.

Planning and organizing lead to task accomplishment; but without control processes in place, things can become derailed over time. Control processes are important, not only to ensure that processes are maintained, but also to serve as a warning light when processes first begin to go awry.

Chapter 9

Performance Appraisals

INTRODUCTION

The major purpose of management controls is to ensure that work is progressing according to the FLM's plans. Controls should, therefore, be designed to alert FLMs to problems or potential problems before they become critical and to give FLMs time to take corrective actions. Controlling is similar to planning in many ways. The major difference between controlling and planning is that planning takes place before work is done and controlling usually takes place while work is ongoing.

In this chapter, we shall first outline the control process and briefly discuss benchmarking as a contemporary tool for monitoring and measuring performance. The chapter will then provide an in-depth discussion of performance appraisals as an FLM tool for monitoring and improving employee performance and will conclude with a discussion of discipline.

THE CONTROL PROCESS

As described in Chapter 8, controlling is the management function concerned with monitoring performance to ensure that it conforms to plans. FLMs carry out this process in many ways. Consider the following fictional examples:

- Arnold Blank told his crew, "I expect the work area to be clean when you leave each day. That means the floors should be swept and all the tools should be put away."
- Once or twice each day, Fran Freedom took time to check the documents pro-

duced by the printing operators she managed. Fran would look over a few pages each employee had produced that day. If one of the employees seemed to be having trouble with a task—for example, writing legibly or preparing neat tables—Fran would discuss the problem with that person.

• Ted Tyler learned that customers calling his department complained that they were spending an excessive amount of time on hold. He held a meeting at which the employees discussed how they could handle calls more quickly.

As shown in these examples, FLMs need to know what is going on in the area they manage. Do employees understand what they are supposed to do and are they able to do it? Is all the machinery and equipment— from computer-operated machines to touch-tone telephones—operating properly? Is work being done correctly and on time?

To answer these questions, an FLM could theoretically sit back and wait for disaster to strike, assuming that where there is no problem, there is no need for correction. However, FLMs have a responsibility to correct problems as soon as possible, which means that they need some way to detect problems quickly. Detection and correction of problems is at the heart of the control function.

By controlling, the FLM can take steps to ensure quality and manage costs. By setting standards for a clean workplace, Arnold Blank reduced the costs related to spending time looking for tools or slipping on a messy floor. By visiting the work area and checking on performance, Fran Freedom made sure that her employees were producing satisfactory work and correcting problems before they became severe. By engaging his employees in improving work processes, Ted Tyler responded effectively to customer concerns. In many similar ways, FLMs can benefit the organization through the control process.

STEPS IN THE CONTROL PROCESS

Control is accomplished by comparing actual performance with predetermined standards or objectives and then taking action to correct any deviations from the standards. The control process has three basic steps:

1. Establishing performance standards.
2. Monitoring performance and comparing it with those standards.
3. Taking necessary corrective actions.

The first step is part of the planning process while the other two are unique to the control process.

Establishing Performance Standards

Once organizational objectives have been set, they generally are used as standards that outline expectations for performance. Standards are used to set expected performance levels for machines, tasks, individuals, groups, or the organization as a whole. Usually standards are expressed in terms of quantity, quality, or time limitations. For example, standards may cover production output per hour, product quality as reflected by the level of customer satisfaction, or production schedule deadlines.

Performance standards attempt to answer the question, "What is a fair day's work?" or "How good is good enough?" Standards take many factors into account that may impact outcomes, such as inevitable delays and time for equipment maintenance. Several types of performance standards are described below:

- *Productivity standards*—designed to reflect the output per unit of time. Example: numbers of units produced per work hour.
- *Material standards*—designed to reflect the efficiency of material usage. Examples: amount of raw materials used per unit, or average amount of scrap produced per unit.
- *Resource usage standards*—designed to reflect how efficiently organizational resources are being used. Examples: return on investment, percent of capacity, asset usage.
- *Revenue standards*—designed to reflect the level of sales activity. Examples: dollar sales, average revenue per customer, per capita sales (i.e., sales per person).
- *Cost standards*—designed to reflect the level of costs. Examples: dollar cost of operation, cost per unit produced, cost per unit sold.

Many methods for setting standards are available. The choice of the most appropriate method depends on the type of standard in question. A common approach is to use the judgment of the FLM or other recognized experts to set the standard, but this approach can be very subjective. A variation is for the FLM and the persons performing the job to set the standard together, thus allowing the employees who actually perform the job to provide input. The most objective approach is to use industrial engineering methods, which usually involve a detailed and scientific analysis of the work to be done.

Monitoring Performance

The primary purpose of monitoring performance is to provide information on what is actually happening in the organization. Monitoring should be preventive and not punitive. In this light, the reasons for monitoring should always be fully explained to employees.

The major problem in monitoring performance is deciding when, where, and how often to monitor. Timing is important. For example, raw materials or parts like those that took four days to be delivered to Ted Tyler's unit must be reordered before they run out so as to allow for delivery time. Monitoring must, therefore, be done often enough to provide adequate information. If it is overdone, however, it can become expensive and can annoy employees. The key is to view monitoring as a means of providing needed information and not as a means of checking up on employees.

There are several tools and techniques FLMs can use to monitor performance. Budgets, reports, audits, and personal observations are the methods most commonly used for this purpose.

Budgets express plans, objectives, and programs of the organization in numerical terms. The administration of the budget is an important controlling function for an FLM. However, excessive reliance on a budget can result in inflexibility or inefficiency. Take, for example, John Smith, a manager in a high tech computer company. John has determined that adherence to his budget is his most important goal. When Sue, his subordinate, comes to him with a new technology in which she thinks they should invest, John says it is not in this year's budget. Despite Sue's information that this technology will speed up the manufacturing process and ultimately reduce overhead, John still insists they can't afford it this year. John meets his budget goals, but quickly falls behind his competitors in terms of efficiency. In the long run, John's decision hurt the company. Thus, budgets should be used as a standard guideline and not as a fixed goal.

Reports are designed to provide important summary information as a second means of monitoring organizational or unit performance. Written reports can be prepared on a periodic or an as-needed basis. These reports may summarize information or interpret the data provided and make recommendations. Reports should be simple and provide information in the most useful way (e.g., by using tables or graphics when appropriate). FLMs should continually monitor a report's usefulness in terms of its timeliness, cost effectiveness, acceptability, and flexibility, among other factors.

Personal observation is sometimes the only way for an FLM to get an accurate picture of what is really happening in an organization, particularly with respect to individual employees. One type of personal observation is management by walking around (MBWA). When this method is used, FLMs are encouraged to walk around and mingle with one another and with the employees. If used appropriately (and not too much!) observations not only provide information to the FLM but also communicate to employees the FLM's interest in them. However, FLMs should remember that what they are observing may be employees on their "best" behavior. It is important also to consider how employees work when the FLM is not watching.

In addition to personal observation, many organizations collect performance information electronically. Examples include electronic cash registers that keep a record of what items are sold and when, video cameras that record employee and customer movements, and phones that record how long each customer is engaged. FLMs then can establish appropriate goals for the unit's performance on these measures, such as the average number of minutes for processing an insurance claim. Organizations such as Bell Canada, Federal Express Corporation, and Northwest Airlines have successfully used these types of monitoring systems. However, FLMs also should note that there are legal risks associated with hidden surveillance and that this type of system may be perceived as overly controlling by employees. Further, focusing too heavily on electronic monitoring may encourage employees to focus more on quantity than quality. Take, for example, Kathy Pearce, an FLM in a grocery store. In an effort to monitor performance, Kathy began tracking the number of customers processed by each cashier and told all of her cashiers that they should process 45 customers per hour. Three months later, they were processing 45 customers per hour, and customer complaints tripled. Upon further investigation, Kathy found that the cashiers were rushing people through the lines, making numerous errors, and responding poorly to customers with large orders in order to meet their per customer goals.

Management by Objectives

Management by objectives (MBO) was discussed in Chapter 8 as a means for setting objectives. The development of an MBO system is part of the planning function. Once such a system has been developed, however, it can be used for control purposes.

Taking Corrective Action

Only after the actual performance has been assessed and compared with the performance standards can FLMs take proper corrective action. All too often, however, FLMs set standards and monitor performance but do not follow up well. A major problem is determining when and why a deviation from the standard is occurring. How many mistakes should be allowed? Have the standards been set correctly? Is the poor performance due to the employee or some other factor such as a lack of proper equipment or training? The key here is the FLM's timely intervention. An FLM should not allow an unacceptable situation to exist for long but should promptly determine the cause and take action.

INDIVIDUAL PERFORMANCE APPRAISALS

Ted Tyler has just been informed by the human resources management (HRM) department that it is time to conduct performance appraisals of his employees. Prior to becoming an FLM, Ted had always felt uncomfortable during his own performance appraisal; he had always felt on the defensive. His manager never seemed to reward his good performance or give him enough specifics to know how to improve. Now that he is an FLM, he does not want his employees to feel the same way. Ted knows that some of his employees deserve an unfavorable appraisal, however, and he certainly is not looking forward to discussing their appraisals with them.

Ted's attitude about performance appraisals is all too common among FLMs. The need to evaluate individual, maintenance team, or departmental performance effectively is as important as ever in today's organizations. FLMs like Ted should think of appraising performance as a kind of compass—one that indicates an individual's or team's actual direction compared to the desired direction. Like a compass, the job of Ted and other FLMs is to indicate where the individual or team is now and to help focus attention and effort on the desired direction.

Unfortunately, many FLMs view performance appraisal as a once a year event when as a supervisor, he or she completes the company appraisal form for each employee. This approach is a mistake. Appraising employee performance should be part of a continuous improvement process that demands daily, not annual, attention. Think of it this way: Why are weekend golfers willing to pay handsomely for private lessons? So that a professional who understands and can demonstrate good performance will observe their performance, evaluate it, and then provide feedback to build sound habits and eliminate unsound ones. Subsequent lessons focus on the overall objective, such as a smooth, accurate swing, while recalling information about performance given in earlier lessons. This type of golf instruction is similar to supervising for maximum performance.

THE PURPOSE OF EMPLOYEE PERFORMANCE APPRAISALS

Twenty years ago, the typical FLM would sit down annually with individual employees and critique their job performances. The purpose of these appraisals was to review how well the employees were progressing toward achieving their goals. The employees found that the performance appraisals gave them little more than a documented list of their shortcomings. Of course, since the performance appraisal is a key determinant in pay adjustments and promotion decisions, anything to do with appraising job performance struck fear into the hearts of employees. Not surprisingly, in this climate FLMs often wanted to avoid the whole appraisal process, and in many instances formal appraisal programs yielded disappointing results. Their failure was often due to a lack of top-management information and support, unclear performance standards, lack of important skills for FLMs, too many forms to complete, or the use of appraisals for conflicting purposes.

Today, effective FLMs treat performance appraisals as an evaluation and development tool, as well as a formal legal document. Appraisals review past performance—emphasizing positive accomplishments as well as deficiencies and drafting detailed plans for development. By emphasizing the future as well as the past, documenting performance effectively, and providing feedback in a constructive manner, employees are less likely to respond defensively to feedback, and the appraisal process is more likely to motivate employees to improve where necessary. The performance evaluation also serves as a vital organizational need by providing the documentation necessary for any personnel action that might be taken against an employee.

WHEN SHOULD APPRAISALS OCCUR?

Ideally, performance appraisals should occur both formally and informally. Formal performance reviews should be conducted once a year at minimum, but twice a year is better. Informal performance appraisals and feedback should complement the formal appraisal system. The ultimate goal is to establish an effective "performance management system" where performance is monitored and managed overall, not just appraised in a once a year session.

Continuous feedback is primarily important in letting employees know how they are doing. Without constructive feedback, employees tend to assume that their performance is acceptable, and problems may continue. Without positive feedback or praise, employees begin to feel that their hard work is unappreciated and may decide to stop putting forth so much effort. Employees need and expect frequent communication and feedback about their performance—not just during the formal appraisal interview session. FLMs must make it a habit to get out among their employees throughout the day or week and do not wait for their employees to come to them. This type of frequent interaction also tells employees that their FLM thinks they are important.

RESPONSIBILITY FOR FORMAL PERFORMANCE APPRAISALS

An immediate FLM, who is usually in the best position to observe the employees and evaluate how well they perform their jobs, should complete a performance appraisal. There are some situations in which a "consensus" or "pooled" type of appraisal may be done by a group of FLMs, such as when an employee works for several FLMs. In organizations that have implemented a work team concept or large spans of management control, it is important to consider how information can be gathered so that the performance appraisal ratings are based on observation of job performance and are fair to all employees.

COMPONENTS OF AN EFFECTIVE PERFORMANCE MANAGEMENT SYSTEM

One key component of a performance management system is the form used to document and appraise performance. There are numerous types of performance appraisal forms that organizations use. Some organizations use graphic rating scales that describe competencies that are important for success (e.g., teamwork) and ask FLMs to rate an employee's level of proficiency or effectiveness (e.g., on a 5-point scale) on each competency. Similarly, behaviorally anchored rating scales (BARS) outline competencies of performance and provide behavioral descriptors of key anchors on the rating scale FLMs use to evaluate performance (e.g., behavior representing a "1," behavior representing a "5," etc.). Forms also may ask FLMs to rank order or compare employees in a workgroup or to mark statements that are most or least characteristic of an employee. Essay forms ask FLMs to write a narrative description of an employee's performance. Critical incident appraisal, on the other hand, asks FLMs to record specific instances of very effective or very ineffective performance for an employee. Finally, several approaches to appraisal, such as the work standards approach and management by objectives, ask FLMs to set specific standards for performance, such as quality or timeliness of work produced, and to measure employees against these standards.

In most cases, the HRM department in an organization will dictate the performance appraisal form that must be used by the FLM. Further, each type of appraisal format has its advantages and disadvantages. However, there are principals for conducting effective appraisals that can help FLMs, regardless of the appraisal form they have been provided. Further, even with a good form, FLMs can do a poor job of implementing the system. Consider the following example:

James sits down to complete a yearly review on Pat Taylor. Pat has been a good worker in the past, but lately his work has been a bit sloppy. When Pat arrives, James begins the session and the dialogue goes something like this:

James: Pat, as you know, it is time to conduct your yearly review. Here are your ratings on the appraisal form. You will see that your work has been unacceptable. If this doesn't improve I am going to have to take drastic action.

Pat (startled): This is news to me. I have always worked hard for this organization. I don't know what you mean.

James: Well, I have heard there are problems. Last Tuesday you were late to work.

Pat: I was late to work because of traffic and that is the only day I have been late in years.

James: Well, you don't seem to have your heart in work. Your attitude is a problem.

Pat (agitated): My attitude is a problem!!?? I have given 10 years to this company and worked hard every single day. I think this whole thing is about personalities, not performance.

Unfortunately, interactions like these are not uncommon in performance appraisal sessions. James is willing to give Pat feedback, but fails to document performance effectively or give Pat feedback that he can actually use to improve. As a result, Pat is defensive and attributes everything to a personality conflict. Clearly this is not how an FLM would like the interaction to happen. A good performance appraisal form, coupled with proper implementation, can help avoid disastrous appraisal sessions like this. A good performance management system should include:

Job- and organization-relevant dimensions. FLMs should be rating job-relevant dimensions or items that are clearly observable and defined in terms of behavior (i.e., how does the organization define teamwork in terms of what you expect people to do).

Clearly defined rating system. The system should have a clearly defined rating scale for FLMs to rate performance.

Integration with other systems. The appraisal system should be integrated with other performance monitoring systems, such as overall units produced or quality indices the FLM has established for the unit overall. Employees need to be evaluated on their contributions to these overall objectives.

Developmental focus. Effective performance management includes not only appraising performance but also establishing specific development plans for employees which include outlining how an employee can im-

prove (e.g., what specific steps he/she will take, what training or resources the FLM will provide, etc.).

Documentation. Effective FLMs will document instances of performance
throughout a rating period so that when they complete an appraisal
form, they have specific information to provide to employees. Further,
this enables FLMs to ensure they are considering performance throughout a rating period, not just what happened (good or bad) this week.

Rater training. FLMs should receive training on the appraisal system
(e.g., how to document and rate performance, complete the forms, and
comply with the requirements of the appraisal system). This training also
may include sources of bias in appraisal, which will be discussed later
in this chapter.

Clear expectations. Regardless of the appraisal form or system in place
in an organization, the expectations for performance should be clearly
defined and communicated to employees.

Ongoing feedback. As has been mentioned previously, managing performance occurs every day, not just once a year. Regardless of the appraisal system in place, FLMs should continually provide feedback to
employees about both their successes and the things they need to do to
improve.

ASSESSMENTS BY SOMEONE OTHER THAN THE FLM

FLMs cannot know how an employee behaves at all times or in all
situations. Nor can FLMs always appreciate the full impact of an employee's behavior on others, inside and outside the organization. To gain
more insight into an employee, FLMs may supplement their appraisals
with self-assessments by the employee or with appraisals by peers and
customers. Their employees may also evaluate FLMs and other managers. Combining several sources of appraisals is called *360-degree feedback*.

To use self-assessments, an FLM can ask each employee to complete
an assessment form. During the appraisal interview, the FLM and employee would then compare the employee's evaluation or his or her behavior with the FLM's assessment. This can stimulate discussion and
insights in areas where the two are in disagreement.

The following are examples of questions employees should ask themselves and their FLMs when completing a self-assessment:

- On a scale of 1 to 10, how does my performance rate?
- What are the strongest elements of my work?
- What are the weakest elements of my work?
- Where can I go in my job or career in the next eighteen months to four years?
- What skills, training, or education do I need to get to that point?

Appraisals by peers—often called *peer reviews*—are becoming more common, especially in team-based environments. Peers often have a valuable perspective on the performance of their coworkers and may witness things (good or bad) that the FLM does not. They may be in the best position to rate some dimensions, such as attendance and timeliness, teamwork and cooperation, or planning and coordination. Peer evaluations may be done in meetings in which the team discusses each team member's strengths and areas needing improvement. They may also be collected in an anonymous survey which an external source, such as human resources, summarizes (e.g., provides an average rating for a person from peers). Employees often find the information from peers credible because it comes from multiple people who work with them every day.

Customer evaluations of employees also are increasing. The drive to please customers in a highly competitive market, coupled with a desire for practical information on performance, has encouraged some organizations to institute programs in which customers appraise employees' performance. Major companies using customer appraisals include IBM, Sears, and Motorola.

Combining several sources of performance evaluations can correct for some of the appraisal biases described in the next section. It also can provide information that is more useful for problem solving and employee development than the results of a traditional supervisor only appraisal.

SOURCES OF BIAS IN PERFORMANCE APPRAISALS

Ideally, FLMs should be completely objective in their appraisals of employees. Each appraisal should reflect only an employee's performance and not any biases of the FLM. Of course, this is impossible to do perfectly. We all have biases that affect our evaluations of other people. FLMs need to be aware of these biases and limit their effects on appraisals. This section discusses some sources of bias that commonly influence performance appraisals.

Some FLMs are prone to a *harshness bias*, that is, rating all employees more severely than their performance merits. New FLMs are especially susceptible to this error, because they may feel a need to be taken seriously. Unfortunately, the harshness bias also tends to frustrate and discourage employees, who resent the unfair assessment of their performance. Further, if ratings are tied to pay, employees in one department may feel, justifiably, that they are being penalized unfairly because their FLM is a more harsh rater than others.

At the other extreme is the *leniency bias*. FLMs with this bias rate all of their employees more favorably than their performance merits. An

FLM who does this may want credit for developing a department full of "excellent" employees or may simply be uncomfortable confronting employees with their shortcomings. The leniency bias may feel like an advantage to the employees who receive the favorable ratings, but it actually cheats them and their department. By not recognizing the benefits of developing and coaching employees, a lenient FLM may actually hinder the employees' progress.

A bias that characterizes the responses of some FLMs is *central tendency*, which is the tendency to select ratings in the middle of the scale. Some people seem more comfortable on middle ground than taking a strong stand at either extreme. This bias also causes an FLM to miss important opportunities to praise or correct employees.

The *similarity bias* refers to our tendency to judge others more positively when they are like us. Thus, FLMs may tend to look more favorably on people who share their interests, tastes, background, or other characteristics. For example, an FLM may view a person's performance in a favorable light because the employee shares his or her interest in sports. On the other hand, an FLM might give a negative assessment of the performance of an employee who is much more shy than the FLM.

The *recency syndrome* refers to the human tendency to place the most weight on events that have occurred most recently. In a performance appraisal, an FLM might give particular weight to a problem the employee caused last week or to an award the employee just won, whereas the FLM should be careful to consider events and behavior that occurred throughout the entire review period. The most accurate way to make a complete evaluation is to document events as they happen (e.g., keep a running log of good and poor incidents of performance) and keep these records throughout the year.

The *halo effect* refers to the tendency of an FLM to generalize one positive or negative aspect of a person to the person's entire performance. Thus, if FLM Ted Tyler thinks that a pleasant telephone manner makes a good customer service representative, he is apt to give high marks on everything to Alice Atkins, who has an extremely pleasant voice, no matter what she actually says to the customers or how reliable her performance.

Finally, the FLM's *prejudices* about various types of people can unfairly influence a performance appraisal. An FLM needs to remember that each employee is an individual, not merely a representative of a group. An FLM who believes that one group of employees generally has poor skills in using standard English needs to recognize that this is a prejudice about a group, not a fact to use when evaluating actual employees.

PERFORMANCE APPRAISALS AND THE LAW

It may seem unnecessary to emphasize that performance appraisals must be job-related, because appraisals are supposed to measure how well employees are doing their jobs. Yet in numerous cases, courts have ruled that performance appraisals were discriminatory and not job related.

The elements of a performance appraisal system that can survive court tests can be determined from existing case law. A legally defensible performance appraisal includes:

- performance appraisal criteria based on an analysis of the job;
- measurements relevant to job performance;
- formal evaluation criteria that limit management discretion;
- formal rating instruments;
- personal knowledge of and contact with the employee being evaluated;
- training of FLMs in conducting appraisals;
- a review process that prevents one FLM acting alone from controlling an employee's career;
- counseling to help poor performers improve.

HOW TO CONDUCT A FORMAL APPRAISAL

Conducting performance appraisals is one of the FLM's most important and difficult functions. The first thing an FLM can do to conduct an effective formal performance appraisal is to make sure that there are no surprises in store for employees. This means that, as discussed previously, FLMs should communicate with their employees on a regular basis about how they are doing with their assignments and how well they are collaborating with others. FLMs also should be using the techniques discussed in the chapters on leadership, communication, motivation, teams, and planning.

The formal appraisal session, therefore, should be primarily a way to summarize and continue the informal interaction that has previously taken place between the FLM and the employee. It should also be a time to look at how the FLM and the employee can continue to work well together in the future. The FLM's job in this session is not to tell the employee all the things the employee did wrong over the past year. One reason employees dread these sessions is that FLMs feel they have to find something to criticize as well as praise. The FLM might then mention a negative comment the employee made or similar trivial points. This hypercritical approach will merely increase the employee's resentment and defensiveness and will make employees feel as though they are powerless to improve.

To make sure the session goes as well as possible and to avoid making it uncomfortable for both the FLM and the employee, five general steps should be followed:

1. Refer to past feedback and documented observations of performance.
2. Describe the current performance.
3. Describe the desired performance.
4. Get a commitment to any needed change.
5. Follow up.

Specific guidelines for conducting performance appraisals are described below.

PREPARING FOR THE APPRAISAL INTERVIEW SESSION

Today's FLM must recognize that failure to plan for the performance appraisal is planning to fail. Being prepared is key to making sure the discussion with each employee goes smoothly. Before the meeting, do the documentation and planning:

- Create and maintain logs or notes on each employee that include observations of the employee's behavior and the results of his or her work. Write down incidents with the date and whether there were problems or successes at the time. Don't rely on memory to recreate what you saw.
- If a rule infraction has occured, describe it in writing and have the employee sign the written record at the time of the infraction. Keep a record of all discussions that deal with problems that are directly attributable to the employee's performance.
- Review your documentation before the formal appraisal session and highlight important points.
- List the points you want to make, focusing on both strengths and areas for improvement. Be prepared to discuss problems in a manner that focuses on the behavior that caused the problem and on solutions, not on the person. Be sure to distinguish between problems that are related to the system (e.g., too many assignments) and those that are attributable to the individual.
- Consider the follow-up actions you think might be appropriate to help the employee improve, but be prepared to take the employee's feelings into consideration.
- Think about how you have interacted with the employee and how these inter-

actions might have affected his or her performance. Be prepared to discuss how you and the employee might improve your interactions.

- Set up an appointment with the employee about a week before the performance appraisal session.
- If the employee needs to fill out a self-assessment form, give it to him or her at the time you set up the appointment to meet.

DURING THE APPRAISAL INTERVIEW SESSION

Here are some ways to make the appraisal session go smoothly:

- Put the employees at ease at the start of the session. Acknowledge that these sessions can be a little nerve-wracking but that their purpose is to help everyone in the team or work group improve and to gather information on how to help these improvement efforts.
- Ask employees what they think of their total performance—not just their strong or weak areas.
- Question employees about what they think are their personal strengths. This gives employees a chance to describe what they do best, which helps them feel positive about the appraisal.
- Tell employees what you believe are their strengths. This demonstrates that you are paying attention to their performance and appreciating their good qualities.
- Describe those areas that you think employees might improve, and use documentation to demonstrate why you are making these observations. Then ask employees what they think of your assessment and listen silently to what they have to say. Consider their reasons for poor performance (e.g., lack of equipment, lack of training) in determining appropriate actions to take.
- Assuming that you identify the cause of poor performance, ask employees what you can do together to take care of it.
- Regardless of whether or not an employee receives an average or a good rating, explain why he or she did not get a higher rating. The employee should understand what needs to be done during the next performance period to get a higher rating.
- Set new goals for performance for the next appraisal period.
- Keep a record of the meeting, including a timetable for performance improvement and what each of you will do to work toward your goals.
- Be open and honest, yet considerate of the employee's feelings. The goal is to facilitate improvement, not to make the employee feel bad.
- Be sure to give positive reinforcement to the employee during the discussion, preferably near the end. Being positive helps to motivate the employee to make any necessary change.

AFTER THE APPRAISAL INTERVIEW SESSION

It is vital to follow up on any agreements made during the appraisal sessions. Follow up indicates that the FLM and the organization are serious about improvement. The FLM should

- make appointments to meet with employees individually to review their progress;
- set up development opportunities as needed to address skill deficiencies;
- arrange for the employee to get counseling, when available, if a personal problem is involved;
- provide positive feedback when you see improvements in performance;
- make him or her aware of the consequences, such as demotion or dismissal, if the employee continues to perform poorly.

Follow up means more than just working with employees. FLMs also have to follow up on themselves. An effective appraisal process requires an ongoing and candid self-assessment by the FLM of his or her performance and its effect on employees. FLMs can use the following questions to evaluate themselves:

- Do your employees know specifically what you expect?
- Do your employees have written goals and results?
- Have you tracked your employees' performance to see if the trend is up, down, or about the same?
- Have you updated your employees recently about your own work and how it affects them?
- Are you maintaining performance documentation?
- Have you scheduled interim reviews with all of your employees?
- Do you frequently—even daily—discuss employee performance?
- Do you frequently "catch" your employees doing something right—and tell them about it?

PERFORMANCE PROBLEMS DUE TO SPECIAL CAUSES

Individual performance problems can harm the productivity of an organization. Some of these performance problems are due to special causes, and they arise through specific actions of the individual employees. Rather than blame the individual for these problems, which usually does nothing to improve performance and can lower employee morale and motivation, the FLM needs to deal with the underlying causes. If an FLM deals effectively with performance problems due to these special causes, there is a good chance the FLM will eliminate the problems and help assure that the organization operates effectively. These performance problems may include absenteeism and tardiness, disrespect or lack of cooperation, substance abuse, theft, unsafe practices, or personality problems. An effective FLM will recognize these potential problems, take steps to identify the cause, and take actions toward resolving problems. In some cases this may mean referring an employee to a company's employee assistance program or taking disciplinary action if things do not improve.

DISCIPLINING EMPLOYEES

"I can't stand Fran's surly attitude any longer!" fumed Ted Tyler, her FLM. "If she doesn't cut it out, she's going to be sorry." This FLM is eager for the employee to experience the consequences of her behavior. Despite his anger and frustration, however, Ted needs to apply discipline in constructive ways. In many cases, effective discipline can quickly bring about a change in an employee's behavior.

ADMINISTERING DISCIPLINE

FLMs must exercise discretion when recommending or imposing penalties on employees. In dealing with mistakes, FLMs must consider what the mistakes were and under what circumstances they were made. Mistakes resulting from continued carelessness call for disciplinary action. Honest mistakes should be corrected by counseling and positive discipline, not by punishment. These corrections should help the employee learn from the mistakes and become more proficient and valuable to the organization.

The specific ways in which an FLM disciplines employees may be dictated by company policies or the union contract, if any. An FLM must, therefore, be familiar with all applicable policies and rules, which include respecting the rights of employees in the discipline process. Employees' rights include the following:

- the right to know job expectations and the consequences of not fulfilling those expectations;
- the right to receive consistent and predictable responses to violations of the rules;
- the right to receive fair discipline based on facts;
- the right to question management's statement of the facts and to present a defense;

- the right to receive progressive discipline;
- the right to appeal a disciplinary action.

THE DISCIPLINE PROCESS

Before administering discipline in response to problem behavior, FLMs need to have a clear picture of the situation. Usually FLMs become aware of a problem either through their own observations or from another employee. In either case, FLMs need to collect the facts before taking further action. Often this will result in a resolution to the problem. For example, Ted Tyler believes that one of his employees is using the office telephone for personal business. The employee has a girlfriend in another state, and Ted suspects the company is paying for the employee's long-distance calls. To solve the problem, Ted should not make hasty accusations or issue a general memo about company policy. Ted should instead ask the employee directly and privately about his telephone conversations. In getting the employee's version of the problem, Ted should use good listening practices and resist the temptation to get angry.

When an FLM observes and understands the facts behind problem behavior, the discipline process takes place in four steps: verbal or written warning, suspension, demotion, and dismissal. These steps can be used one after the other in a "progressive" pattern of discipline, indicating that the steps progress from the least to the most severe action an FLM can take.

In following steps in the discipline process, an FLM should keep in mind that the objective is to end the problem behavior. The FLM should take only as many steps as are necessary to bring about a change in that behavior: the ultimate goal is to solve the problem without dismissing the employee.

GUIDELINES FOR EFFECTIVE DISCIPLINE

The guidelines for effective discipline are

- Act immediately.
- Focus on solving the problem.
- Keep emotions in check.
- Administer discipline in private.
- Be consistent.

These are described further below.

Act Immediately

When an employee is causing a problem—from tardiness to theft to lack of cooperation—the FLM needs to act immediately. This is not always easy to do. Pointing out poor behavior and administering discipline are unpleasant tasks, but FLMs who ignore problem situations are effectively signaling that the problem is not serious. As a result, the problem often gets worse.

Focus on Solving the Problem

When discussing a problem with an employee, an FLM should focus on learning about and resolving the issue at hand. This meeting is no time for name-calling or for dredging up instances of past misbehavior. Nor is it generally useful for an FLM to dwell on how patient or compassionate he or she has been. Instead, an FLM should listen to the employee and be sure he or she understands the problem and then begin discussing how to correct it in the future. Talking about behavior instead of personalities helps the employee understand what is expected.

Keep Emotions in Check

An FLM should avoid becoming emotional. Although it is appropriate to convey sincere concern about a problem, an FLM's other feelings are largely irrelevant and can even stand in the way of a constructive discussion. Being calm and relaxed when administering discipline tells an employee that the FLM is confident about what he or she is doing.

Administer Discipline in Private

Discipline should be a private matter. The FLM should not humiliate an employee by issuing a reprimand in front of other employees. Humiliation only breeds resentment and may actually increase problem behavior in the future.

Be Consistent

An FLM also should be consistent in administering discipline. One way to do this is to follow the four steps of the progressive discipline process. An FLM should also respond to all instances of misbehavior equitably rather than, for example, ignoring a longstanding employee's misdeeds while punishing a newcomer.

DOCUMENTATION OF DISCIPLINARY ACTIONS

Employees who are disciplined sometimes respond by filing a grievance or suing the employer. To be able to justify their actions, therefore, FLMs must have a record of the disciplinary actions taken and the basis for the discipline. These records may be needed to show that the actions were not discriminatory or against company policy.

While documentation is important for any disciplinary action, it is especially important when an FLM must dismiss an employee. Because the experience is so emotional, some former employees respond with a lawsuit against the employer. The employee's file should show the steps the FLM took leading up to the termination and a record of the specific behaviors that led the FLM to dismiss the employee to protect the organization against this type of legal action. The performance appraisal ratings should correspond to other documentation about problematic performance.

POSITIVE DISCIPLINE

Ideally, discipline should not only end problem behavior but should also prevent problems from occurring. Discipline designed to prevent problem behavior from starting is known as positive discipline, or preventive discipline. One important part of positive discipline is making sure employees know and understand the rules they must follow and the consequences of violating those rules.

Employees may engage in problem behavior when they feel frustrated or unhappy. Therefore, an FLM also can administer positive discipline by working to create positive working conditions under which employees will be unlikely to cause problems. This includes setting realistic goals, being aware of and responsive to employees' needs and ideas, and making sure employees feel that they are important to the organization.

SUMMARY

Control is accomplished by comparing actual performance with predetermined standards or objectives and then taking action to correct any deviations from the standards. The control process has three basic steps:

1. establishing performance standards;
2. monitoring performance and comparing it with standards;
3. taking necessary action.

Among the tools and techniques most frequently used by FLMs to exercise control are budgets, written reports, personal observation, electronic monitors, and management by objectives. Benchmarking is a control tool that organizations use to improve different types of performance.

Performance appraisal is a process that involves determining and communicating to an employee how well he or she is performing the job and also establishing a plan for improvement. While there are many types of appraisal forms, effective management of performance involves continually monitoring performance and giving feedback to employees. Further, when conducting performance appraisals, FLMs must avoid the biases discussed earlier: harshness bias, leniency bias, central tendency, similarity bias, recency syndrome, and the halo effect.

Problems that an FLM can attribute to individuals are special cause problems and include absence and tardiness, disrespect and lack of cooperation, substance abuse, use of unsafe practices, and theft. One way of dealing with special cause performance problems is discipline. Discipline is action taken by an FLM to prevent employees from breaking rules.

Effective ways of administering discipline require the FLM to meet with the employee(s) involved and ask for his or her version of what has happened after collecting the facts of the situation. The FLM should use good listening techniques and, if necessary, let the employee experience the consequences of unsatisfactory behavior through verbal or written warning, suspension, demotion, and ultimate dismissal. The FLM takes as many steps as are necessary to resolve the problem behavior.

Positive discipline focuses on preventing problem behavior from ever beginning. It can include making sure employees know and understand the rules, creating conditions under which employees are least likely to cause problems, using decision-making strategies when problems occur, and rewarding desirable behavior. Effective positive discipline results in self-discipline among employees; that is, employees voluntarily follow the rules and try to meet performance standards.

Chapter 10

Safety and Health

INTRODUCTION

Organizations have become involved in safety and health management in response to many compelling influences, the most basic of which is a sense of social and humanitarian responsibility. Other influences include government intervention, pressure from labor unions, and an increased awareness of safety and health issues among the general public. Finally, their experiences in issues of worker protection have led organizations to appreciate the direct relationship between safety and health management and organizational effectiveness. When a company protects the well-being of its employees, it is protecting the organization's most valuable resource and avoiding the staggering costs and negative public image associated with safety neglect. Before taking a closer look at the key points of this chapter, consider the experience of one FLM, Clarence Williams.

CLARENCE'S EXPERIENCE

Clarence Williams has just filled out an OSHA accident report concerning the second major injury in his department this year. Both injuries occurred when an employee was trying to reach for something on a high shelf. First, Teresa Mason, standing on the top step of a stepladder in the storage room, lost her balance and fell. She was out for three weeks with a strained back. Next, Terence Foster tried to reach a hammer on a shelf and fell to the floor after the chair he was standing on slipped. He broke his arm in the fall and missed 12 days of work.

Clarence sighs in frustration. If he had talked to his employees once about being careful, he had talked to them a dozen times! Clarence simply cannot believe the stupid things his employees do. Why only yesterday he himself tripped over a wrench someone had left on the floor. Fortunately, he caught himself in time. Whatever can he do to prevent more "useless" accidents? Clarence Williams' impromptu talks with his employees have had little effect on reducing accidents. He now needs to implement a safety program in his department and encourage employee participation in the program.

A successful safety program starts at the very top of the organization. The owners, top executives, and middle managers must all be committed to safety. FLMs like Clarence Williams are the representatives of management who have daily contact with the employees and are therefore critical to the program's success. A safety program is only one way FLMs contribute to safety and health in the workplace. Even in organizations that have a safety engineer or safety director, the FLM is responsible for seeing that any safety directives are carried out. It is the FLM who shapes the employees' attitudes toward safety: employees take their cues from FLMs as to what is important.

As an FLM, Clarence has a legal responsibility to ensure that the workplace is free from unnecessary hazards and that working conditions are not harmful to employees' physical or mental health. Although accidents can and do happen, Clarence and other FLMs are on the front line to prevent them from occurring. Clarence must be concerned about safety and health if for no other reason than unsafe and unhealthy work sites cost money. He therefore needs to focus his efforts on both preventive and corrective safety controls.

Today, safety and health management concerns go beyond the physical condition of the workplace to a regard for employees' mental and emotional well-being and a commitment to protecting the surrounding community from pollution and exposure to toxic substances. Consequently, employees at all levels of the company are now involved in promoting safety. Some of the health and safety activities of FLMs, HRM professionals, and other employees are listed below:

FLMs

- Make safety and health a major objective of the organization.
- Support the HRM professionals' efforts to train all employees in safety and health.

HRM Professionals

- Work with other professionals such as medical doctors and industrial engineers to develop new programs.

- Create HRM programs that train employees for safe and healthy behaviors and reward them for their success.

Employees

- Participate in the development and administration of safety and health programs.
- Perform in accordance with established safety and health guidelines.

The importance of these activities is evident when one thinks of the benefits and costs of safety and health.

THE BENEFITS OF SAFETY AND HEALTH PROGRAMS

If organizations can reduce the rates and severity of work-related accidents, diseases, and stress levels, and improve the quality of work life for their employees, they can become more effective. The benefits of improved health and safety include

- more productivity due to fewer lost workdays;
- increased efficiency from a more committed workforce;
- reduced medical and insurance costs;
- lower workers' compensation rates and direct payments because fewer filed claims;
- greater flexibility and adaptability of the workforce as a result of increased participation and an increased sense of ownership;
- better selection ratios when hiring new employees because of the enhanced image of the organization;
- a substantial increase in profits.

COSTS OF WORK-RELATED ACCIDENTS AND ILLNESSES

The costs of work-related accidents and occupational diseases to American industry are known to be in the billions of dollars annually and are increasing in certain areas. These costs are both tangible and intangible. The tangible costs are measurable financial expenses. One major category of these costs is directly related to lost production. This category includes costs incurred as a result of work slowdown, damaged or idle equipment, damaged or ruined products, excessive waste, and any profit forgone due to lost sales. A closely related cost is the cost incurred for training new or temporary replacements. Another category covers insurance and medical costs. These costs are increasing due to large claims and other expenses incurred as a result of work-related accidents. This category includes the costs of worker's compensation insurance, accident insurance, and disability insurance.

The intangible costs of work-related accidents and illnesses include lowered employee morale, less favorable public relations, and a weakened ability to recruit and retain employees. It is only natural that employee morale will suffer in an unsafe environment. If a member of a work team is injured, the harmony of the team may be impaired by the absence of the injured employee. A bad safety record may also be a major reason for poor employee relations with management. If employees perceive that their FLMs are unconcerned about their physical welfare, employee-FLM relations can deteriorate. In fact, safety is often a primary reason for unionizing. For example, in the months after the crash of Atlanta-based ValuJet Flight 592 in the Everglades that killed 110 people due to improperly stored oxygen containers in the cargo hold, the company experienced three times its average monthly turnover rate. A poor safety record is also harmful to an organization's public relations. It may deter customers from purchasing a business' products or services.

Frequently, organizations ignore or are not aware of these and other "hidden" costs of occupational illness or injury. The following list summarizes some of the costs that can be associated with a single accident in the workplace. In general, the more serious the accident, the greater the costs:

- the cost of wages paid to workers who are attracted to the accident site and therefore not working;
- the cost of slowdowns at later production stations caused by interruptions in the work of both the injured person and those who come to the scene;
- the cost of repairing damaged equipment;
- cleanup costs;
- payments to the injured employee in excess of workers' compensation;
- the cost of dispensary services provided by the plant nurse or infirmary;
- diminished productivity of injured employees after they return to the job, but before they regain the ability to produce their full work output;
- the cost of management time incurred to investigate accidents;
- extra overtime costs occasioned by the interruption of work;
- the cost associated with the recruitment, selection or transfer, and training of replacements for the injured workers;
- the costs due to the generally lower efficiency of replacement workers;
- legal costs for advice with respect to any potential claims;
- the costs of rental equipment placed temporarily in service while unsafe equipment is repaired or replaced;

- increased insurance payments that reflect the degree of safety and health risk containment;
- the costs associated with any loss of accreditation by national or international marketing or business associations, or any adverse impact on competitiveness within the global market;
- the loss of market share from adverse publicity.

THE OCCUPATIONAL SAFETY AND HEALTH ACT (OSHA)

In 1969, in the aftermath of a tragic explosion that claimed the lives of 78 coal miners and amid reports of a high incidence of black-lung disease among miners, Congress passed the Coal Mine Health and Safety Act. The following year, continuing public and governmental concern about safety and health in the workplace was reflected in passage of the Occupational Safety and Health Act (OSHA). Its stated purpose is "to assure so far as possible every working man and woman in the nation safe and healthful working conditions and to preserve our human resources." Thus OSHA was designed to enforce safety and health standards to reduce the incidence of occupational injury, illness, and death. The Occupational Safety and Health Administration of the U.S. Department of Labor (DOL) enforces OSHA, which covers nearly all businesses with one or more employees. OSHA was created to

- encourage employers and employees to reduce workplace hazards and to implement new or improve existing safety and health programs;
- provide for research to develop innovative ways of dealing with occupational safety and health problems;
- establish "separate but dependent responsibilities and rights" for employers and employees to achieve better safety and health conditions;
- maintain a reporting and record-keeping system to monitor job-related injuries and illnesses;
- establish training programs to increase the number and competence of occupational safety and health personnel;
- develop mandatory job safety and health standards and enforce them effectively;
- provide for the development, analysis, evaluation, and approval of state occupational safety and health programs.

Accident prevention is a major goal of safety and health management. OSHA requires employers to keep a log of on-the-job accidents, and accident investigation and measurement can supply useful data for developing effective safety programs and improving working conditions.

These data can be useful to company safety specialists as well as to worker-management safety committees. State OSHA programs are found in those states that have assumed responsibility for administration of OSHA. Under special plans negotiated with the DOL, states agree to establish programs of inspection, citation, and training that meet or exceed the minimum standards enforced on the federal level.

Few laws have evoked as much negative reaction as OSHA. While most people would support its intent, many have criticized the manner in which it has been implemented. The sheer volume of regulations has been staggering, and many of them are vaguely worded. For example, the Occupational Safety and Health Administration developed the following 39-word single-sentence definition of the word exit: "That portion of a means of egress which is separated from all other spaces of the building or structure by construction or equipment as required in this subject to provide a protected way of travel to the exit discharge."

In addition, many OSHA standards have been criticized as unacceptable, arbitrary, trivial, unattainable, excessively detailed, costly, or petty. For example, one regulation states: "Where working clothes are provided by the employer and become wet or are washed between shifts, provision shall be made to ensure that such clothing is dry before reuse."

In response to definitions and regulations similar to the examples given above, many organizations have developed a negative attitude toward OSHA. As a result of these critics, legislation was enacted to soften some OSHA requirements. Many of the original standards were also subsequently revoked by the Occupational Safety and Health Administration itself. In spite of these changes to its policies and procedures, OSHA performs a job that today's FLMs must understand.

INSPECTIONS

OSHA inspections are conducted by compliance officers. These inspectors are men and women from the safety and health field who have attended at least four weeks of specialized training at OSHA's Training Institute at Des Plaines, Illinois, or at one of eleven other training centers. They also take additional training courses once each year in specialized areas such as industrial hygiene, construction, or maritime safety and health.

The inspection process starts with the presentation of the compliance officer's credentials and a meeting with the appropriate employer representative. If the inspection has resulted from an employee complaint, the compliance officer should give the employer a copy of the complaint (with the complainant's name withheld), as well as copies of any applicable laws and safety and health standards. Before an inspection tour, the compliance officer will also want to meet with a representative of the employees if the company is unionized. If it is not, an employee representative will be selected by the members of the plant safety committee or by the employees as a whole. Both the employee and employer representatives typically accompany the compliance officer during the inspection. In addition to a plant inspection, the compliance officer is permitted to interview various employees at his or her discretion about safety and health conditions. OSHA gives the compliance officer the right to take photographs, make instrument readings, and examine safety and health records. Compliance officers must keep any trade secrets they observe confidential or face a $1,000 fine and/or one year in jail.

After the inspection, the officer should discuss any observations with the employer and review possible OSHA violations. The employer should estimate the time needed to correct any hazardous conditions noted by the officer. Citations and penalties are not issued at this time, nor can the officer order that any part of the business be closed down immediately. If an imminent danger exists, the compliance officer will ask the employer to abate the hazard and remove endangered employees. If the employer does not comply, OSHA administrators can go to the appropriate Federal District Court for an injunction prohibiting further work as long as unsafe conditions exist.

VIOLATIONS AND CITATIONS

If after the inspection tour an OSHA standard is found to have been violated, the OSHA area director determines what citations and penalties, if any, will be issued as well as a proposed time period for abatement. An employer who believes the citation is unreasonable or the abatement period is insufficient may contest it. The act provides an appeal procedure and a review agency, the Occupational Safety and Health Review Commission, which operates independently from OSHA. OSHA may impose civil penalties up to $7,000 for each violation.

Criminal penalties are levied in the most serious cases. For example, a willful violation that results in the death of an employee can bring a court-imposed fine of up to $250,000 (or $500,000 if the employer is a corporation) or imprisonment for up to six months, or both. A second conviction can double these penalties. Falsifying records can result in a fine of up to $10,000 and six months in jail. Multiple violations or failure to correct prior violations can add up to enormous fines.

OSHA has levied fines in the millions of dollars, although settlements have tended to be for lesser amounts and do not always include an admission of wrongdoing. Companies usually can negotiate with OSHA on the final amount of fines levied. Companies also can reduce the amount of fines they pay by cooperating with OSHA and especially by being proactive in responding to OSHA investigations and recommendations. For example, the Doe Run Company agreed to a $1.3 million settlement over OSHA allegations that the company violated federal health and safety standards at its Herculaneum, Missouri, smelter. OSHA originally proposed penalties of $2.8 million, alleging 313 violations, 283 of them willful. The Phillips 66 Company agreed to a $4 million settlement after OSHA had proposed a $5.7 million fine for some 575 willful and serious safety violations.

Other settlements—many of which do not include an admission of wrongdoing on the part of the company—include United Parcel Service agreeing to a $3 million fine and intensifying its training programs to settle a hazardous-material handling case. Large fines that were initially levied and then appealed involved General Motors ($1.9 million in the case of a worker killed when a pneumatic lift he was repairing started up unexpectedly), a Bridgestone/Firestone unit ($7.5 million in the death of a worker crushed in a machine that started up during repairs), and Samsung, Guam, Inc. ($8.3 million after a worker fell 50 feet to his death).

OSHA's HAZARD COMMUNICATIONS STANDARDS

Approximately 32 million U.S. employees are potentially exposed to one or more chemical hazards in the workplace. There are an estimated 650,000 chemical products at present, and hundreds of new ones are being introduced annually. Because of the threats posed by these chemicals, OSHA has established a Hazard Communications Standard. This standard is also known as the "right to know" rule. The basic purpose of the rule is to ensure that employers and employees know what chemical hazards exist in the workplace and how to protect themselves against those hazards. The goal of the rule is to reduce the incidence of illness and injuries caused by chemicals.

The Hazard Communications Standard establishes uniform requirements to ensure that the hazards of all chemicals imported into, produced by, or used in the workplace are evaluated and that the results of these evaluations are transmitted to affected managers and exposed employees.

The Hazard Communications Standard specifically requires that employers maintain complete and updated Material Safety Data Sheets (MSDSs) for each hazardous material. MSDSs provide information on the nature of the hazards involved and include appropriate handling procedure and remedies for unexpected exposure. Employers, manufacturers, or importers involved with the hazardous material may prepare MSDSs.

OSHA has developed a variety of materials to help employers and employees implement effective hazard communications programs. FLMs play a key role in these programs. FLMs should make certain that MSDSs are available for chemicals that are brought into, used in, or produced at the workplace they supervise. If FLMs find that some information is missing, the suppliers of the chemicals and other hazardous substances should be able to provide it.

THE FLM's ROLE UNDER OSHA

While OSHA has an impact on the entire organization, it also places certain responsibilities on the FLM. Although FLMs cannot be familiar with all of the thousands of pages of OSHA regulation interpretations, they do need to understand what kinds of practices are required to preserve health and safety in their departments. In addition, OSHA imposes some specific responsibilities on FLMs.

First, OSHA requires that FLMs keep specific records. One of these is OSHA Form 200—Log and Summary of Occupational Injuries and Illnesses. Each occupational injury and illness must be recorded on this form within six working days from the time that the employer learns of it. Furthermore, if fatalities occur or five or more employees require hospitalization, the organization must report them to OSHA within 48 hours. FLMs must also complete OSHA Form 101—Supplemental Record of Occupational Injuries and Illness within six working days from the time that the employer learns of the accident or illness. This form contains much more detail about each injury or illness required to be recorded. These are injuries and illnesses resulting in death, lost workdays, loss of consciousness, restriction of work or motion, transfer to another job, or medical treatment other than first aid. Injuries requiring temporary first aid do not have to be recorded.

Second, FLMs are often asked to accompany OSHA officials while they inspect the organization's facilities. Because many organizations and FLMs feel threatened by OSHA officials, they may tend to behave antagonistically toward them. This is not advisable. An uncooperative FLM could cause these officials to be more hard-nosed than usual, resulting in stiffer penalties than would have been imposed otherwise. It is in the best interests of the FLM and the host organization for the FLM to cooperate with visiting OSHA officials. During the inspection, it is important to be polite and cooperative. This is not always as easy as it sounds, because the inspection may come at an inconvenient time and may be viewed as unwanted interference.

Third, FLMs should be familiar with the OSHA regulations affecting their departments. They should constantly be on the lookout for safety violations. It is the FLM's responsibility to see that the employees follow all safety rules. Naturally, these include all OSHA rules and regulations. As part of this role, FLMs must ensure that, as mentioned above, MSDSs are available for all hazardous substances.

EMPLOYEE'S RIGHTS UNDER OSHA

It appears that OSHA will continue to be important in regulating health and safety in the workplace. As its provisions become more generally known, more employees are likely to exercise their rights concerning business hazards under OSHA. These include

- the right to request an OSHA inspection;
- the right to be present during the inspection;
- the right to protection from reprisal for reporting the company to OSHA;
- the right to access the individual's personal medical records held by the company;
- the right to refuse to work if there is a real danger of death or serious injury or illness from job hazards.

UNSAFE PERSONAL ACTS

Experts believe that unsafe personal acts cause mostly—85 percent— workplace accidents. These unsafe acts include taking unnecessary chances, engaging in horseplay, failing to wear or use protective equipment, using improper tools or equipment, taking unsafe shortcuts, operating equipment too quickly, and throwing materials. It is difficult to determine why employees behave unsafely. There probably is no single reason. Some employees may be suffering from fatigue, haste, boredom, stress, poor eyesight, daydreaming, or physical limitations. However, these reasons do not explain why some employees intentionally neglect to wear prescribed safety equipment or to follow safety procedures. These employees may wish to impress others or project a certain image. They may think that accidents always happen to someone else. That attitude can easily lead employees to be careless or show off. Employees with low morale also tend to have more accidents than employees with high morale; low morale is likely to be related to employee carelessness. A company's poor safety record can adversely affect morale.

Finally, a reason often given for accidents is that certain people are accident-prone. It seems to be true that due to their physical and mental makeup, some employees are more susceptible to accidents than are others. The tendency to be accident-prone may derive from inborn traits, but it often develops as a result of the individual's environment. Given the right set of circumstances, anyone can be accident-prone. For example, an otherwise normal employee who was up all night with a sick child might very well be accident-prone the next day. A tendency to be accident-prone should not be used to justify an accident, however. Employees who appear to be accident-prone, even temporarily, should be identified and receive special attention.

UNSAFE PHYSICAL ENVIRONMENT

Accidents can and do happen in all types of environments: in offices, retail stores, factories, and lumberyards. Accidents are more likely to occur in certain locations than others, however. Listed in order of decreasing accident frequency, these locations are

1. wherever heavy awkward material is handled, using hand trucks, forklifts, cranes, and hoists;
2. improper handling and material lifting (about one-third of workplace accidents);
3. around any type of machinery that is used to produce something else, the most hazardous being metalworking and woodworking machines, power saws, and machines with exposed gears, belts, chains, and the like (even a paper cutter or an electric pencil sharpener has a high accident potential);
4. wherever people walk or climb, including ladders, scaffolds, and narrow walkways (falls are a major source of accidents);
5. wherever people use hand tools, including chisels, screwdrivers, pliers, hammers and axes;
6. wherever electricity is used other than for the usual lighting purposes, especially near extension cords, loose wiring, and portable hand tools;
7. near outdoor power lines.

Just as there are certain locations where accidents occur more frequently, certain conditions of the work environment also seem to result in more accidents. Some of these unsafe conditions are

1. serious understaffing;
2. unguarded or improperly guarded machines;
3. defective equipment and tools;
4. poor lighting;
5. poor or improper ventilation;
6. improper dress, such as clothing with loose and floppy sleeves worn when working on a lathe or any machine with moving parts;
7. loose tile, linoleum, or carpeting;
8. sharp burrs or edges of material;
9. reading while walking;
10. poor housekeeping (e.g., cluttered aisles and stairs, dirty or wet floors that

are slippery or have small, loose objects lying on them, improperly stacked materials, etc.).

HOW TO MEASURE SAFETY AND HEALTH RATES

OSHA requires organizations to maintain records of the incidence of injuries and illnesses. Some organizations also record the frequency and severity of each.

Incidence rate. The most explicit index of industrial safety is the incidence rate. It is calculated by the following formula:

$$\text{Incidence rate} = \frac{\text{Number of injuries and illnesses} \times 200{,}000}{\text{Number of employee hours worked}}$$

The figure 200,000 is the base for 100 full-time workers (40 hours per week, 50 weeks). Suppose an organization had 10 recorded injuries and illnesses and 500 employees. To calculate the number of yearly hours worked, multiply the number of employees by 40 hours and by 50 weeks: $500 \times 40 \times 50 = 1$ million. The incidence rate thus would be 2 per 100 workers per year.

Severity rate. The severity rate reflects the hours actually lost due to injury or illness. It recognizes that not all injuries and illnesses are equal. Four categories of injuries have been established: deaths, permanent total disabilities, permanent partial disabilities, and temporary total disabilities. An organization with the same number of injuries and illnesses as another but with more deaths would have a higher severity rate. The severity rate is calculated as follows:

$$\text{Severity rate} = \frac{\text{Total hours charged} \times 1 \text{ million (hours)}}{\text{Number of employee hours worked}}$$

Frequency rate. The frequency rate reflects the number of injuries and illnesses per million hours worked rather than per year as in the incidence rate. It is estimated as follows:

$$\text{Frequency rate} = \frac{\text{Number of injuries and illnesses} \times 1 \text{ million (hours)}}{\text{Number of employee hours worked}}$$

None of these rates would mean much unless they are compared with similar figures. Useful comparisons can be made with similar figures from other departments or divisions within the same organization, from previous years, or from other organizations. These comparisons make it possible to evaluate an organization's safety record more objectively.

OTHER SAFETY AND HEALTH CONCERNS

Besides accidents, several common concerns about safety and health in the workplace are especially significant because they are widely occurring, or at least widely discussed. These include HIV-AIDS in the workplace, substance abuse, occupational diseases including stress, and violence. Alcohol and drug abuse, prolonged job stress, and emotional illness are among the enormously costly problems that need to be addressed through programs within organizations as well as through broader community programs. A few years ago, the Alcohol, Drug Abuse and Mental Health Administration estimated that alcohol and drug abusers were costing the country more than $140 billion per year in direct costs, of which $100 billion was attributed to lost productivity. As of 1996, the International Labor Organization estimated that excessive job stress was costing American organizations some $200 billion each year. More than a decade ago, mental health problems were estimated to cost employers $17 billion annually. These costs are of various kinds, and they include losses stemming from absenteeism, lowered productivity, and treatment expenses. What cost figures do not show, of course, is the mental and emotional anguish these problems cause fellow workers, friends, family members, and others. Obviously, drug, alcohol, and emotional problems off the job carry over into the job setting and vice versa.

HIV-AIDS in the Workplace

Human immunodeficiency virus (HIV) and acquired immune deficiency syndrome (AIDS) were first reported in the United States in the late 1970s. HIV-AIDS is transmitted by blood, body products, or sexual activity; it is a disease caused by the HIV retro virus. It is not spread through casual contact, but infected blood products can lead to infection if the individual is exposed through an open wound.

Individuals infected with HIV-AIDS are protected under the Americans with Disabilities Act discussed in Chapter 3. But the disease is quite different from most other disabilities. Because of the complex nature of the infection and the multiplicity of AIDS-related illnesses, greater understanding is required of the general medical symptoms of AIDS, and it may be difficult for FLMs and other managers to determine just how to comply with the law. It must be noted, however, that few jobs exist where having HIV-AIDS prohibits an employee from performing essential job functions. Should such a situation arise, the employer is expected to provide reasonable accommodations, which might include changes in equipment or work assignments.

American businesses have already faced significant productivity losses due to illness, disability, and premature death as a result of AIDS. Fear of the disease by co-workers has also contributed significantly to lost productivity. A case of AIDS at work is a serious issue for both afflicted employees and their fellow employees. The primary job of any FLM who knows that an employee has HIV-AIDS is to preserve the individual's privacy. Disclosure raises a potential for retaliation from peers, FLMs, and other employees in general.

At one organization, for instance, an employee told his FLM that he had AIDS. The FLM allegedly passed the information along to co-workers. Some of them began to threaten the employee, and he was fired. He sued his employer, charging disability discrimination, breach of privacy, and other violations of state law. The case was settled out of court, and the employee was reemployed. When he returned to work, his co-workers walked out. Medical experts had to be called in to discuss HIV-AIDS and how it was transmitted before the other employees would return to work.

A company can choose one of three approaches when dealing with AIDS:

- including AIDS under a comprehensive life-threatening illness policy. For example, one organization identifies all resources available through the company's HRM department for any employees facing a life-threatening illness and has adopted 10 guidelines for FLMs of stricken employees
- forming an AIDS-specific policy, which includes guidelines created especially to deal with AIDS-afflicted employees.
- deciding not to adopt an AIDS-specific policy. If the no-policy approach is chosen, the workforce must be kept informed about AIDS and told that people with AIDS are entitled to remain employed.

Hotlines, job flexibility, part-time work, flexible hours, and working at home are other approaches adopted by employers to keep the employee with AIDS gainfully employed. In addition, the federal government suggests that employers establish guidelines on accidents involving the handling of blood or other body fluids to control the spread of the infection.

Substance Abuse

Substance abuse in the workplace was briefly discussed in Chapter 9 as a source of employee performance problems. It is estimated by the National Institute on Drug Abuse and the National Institute on Alcohol Abuse and Alcoholism that at least 15 percent of the workforce is afflicted with drug addiction or alcoholism. Another 10 to 15 percent is affected by the substance abuse of a member of the immediate family. At least one in every four members of the workforce is directly affected by substance abuse, posing a potential major health and productivity problem for any organization.

Increasingly, alcohol abuse is seen as a disease. In cases where alcohol abuse is suspected, many organizations refer the employees for counseling prior to subjecting them to disciplinary action. In discharge cases involving alcoholism, arbitrators tend to disapprove of the imposition of severe penalties unless counseling and treatment have been tried first. On the other hand, arbitrators tend to support discipline in cases involving drugs.

Denial is a typical response of the alcoholic or addicted person. But the problem must be confronted before treatment can be effective. Below are some suggested steps for dealing with an employee whose performance is below standard and alcohol or drug abuse is suspected to be the cause. Notice that there is an emphasis on job performance throughout the process.

- Establish levels of work performances you expect.
- Be specific about supportive behavioral criteria (i.e., absenteeism, poor job performance, and others).
- Be consistent.
- Restrict criticism to job performance.
- Be firm.
- Be prepared to cope with the employee's resistance, defensiveness, or hostility.
- Try to get the employee to acknowledge the problem.
- Show the individual that you cannot be played against higher management and/or union.
- Point out the availability of counseling services.
- Discuss drinking only if it occurs on the job or the employee is obviously intoxicated.
- Get a commitment from the employee to meet specific work criteria and monitor this with a plan for improvement based on work performance.
- Explain that the employee must decide for himself [or herself] whether or not to seek assistance.
- Emphasize confidentiality of the program. (Filipowicz, 1979)

THE DRUG-FREE WORKPLACE ACT

Recognizing the huge direct and indirect costs of substance abuse to the American society, Congress in 1988 passed a law that is having far-reaching implications for organizations with federal contracts and their FLMs. The Drug-Free Workplace Act of 1988 (a subsection of the Anti-Drug Abuse Act) requires federal contractors to establish antidrug policies and procedures and to make a "good-faith" effort to sustain a drug-free working environment.

Under this act, contractors must publish company rules prohibiting the "manufacture, distribution, dispensation, possession, or use" of controlled substances in the workplace, administer appropriate discipline or require participation in a rehabilitation program in the event an employee is convicted of violating any criminal drug statute in the work setting, and establish a drug-free awareness program. In the awareness program, employees must be informed of

1. the dangers of drug abuse in the workplace;
2. the organization's policy of maintaining a drug-free workplace;
3. any available drug counseling, rehabilitation, and employee assistance programs;
4. the penalties that the employer may impose for drug abuse violations.

Employees are required to notify the employer within five days after any substance abuse conviction, and the employer is required to notify the appropriate federal government agency within ten days after receiving notice from the employee of any such conviction.

DRUG TESTING

Although the Drug-Free Workplace Act does not specifically mention drug testing, it is likely that compliance with the law will result in the establishment or enlargement of drug-testing programs by government contractors. Drug testing is controversial, but its use is increasing. Eighty-one percent of major U.S. corporations now test employees or new hires for illegal drug use, in contrast to 22 percent of firms surveyed in 1987. Ninety percent of firms will withdraw job offers from job applicants who were offered employment and then tested positive. Four percent of firms allow for other options, including retesting at a later date.

What happens to employees who test positive? An American Management Association survey found that almost one-quarter of companies that test employees will immediately dismiss a worker who tests positive for illegal substances and an additional 14 percent fire workers who repeatedly fail a drug test. Nearly two-thirds refer test-positive employees for counseling and treatment. One-fifth enforce a suspension or probation period for test-positive workers, and two percent reassign them to other duties.

The legal issues surrounding drug testing are complex and still evolving. In the public sector, some of these issues center on constitutional rights pertaining to search and seizure, privacy, and due process. In the private sector, legal issues center on equal employment opportunity laws, disability discrimination laws, and liability for defamation and wrongful discharge. The courts clearly tend to approve drug testing when there is a "reasonable individualized suspicion" that an employee's performance is being affected by drugs.

OCCUPATIONAL DISEASE

Occupational disease can be defined as a job-related disturbance of the normal functioning of the body or of a person's mental and emotional capacities. Examples of common occupational diseases are silicosis from breathing silica dust, rashes from handling insecticides, impaired hearing from exposure to noisy machines, and lead poisoning from exposure to lead in paint. Excessive and prolonged job stress, which is beginning to be recognized as a serious problem in many contemporary organizations and is discussed separately in the next section, can also be considered an occupational disease. Potential lawsuits and criminal charges are reason enough to interest organizations in the prevention of occupational disease. The costs of occupational diseases are also of major concern. It has been estimated that American businesses pay half of the nation's health care bills, and any reasonable preventive measures they can take would seem to make economic sense.

CAUSES OF OCCUPATIONAL DISEASE

Some of the common causes of occupational illness are exposure to toxic substances, dangerous chemicals, radiation, cigarette smoke, excessive noise, inadequate lighting, and harmful fumes and vapors aggravated by poor ventilation. The rapidly growing use of visual display terminals (VDTs) is associated with such ailments as eyestrain, neck pain, and disorders of the hand and wrist nerves, including carpal tunnel syndrome, a painful wrist disorder caused by repeated hand or wrist motions.

INDOOR AIR QUALITY (IAQ)

Over the last 10 years, more and more employees have expressed concerns over the quality of indoor office environment. Two terms you should be familiar with in this context are indoor air quality (IAQ) and sick-building syndrome. IAQ refers to the quality of the air in a business environment. Sick-building syndrome refers to illnesses with a wide range of symptoms that are believed to be caused by the building itself. The reason that employees blame poor IAQ for their symptoms is that those symptoms are often alleviated by leaving the building. For example, one office building near Washington, D.C., had to be evacuated several times because of a noxious odor that was making employees violently ill.

Sick-building syndrome has been linked to several factors. These include inadequate ventilation and chemical contaminants from indoor sources like adhesives, carpeting, upholstery, copy machines, pesticides, and cleaning agents. One employee recently developed a recurrence of asthma due to a solvent used to remove old carpet and the glue used to lay the new carpet. Other factors are chemical contaminants from outdoor sources (motor vehicle exhaust fumes, etc.), biological contaminants (bacteria, molds, pollen, and viruses), uncomfortable temperatures, and high levels of humidity. Pollutants that are most frequently in the news include secondhand smoke, asbestos, and radon. Poor building environment can also be caused by discomfort, noise, poor lighting, ergonomic stresses (such as poorly designed equipment), and job-related psychological stresses.

Workers' compensation claims based on IAQs have become increasingly frequent. Typically, a wide spectrum of symptoms are reported: headaches, unusual fatigue, itching or burning eyes or skin, nasal congestion, dry throat, and nausea. There are many reasons why IAQ problems may be increasing. One primary cause is that ventilation requirements were changed in the 1970s to help preserve fossil fuels, making new buildings virtually airtight and so more likely to be unhealthy. Computers and other new technologies forced changes in the way work was accomplished, creating ergonomic and organizational stress.

The National Institute for Occupational Safety and Health (NIOSH) evaluates potential health hazards in the workplace through its Health Hazard Evaluation (HHE) Program. Any employer, employee, employee representative, state or local government agency, or federal agency can ask NIOSH investigators to conduct an evaluation. Solutions to problems with IAQ and sick-building syndrome usually include combinations of the following: removal of the pollutant, modification of ventilation through increasing rates and locations of air distribution, cleaning the air, installing particle control devices, and banning smoking. Education and communication are also important elements of both remedial and preventive IAQ control.

MINIMIZING OCCUPATIONAL HEALTH RISKS

In some ways, avoiding occupational disease is more difficult for organizations than avoiding accidents. In the first place, occupational diseases are frequently diagnosed only in their advanced stages. Workers may not notice the small, incremental changes in their physical condition that may occur from week to week or even year to year. There is often no way to identify with certainty the precise moment the disease began or what were the precise circumstances at that time. It may be unclear whether an occupational disease is attributable to repeated exposure and progressive debilitation over time, or whether one exposure produced the disease. Thus, the organization's strategy for minimizing health risks may need to be very complex and expensive, and may not be recognized as necessary until some damage has been done.

Once the nature of a health hazard is understood, a hierarchy of approaches to resolve it, in order of preference, is listed below:

- Substitute less toxic materials.
- Enclose the process, using automatic or remote operation, locating employees as far away as possible.
- Isolate the harmful process from the rest of the facility and provide special protection for everyone who works in that operation.
- Provide local exhaust ventilation.
- Provide good general ventilation.
- Use wet methods to keep dust down.
- Provide necessary training for safe handling of chemicals and substances.
- Provide training on use of personal protective equipment and safety devices (i.e., eyewash stations and personnel showers).
- Use personal protection devices, particularly personal respiratory protective gear.
- Decrease daily exposure to hazards through shorter work periods or rotating job assignments.
- Promote personal hygiene.
- Require high standards of housekeeping and general maintenance.
- Make use of warnings and publicity.

As more is learned about the connections between industrial environments and medical consequences, employers will undoubtedly be required to shoulder more of the responsibility for both initial and cumulative exposure prevention, as well as for compensation of victims. It is also likely that health and safety departments will need to devote more time and expense to maintaining records of employees' exposure to hazardous materials, monitoring cumulative exposure effects on a routine basis, and checking the degree to which safety measures are routinely applied.

STRESS

Concerns about stress and how to manage it have become major safety and health issues. Hans Selye (1974), one of the foremost authorities on this subject, defines stress as follows:

> by stress the physician means the common results of exposure to any stimulus. For example, the bodily changes produced whether a person is exposed to nervous tension, physical injury, infection, cold, heat, X-rays or anything else are what we call stress. The problem is not stress itself but prolonged and unchecked stress. When the body remains in an excited state after a crisis has passed, harmful effects begin to set in. (p. 151)

Studies indicate that prolonged stress is linked to subsequent physical injury, debilitation, and disease, including heart disease. Cardiovascular diseases are responsible for more than half of all deaths in the United States, and heart attacks are the leading cause of death among males over the age of thirty-five. Further, there are links between stress and gastrointestinal diseases, arthritis, and rheumatism, which are major sources of employee disability.

Some of the causes of excessive stress in organizations are

- work overloads due to downsizing;
- poor organization;
- information overloads from voice mail, e-mail, the cellular phone, the fax machine, and the laptop computer;
- unresolved conflicts at work;
- overly demanding or autocratic FLMs;
- harassment of various kinds;
- intense and prolonged competition.

Excessive stress tends to occur in jobs in which there are heavy psychological demands, but the employee has little control over how to get the job done. These include jobs in which employees have little control over how to relate to the client, such as telephone operators, nurse's aides, and cashiers. Postal work also appears to be a high-stress job. Stress appears to be a factor in—and certainly a result of—homicides that have occurred at post offices.

Much of the heightened concern about dealing with the consequences of workplace stress stems from the increasing incidence and severity of stress-related workers' compensation claims and their associated costs. In Japan, work related stress (karoshi) has come to be seen as a deadly national problem. FLMs can help to prevent stress from turning into a serious health problem if they

- allow employees to talk freely with one another;
- reduce personal conflicts on the job;
- give employees adequate control over how they do their work;
- ensure that staffing budgets are adequate;
- talk openly with employees about bad news as well as good news;
- support employees' efforts by listening to employees and addressing any issues they raise;
- provide competitive personal leave and vacation benefits;
- maintain current levels of employee benefits, since employees' stress levels increase when their benefits are reduced;
- reduce the amount of red tape by ensuring that employees' time isn't wasted on unnecessary paperwork and procedures;
- recognize and reward employees for their accomplishments and contributions.

VIOLENCE IN THE WORKPLACE

Historically, safety prevention has focused on the prevention of accidents in the workplace. Recently, however, violence in the workplace has become an increasing concern, as previously discussed in Chapter 10. Reports show that some form of violence has occurred in nearly one-third of all companies within the last five years. The same reports indicate that approximately one million workplace incidents of violence result in some two million victims annually. While there is no way to guarantee that an organization will be free from violence, a violence prevention program can greatly increase that probability. Violence prevention programs are described in the next section.

PROGRAMS TO PROMOTE SAFETY AND HEALTH

Management's first duty should be to formulate a safety policy and then implement and sustain this policy through a safety or loss control program. The heart of any safety program is accident prevention. It is obviously much better to prevent accidents than to react to them. A major objective of any safety program is to get the employees to "think safety"—to keep safety and accident-prevention on their minds. These programs may include training, safety meetings, the posting of safety statistics, awards for safe performance, contests, and safety and health committees. Although these programs may be time-consuming, FLMs will ultimately benefit if their employees use good safety practices. Not only will there be budgetary and morale advantages, but increased safety will decrease the time an FLM spends filling out accident reports, attending meetings to investigate injuries, and making recommendations.

Many approaches are used to make employees more safety conscious. However, the following elements are present in most successful safety programs:

- *Clear terms and procedures.* Employees and FLMs should be trained in safety procedures and understand all relevant company rules.
- *A safety budget.* To reduce the frequency of accidents, management must be willing to spend money and to budget for safety. As discussed above, accidents involve direct as well as indirect costs. Money spent to improve safety is returned many times over through the control of accidents.
- *The support of management.* Safety programs need the support of top and middle management. That support must be genuine, not casual. If upper management takes an unenthusiastic approach to safety, employees will be quick to realize it. Management's personal concern helps to show this support. This includes meeting with department heads over safety issues, on-site visits by top executives to discuss the need for safety, appointing high-level safety officers where appropriate, and offering rewards to FLMs based on their employees' safety records.
- *Good example set by management.* Management's good example is critical. If safety glasses are required at a particular operation, then all managers should wear safety glasses at the required work locations. If employees see FLMs or other managers disregarding safety rules or treating hazardous situations lightly by not conforming to regulations, some may feel that they, too, have the right to violate the rules.
- *Responsibility for safety.* One person should be in charge of the safety program and responsible for its operation. Typically this is the safety engineer or the safety director, but it may also be a high-level manager or the human resources manager. Safety should also be clearly established as a line organization responsibility. All line FLMs should consider safety an integral part of their jobs, and operating employees should be responsible for working safely.
- *Positive attitude.* A positive attitude toward safety should exist and be maintained throughout the organization. The employees must believe that the safety program is worthwhile and that it produces results.

In short, organizations show their concern for loss control by establishing a clear safety policy and by assuming the responsibility for its implementation. Organizations that fail to implement safety policies or fail to report job-related illnesses and injuries face being fined by OSHA for unsafe practices, as well as potential lawsuits or workers' compensation claims by employees.

STRATEGIES FOR PROMOTING SAFETY

Uninteresting work often leads to boredom, fatigue, and stress, all of which can cause accidents. In many instances, job enrichment, discussed in Chapter 6, can be used to make the work more interesting and result in fewer accidents. Simple changes can often make work more meaningful to the employee. Job enrichment attempts are usually successful if they add responsibility, challenge, and similar qualities that contribute to the employee's positive inner feelings about the job.

The safety committee is a way to get employees directly involved in the operation of the safety program. A rotating membership of 5 to 12 members is usually desirable, including both management and operating employees. The normal duties of a safety committee include inspecting the work site, observing work practices, investigating accidents, and making recommendations. The safety committee also may

- sponsor accident-prevention contests;
- help prepare safety rules;
- promote safety awareness;
- review safety suggestions from employees;
- supervise the preparation and distribution of safety materials.

Reinforcing behaviors that reduce the likelihood of accidents can be highly successful. Reinforcers include non-monetary reinforcers such as feedback; activity reinforcers such as time off; material reinforcers such as company-purchased doughnuts during the coffee break; and financial rewards for attaining desired levels of safety. The behavioral approach relies on specifying and communicating the desired performance to employees, measuring that performance before and after interventions, monitoring performance at unannounced intervals several times a week, and reinforcing desired behavior several times a week with performance feedback.

Management by objectives was introduced in Chapter 8. This approach can be used in the safety area. Behavior modification programs are often linked successfully to management by objectives programs that deal with occupational health. The seven basic steps of these programs are to

1. Identify hazards and obtain information about the frequency of accidents.
2. Based on this information, evaluate the severity and risk of the hazards.
3. Formulate and implement programs to control, prevent, or reduce the possibility of accidents.
4. Set specific goals that are challenging but attainable regarding the reduction of accidents or safety problems.

5. Consistently monitor results of the program.
6. Provide positive feedback to promote correct safety procedures.
7. Monitor and evaluate the program against the goals.

THE FLM's ROLE IN PROMOTING SAFETY

Because FLMs are the link between management and the operating employees, they are in the best position to promote safety. In addition to fostering a healthy attitude toward safety, an FLM who observes unsafe conditions should take one of the following actions, listed in order of priority:

1. Eliminate the hazard.
2. If the hazard cannot be eliminated, use protective devices, such as guards on machinery.
3. If the hazard cannot be protected, provide warnings, such as labels on parts of equipment.
4. If the hazard cannot be removed, notify the proper authority.

Recommend a solution, and then follow up to make sure that the unsafe condition has been corrected.

FLMs should always take a proactive stance towards preventing accidents and promoting safety. It is up to FLMs to see that employees follow safety. It is up to FLMs who observe and are responsible for the day-to-day performance of employees. Unfortunately, some FLMs must witness a serious injury before they appreciate why they must enforce safety rules and procedures. FLMs who avoid enforcing these rules because they are afraid employees will react negatively do not understand why the rules exist. They fail to recognize the importance of their role in maintaining a safe and healthy workplace.

VIOLENCE PREVENTION PROGRAMS

A set of OSHA guidelines released in 1995, "Guidelines for Preventing Workplace Violence for Health Care and Social Service Workers," can serve as a guide for organizations to develop a written workplace violence prevention program as part of an overall safety and health program. Some of the guidelines' main recommendations are to

1. establish a policy of zero tolerance for workplace violence;
2. encourage employees to report incidents of workplace violence;
3. develop a plan for workplace security;

4. appoint a person with program responsibility and provide adequate resources to run the program;

5. ensure management commitment to employee safety;

6. hold employee meetings on safety.

THE FLM'S ROLE IN PREVENTING VIOLENCE

FLMs play an important role in the success of violence prevention programs. FLMs need to take responsibility for reducing or eliminating violence in the workplace. To this end, they must be sensitive to the causes of workplace violence. Many people feel pressured in their jobs and fear layoffs. When other stresses are added to these, such as negative performance appraisals, personality conflicts with co-workers or managers, or personal problems such as divorce, a potentially dangerous person may emerge. While FLMs cannot eliminate all of these pressures, which are realities of everyday life, they can make sure that employees are treated fairly. When employees are treated as though they are expendable, they will not feel a commitment to the company and could respond to such treatment with a violent reaction. FLMs should deal with performance problems by focusing on employee behavior and future improvement, rather than on past performance problems (see Chapter 9 on performance appraisals). FLMs should never discipline employees in front of co-workers. This can be humiliating and incite a violent reaction.

FLMs should also take steps to reduce the possibility of hiring employees who might be prone to violence. For example, interviewers might ask job candidates to describe how they reacted to a past management decision with which they disagreed, and why. The responses to this question and follow-up questions could be quite revealing. Interviewers should also check for evidence of substance abuse or emotional problems, which might be indicated by careless driving or DWI (driving while intoxicated) entries on driving records. Unexplained gaps in a person's employment history should be carefully examined. A profile of the characteristics of those who may be prone to violence and a list of some warning signs are presented below.

Profile of Characteristics

• white men between 30 and 40 years of age
• socially isolated—a "loner," who may avoid socializing during breaks or work functions
• experiencing stress in personal life, such as divorce or death in the family
• low self-esteem with no healthy outlet for anger

- work being the person's primary, or sole, activity and providing him with the opportunity to be "somebody"
- difficulty dealing with criticism or frustration
- difficulty dealing with authority
- fascinated with weapons and the military
- temper-control problems
- abuse of alcohol or drugs
- history of conflict with others

Warning Signs

- may blame others for problems
- a behavioral change, such as becoming withdrawn, depressed, or irritable
- may hold a grudge over a termination, lost promotion, performance feedback, or some other outcome
- may make threats and intimidate other workers
- may exhibit paranoia and believe that management or other employees are out to get him
- may test the limits of policies
- may be fascinated by weapons (Adapted from Missouri Capital Police, 1996; Bensimon, 1994)

Finally, FLMs should learn the proper organizational procedures for reporting and dealing with different types of potentially violent situations. Comprehensive violence-prevention programs can be beneficial. For example, one organization created this type of program, which is run by a full-service loss prevention department and includes extensive training, a 24-hour hotline, and an intervention policy. The program's primary purpose is to reduce violent crime within the organization. It also addresses threats, harassment, and domestic violence targeted toward any member of the organization's workforce. Even though the company spends $3 million a year on violence prevention and safety, its director of loss prevention believes it is a small price to pay.

EMPLOYEE ASSISTANCE PROGRAMS (EAPs)

Employee assistance programs (EAPs) are designed to help employees whose job performance is suffering because of physical, mental, or emotional problems. EAPs address a variety of employee problems ranging from drug abuse, to marital problems, to bereavement. Direct assistance or help through referrals for these employees is essential for humane reasons and for reasons of organizational effectiveness. Many organizations create EAPs because they recognize their ethical and legal obligations to protect not only their workers' physical health but their mental health as well. Ethical obligations stem from the fact that the work climate, job change, work rules, work pace, and style frequently cause behavioral, psychological, and physiological problems for employees. Ethical obligations become legal obligations when employees sue the company or file workers' compensation claims for work-related illness. The success of EAPs depends on how well they are planned and implemented. There is also some evidence that EAPs are more successful with some types of problems than with others. For instance, EAPs appear to be more effective at dealing with alcoholism than with drug addiction.

THE FLM's ROLE IN EAPs

In the traditional alcoholism treatment program, the FLM had to look for symptoms of alcoholism and then diagnose the problem. Under an EAP, however, the FLM is responsible only for identifying declining work performance. If normal corrective measures do not work, the FLM confronts the employee with evidence of his or her performance and offers the EAP. Classic warning signs, such as chronic tardiness and absenteeism, may be difficult to recognize, however, in companies where some employees telecommute, or where workers are geographically separated from their FLMs. Nevertheless, here are some recommendations on how to proceed:

- Once you suspect a problem, begin documenting instances in which job performance has fallen short. Absenteeism (including leaving early or arriving late for work), errors, a slackened commitment to completing tasks, and a rise in conflicts with other employees due to mood swings may be evident.
- Having assembled the facts, set up a meeting. Keep the discussion focused on performance, and do not try to make a diagnosis. Outline the employee's shortcomings, insist on improvement, and then say, "I need to bring you to the medical department . . . something isn't right here . . . I'm taking you to the experts."
- Often FLMs are afraid of being wrong and of potential liability. They worry, "Can the person sue me?" As long as the discussion focuses on declining job performance, legal experts say that a defamation claim is highly unlikely. A focus on job performance is usually necessary for an effective confrontation in any event.

This approach leaves the diagnosis and treatment recommendations to trained counselors. FLMs can increase the odds of success by telling employees that if their performance doesn't improve, they'll be disciplined. As difficult as it is, such intervention often works.

WELLNESS PROGRAMS

As health-care costs have skyrocketed over the last two decades, organizations have become more interested in preventive programs focused on maintaining worker health. Companies are encouraging employees to lead healthier lives and are attempting to reduce health-care costs through formal employee wellness programs. While EAPs focus on treating troubled employees, wellness programs focus on preventing health problems in the first place. A complete wellness program has three components:

1. It helps employees identify potential health risks through screening and testing.
2. It educates employees about particular health risks, such as high blood pressure, smoking, poor diet, and stress.
3. It encourages employees to change their lifestyles through exercise, good nutrition, and health monitoring.

Wellness programs may be as simple and inexpensive as providing information about stop-smoking clinics and weight-loss programs or as comprehensive and expensive as providing professional health screening and multimillion-dollar fitness facilities.

Should FLMs attempt to change employees' bad health habits through a "carrot" or a "stick" approach? That is, should employees be rewarded for healthy behaviors (the carrot) or penalized for unhealthy behaviors (the stick) or both? Some companies prefer the stick approach. For example, Atlanta's Turner Broadcasting refuses to hire workers who smoke, and Best Lock of Indianapolis has fired workers for drinking excessively after their shifts. Both companies claim their actions are justified by their interest in avoiding the higher health-care costs attributable to smokers and drinkers. Other organizations charge smokers more for health insurance. U-Haul and International Paper impose fines on employees with unhealthy lifestyles and make them pay more for insurance.

In contrast, General Mills uses a carrot approach that includes lowering insurance premiums for employees with healthy lifestyles, including nonsmokers who control their weight and blood pressure. Mesa Limited Partnership pays employees to get a computerized health-risk appraisal and awards them up to almost $1,000 per year for participating in weight-loss and exercise plans. Employees at Quaker Oats Company in Chicago can participate in a health incentive plan that provides an annual medical expense allowance of $300 to pay health insurance deductibles or health-care expenses, or can simply take a cash refund at the end of the year. Employees can also participate in a flexible benefits plan in which they can earn $140 each year by pledging to engage in certain healthy behaviors.

A number of organizations have developed fitness programs, which involve employees in some form of controlled exercise or recreation activities. Fitness programs range from subsidized membership at a local health club, to company softball teams, to very sophisticated company-owned facilities. As an example of the latter, Kimberly-Clark Corporation constructed its own $2.5 million fitness center and staffed it with 15 full-time professional employees. By the mid-1980s, Xerox had seven facilities, one which cost $3.5 million and included putting greens, soccer fields, a swimming pool, two gyms, tennis and racquetball courts, a weight room, and 2,300 acres of wooded land with running trails.

EVALUATION OF SAFETY AND HEALTH PROGRAMS

Safety and health programs have begun to receive more attention in recent years. The consequences of inadequate programs are measurable: increased employees' compensation payments, increased lawsuits, larger insurance costs, fines from OSHA, and pressures from unions. Evaluation of a safety management program requires indicator systems, such as accident statistics, effective reporting systems, clear safety rules and procedures, and management of the safety effort.

A safety and health program can be evaluated fairly directly in a cost-benefit sense. The most cost-effective safety programs need not be the most expensive. Programs that combine a number of approaches—identifying safety criteria like improvements in job performance and decreases in sick leave, safety training, safety meetings, providing medical facilities, and strong participation by top management—work when the emphasis is on the engineering aspects of safety. Conducting a cost-benefit analysis can be helpful in improving programs. An organization can calculate the costs of safety specialists, new safety devices, and other safety measures. Savings due to reductions in accidents, lowered insurance costs, and lowered fines can be weighed against these costs. Programs can be judged by other measurable criteria as well, such as improvements in job performance, decreases in sick leave, and reductions in disciplinary actions and grievances. At the same time, FLMs must realize that cause-and-effect relationships may be complex and difficult to measure accurately. In addition, not all benefits of a health and safety program are measurable; many benefits are intangible.

SUMMARY

FLMs' primary responsibility toward safety is to establish an environment where safety is emphasized. FLMs have a legal responsibility to ensure that the workplace is free from unnecessary hazards and that working conditions are not harmful to employees' physical or mental health. FLMs also have responsibilities to listen to employee complaints and suggestions, work closely with the safety committee (if there is one), and provide safety instruction.

The costs to an organization of accidents, injuries, and occupational diseases are both tangible and intangible. The tangible costs are the measurable financial expenses. The intangible costs include lowered employee morale, less favorable public relations, and weakened ability to recruit and retain employees.

The basic purpose of any safety program is to prevent accidents. Since getting employees to "think safety" is one of the more effective ways to prevent accidents, this is a major objective of most programs. Many strategies are available for promoting safety within an organization. These include making the work interesting, establishing a safety committee, periodically holding safety training, and rewarding employee participation.

Indoor air quality, HIV-AIDS, substance abuse, stress, and occupational diseases are common concerns about safety and health. Occupational disease is a particularly difficult problem for many reasons in today's organizations, including the fact that the onset of some disease is gradual and hard to detect. It is likely that organizations will be required to shoulder more responsibility for prevention in the future.

Prolonged stress is associated with enough health and accident problems for stress to be an important area of concern for organizations. Today's FLMs must learn to recognize the following warning signs of potentially violent employees: employees making threats or being threatened, employees with serious problems at home, employees with a chemical dependency, employees showing signs of paranoia, or employees fascinated with weapons.

Employee assistance programs (EAPs) provide avenues for FLMs and organizations to offer help to employees with problems in their personal and work lives. Wellness programs provide opportunities for employers to reduce healthcare costs.

REFERENCES

Bensimon, H. F. 1994. Crisis and disaster management: Violence in the workplace. *Training and Development* 48, 27–32.

Filipowicz, Christine A. 1979. The troubled employee: Whose responsibility? *HR Magazine* (June), 17.

Missouri Capital Police. 1996. Violence in the workplace. http://www.dps.state.mo.us.dps/mcp/study/wkviolnc.htm (June 7), 1–6.

Selye, Hans. 1974. *Stress without distress.* New York: The New American Library.

Chapter 11

Decision Making

INTRODUCTION

One of the primary factors that distinguish front-line managers (FLMs) from operating employees is the type of decisions that they must make. By nature of their role, FLMs must make decisions that impact the people they supervise. They must be concerned with how their decisions might affect their employees and the organization. Operating employees, in contrast, are primarily concerned with how decisions affect them individually.

Like all managers, the quality of the decisions that FLMs make is the measure of their effectiveness. In fact, a manager's skill in making decisions is often a key factor considered in his or her evaluations, promotions, raises, and other rewards. A manager's decision-making ability will ultimately contribute to the success or failure of the organization. All human activities involve decision making. Everyone must solve problems and make decisions at home, at work, and in social groups. When asked to define their major responsibilities, many managers respond that "solving problems" and "making decisions" are the most important and sometimes most challenging parts of their jobs.

Decision making is the process of defining problems and choosing a course of action from among alternatives. Decision making is often associated with problem solving since many FLM decisions focus on solving existing or anticipated problems. "Problems" are not limited to difficult or negative situations but can include opportunities or positive situations that present alternatives.

DECISION MAKING AND THE FLM

Since the day Sarah Johnson became a manager at Carrollton Products, she has been concerned about the many tough decisions she has had to make. Just this morning one of her employees, Thomas Clark, requested a change in the vacation schedule. He had received a last-minute invitation to go on a skiing trip as his cousin's guest. Thomas considered this "the chance of a lifetime." The problem is that Sarah had already approved vacation for three other members of the department for the same week. Even with Thomas on hand, Sarah's department would be operating with a skeleton crew.

Managers must make decisions whenever they perform any of the four management functions—planning, organizing, leading, and controlling—discussed earlier in this book. For example, in planning, the manager must decide which objectives to seek, which policies to establish, and which rules and regulations to institute. In organizing, managers must determine how to delegate authority and how duties and responsibilities should be grouped. As leaders, managers must decide how best to communicate with and motivate employees. In controlling, managers must decide to make actual performance match planned performance.

Decision making is at the center of the manager's job. Managers must continually decide what will be done, who will do it, and how, when, and where it will be done. Although these decisions may appear to be separate, they are often interrelated. Each decision is affected by, and builds upon, previous ones. For example, the goods a department produces or the services it provides determine what types of facilities are needed. Decisions about production, in turn, influence the types of employees needed and the training and compensation they should receive. All these decisions affect the amount of money budgeted for the department.

FLMs—even more than managers at other levels—are involved in directing employees' behavior toward achieving both the organization's and the employees' goals. Employees look to their FLMs for more assistance, guidance, and protection than employees do of managers at higher levels. The lower the level of management, the greater the span of control, which is the number of immediate employees a manager can manage effectively.

FLMs must also make decisions more frequently than other managers must, since they are operating on a day-to-day, person-to-person basis. FLMs frequently must make decisions quickly with little information, or even conflicting information. These decisions involve a variety of activities, as the following example illustrates.

It is Monday morning. Sarah Johnson has been at work for only three hours, but she has already made seven major decisions:

- She signed up to attend a one-day course on time management.
- She completed performance appraisals for five of her new employees.
- She approved vacation requests for two employees in her department.
- She assigned one of her team leaders a work order to schedule the completion of an important project.
- She resolved a dispute between two of her employees.
- She selected an employee to replace her during her vacation.
- She requisitioned supplies needed by her department.

In addition, she made a handful of minor decisions. The newest member of her team said, "Are you always this busy, or is it just because it's Monday morning?" Johnson replied, "It's all a normal part of a manager's job."

Managers can learn how to make more thoughtful decisions and improve the quality of their decisions. Decision making is a skill that can be developed—just as the skills involved in playing golf are developed—by learning the steps, practicing, and exerting effort. At the same time, managers should ensure that their employees learn to make their own decisions more effectively. A manager cannot make all the decisions necessary to run a department. Many daily decisions are made by the employees who do the work. For example, how a job is to be done, what materials to use, when it is to be done, and how to coordinate with other departments are decisions that employees often have to make without their managers. As we discussed in previous chapters, organizations are giving employees and teams a more active role in decision making. Therefore, training employees in the decision-making process should be a high priority for all managers.

TYPES OF DECISIONS AND LEVELS OF MANAGEMENT

All managers must make decisions. Even when the decision-making process is highly participative in nature, with full employee involvement, it is the manager who ultimately is responsible for the outcomes. Regardless of whether the manager makes decisions unilaterally or in consultation with employees, decisions may be classified into two categories: programmed and nonprogrammed, though most decisions fall somewhere between the two extremes.

Programmed decisions produce solutions to repetitive, well-structured, and routine problems. When making a programmed decision, there is a specific procedure, or program, that can be applied to the problem at hand. Many daily problems that confront managers are programmed, and they are not difficult to solve because a more or less set answer is available. Usually the organization has already developed procedures and rules to deal with these problems. Managers can delegate these kinds of decisions to employees and be confident that the decisions will be made in an acceptable and timely manner.

Nonprogrammed decisions are made to address new, unusual, or unstructured problems that are unlikely to recur. They are often caused by changing situations or unusual circumstances. Nonprogrammed decisions tend to be more important, demanding, and strategic than programmed decisions. There are no set answers or guidelines for making these decisions. Managers are called on to use intelligence, good judgment, intuition, and creativity in attempting to solve these problems. They should apply a decision-making process that is consistent and logical, but also adaptable.

THE DECISION-MAKING PROCESS

Step 1: Define the Problem

Before seeking answers, the manager should identify the real problem. Nothing is as useless as the right answer to the wrong question. Defining the problem is not always an easy task. A problem exists when there is a difference between the way things are and the way they should be. Problems that occur frequently and have fairly certain outcomes should be the concern of the lower levels of management, including managers. What appears to be the problem might be merely a symptom of the problem that shows on the surface. It usually is necessary to delve deeper to locate the real problem and define it.

Consider the following scenario: Sarah believes that there is a problem of conflicting personalities within her department. Two employees, David and Susan, are continually bickering and cannot get along together. Because of this lack of cooperation, the department's work is not being done in a timely manner. Sarah needs to develop a clear, accurate problem statement. The problem statement should be brief, specific, and easily understood by others. A good problem statement should address the following questions:

- What is the problem?
- How do you know there is a problem?
- Where has the problem occurred?
- When has it occurred?
- Who is involved in or affected by the problem?

A careful review of answers to the key questions can lead to a problem statement like Sarah's below, which reveals that the major problem is not that there is a personality conflict, but that the work is not getting done in a timely manner. When checking into this situation, Sarah should focus on why the work is not getting done.

> *Problem statement.* The bickering between David and Susan detracts from the completion of work assignments. Last Monday and Tuesday, neither of them completed assigned work. Customers, co-workers, and other departments are all affected.

Defining a problem can be time consuming, but it is time well spent. A manager should not proceed in the decision-making process until the problem relevant to the situation has been specifically identified. The effective manager will use problem solving not only to take corrective action but also as a means to make improvements in the organization.

Step 2: Analyze the Problem Using Available Information

After the problem has been defined, the next step is to analyze it. The manager begins by assembling the facts and other relevant information. This is sometimes viewed as being the first step in decision making, but until the real problem has been defined, the manager does not know what information is needed. Only after gaining a clear understanding of the problem can the manager decide which data are important and what additional information to seek. Information is a fuel that drives organizations. Information is vital to the survival of the organization, but to be useful it must be at the right place at the right time, and it must be used efficiently and effectively.

A major job of a manager is to convert information into action through the process of decision making. The manager is either helped or hindered by the availability of information. Making decisions without knowing enough about a situation is risky and sometimes even dangerous. Having too much information can also be a problem. Simple decisions do not require exhaustive information; but specific information is necessary to decide how to handle a complex problem. The quality of a decision depends greatly on understanding the circumstances surrounding an issue and selecting the appropriate strategy. The better the information, the better the resulting decision is likely to be because there is less risk and uncertainty about the facts.

Managers can stay informed by actively keeping up with everything related to their areas of responsibility and paying careful attention to all kinds of communications. Time spent reading equipment manuals and other technical materials may be helpful. Discussing potential problems with employees and getting their input on possible solutions could eventually lead to a stroke of genius when a problem arises.

Many managers often complain that they must base their everyday decisions on insufficient or irrelevant information. Managers complain that they have too much of the wrong kind of information, information is difficult to locate and/or suppressed by employees or other managers, and vital information often arrives long after it is needed. Historically, managers did not have to deal with an overabundance of information; instead they gathered a bare minimum of information and hoped that their decisions would be reasonably good. By contrast, today's managers often feel buried by the deluge of information and data, much of it useless, confronting them on a regular basis. It is essential that managers learn to manage this deluge of information.

How information is used depends greatly on its quality (accuracy), presentation (form), and timeliness (available when needed). Effective use of information is possible only if the right questions are asked by managers and their employees to determine information needs. The goal is to have the right information at the right time. To this end, timeliness may take precedence over accuracy. If information is not available when it is needed, then its accuracy is not important. In most cases, however, both accuracy and timeliness are critical. Additionally, information should be formally catalogued in some manner to ensure its availability. Managers cannot remember everything. Critical information should be put where it can be found quickly and easily. Personal computers offer a handy way to maintain ready access to a vast body of information.

After gathering information, the manager needs to analyze the problem. In our example, Sarah needs to find out why the work is not getting done. When she gathers information, she discovers that she never clearly outlined her expectations for each employee—where their duties begin and where they end. What appeared on the surface to be a problem arising from a personality conflict was actually a problem caused by the manager. The chances are good that once the activities and responsibilities of the two employees are clarified, the friction will end. Sarah needs to monitor the situation closely to ensure that the new definition of duties results in a more timely completion of work.

A manager will find that personal opinions are likely to creep into decision making. This is particularly true when employees are involved in the problem. For example, if a problem involves an employee who performs well, the manager may be inclined to show this person greater consideration than would be afforded a poor performer. The manager should therefore try to be as objective as possible in gathering and analyzing information.

In the process of analysis the manager should also try to think of intangible factors that play a significant role in the problem, such as reputation, morale, discipline, and personal biases. It is difficult to be specific about these factors; nevertheless, they should be considered. As a general rule, written and objective information is more reliable than opinions and hearsay.

Step 3: Establish Decision Criteria

Decision criteria are the standards used to evaluate alternatives. They typically express what the manager wants to accomplish with the decision and can also be used to evaluate whether the implementation of the decision is producing the expected results. To illustrate, suppose Sarah's initial actions do not remedy conflict between David and Susan. She then needs to establish decision criteria that can be used to evaluate other courses of action. Sarah has identified six criteria for her decision. Her decision

- should result in timely completion of assignments;
- should incur no additional costs;
- must not impede the quality of service to the customer;
- should not put either David's or Sarah's job in jeopardy;
- should not have a negative impact on other employees;
- must alleviate the problem within one week.

Once the decision criteria are established, the manager must determine which criteria are absolutely necessary and their order of priority. Because it is likely that no solution will satisfy all the criteria, the manager needs to know which are most important. The manager will evaluate alternatives based on which and how many important criteria they meet. The FLM may want to consult with upper-level managers, other managers, or employees to assist in prioritizing the decision criteria.

Step 4: Develop Alternative Solutions

After the manager has defined and analyzed the problem and established decision criteria, the next step is to develop various alternative solutions. By formulating and considering many alternatives, the manager is less likely to overlook the best course of action. Stating this another way, a decision will only be as good as the best available alternative. Almost all problems have a number of possible solutions, which may not always be obvious. Managers must work to develop alternatives rather than fall into an "either/or" kind of thinking. They must stretch their minds to develop alternatives even in the most discouraging situations. Although none of the alternatives may be attractive, some should be better than others.

Suppose that Sarah has been ordered to make a 20 percent reduction in employment because the organization is experiencing financial problems. After careful study, she develops the following five alternatives:

- Lay off employees who have the least seniority, regardless of their job position or performance, until the overall 20 percent reduction is reached.
- Lay off employees who have the lowest performance ratings until the overall 20 percent reduction is reached.
- Analyze departmental duties and decide which jobs are essential. Keep the employees who are best qualified to perform those jobs, and lay off the least qualified until the 20 percent reduction is reached.
- Without laying off anyone, develop a schedule of reduced work hours for every employee that would be equivalent to a 20 percent overall reduction.
- Develop proactive alternatives to increase the organization's performance so that no employee has to be laid off.

While the last may be the most attractive, it is not realistic, given the economic situation. Although none of the other alternatives may be an ideal solution to this problem, at least Sarah has considered several alternatives before making a decision. This "no-win" situation unfortunately portrays the realities of organizational life.

When enough time is available, a manager should get together with a group of other managers or employees to brainstorm alternative solutions to a perplexing problem. *Brainstorming* is a free flow of ideas within a group, with judgement suspended, in order to come up with as many alternatives as possible. Using the technique, the manager presents the problem and the participants offer as many alternative solutions as they can develop in the time available. It is understood that any idea is acceptable at this point—even those that may at first appear to be wild or unusual. Evaluation of ideas is suspended so that participants can give free rein to their creativity. Creative approaches and brainstorming meetings are particularly adaptable to nonprogrammed decisions, especially if the problem is new, important, or strategic. One authority on creativity and brainstorming has suggested the following four major guidelines for effective brainstorming by both individuals and groups:

Defer all judgement of ideas. During the brainstorming period, do not allow any criticism by anyone in the group. Although it is natural for people to suppress new ideas, both consciously and unconsciously, this tendency must be avoided. Even if an idea seems impractical and useless at first, it should not be rejected by quick initial judgements because the rejection itself could inhibit the free flow of more ideas. Managers should understand that how people respond to creative ideas affects individual and group actions.

Seek a quantity of ideas. Idea fluency is the key to creative problem solving, and fluency means quantity. The greater the number of ideas, the greater the likelihood that some of them will be viable solutions.

Encourage "free wheeling." Being creative calls for a free-flowing mental process in which all ideas, no matter how extreme, are welcome. Even the wildest idea may, on further analysis, have a germ of usefulness, and therefore should be encouraged.

"Hitchhike" on existing ideas. Combining, adding to, and rearranging ideas often can produce new approaches that are superior to any one original idea. When creative thought processes slow or stop, review some of the ideas already produced and try to combine them, considering additions or revisions.

When a fairly large group of people are brainstorming an unstructured session can become rather long, tedious, and unproductive because many of the ideas are simply not feasible, and conflicts may develop within the group due to individual biases. For this reason, the so-called nominal group technique (NGT) is more useful, as it allows group members to generate ideas more efficiently. Typically under NGT, individual members of the group each develop and write down a list of ideas and alternatives to solve the problem at hand. Afterwards, the group members share their ideas, discussing, evaluating, and refining them. The group's final choice may be made by a series of confidential votes in which the list of ideas is narrowed until a consensus is reached.

Both in the development and the evaluation of alternatives, a manager should consider only lawful options that fall within the organization's ethical guidelines. As noted in Chapter 3, more organizations are encouraging their managers and employees to make ethical decisions because they recognize that good ethics is good business in the long term. Consequently, many organizations have developed handbooks, policies, and official statements that specify the ethical standards and practices expected. The following guidelines, or ethical tests for decision making, while not comprehensive, are relevant in addressing the ethical aspects of most problems.

Legal-compliance test. Legal compliance should be only a starting point in most ethical decision making. Laws, regulations, and policies should be followed, not broken or ignored. The rationale that "everybody's doing it" or "everybody's getting away with it" are poor excuses if you are caught in an illegal or unethical act. If in doubt, ask for guidance from someone who understands the particular law or regulation.

Public-knowledge test. Decisions should be made as if they were going to be publicized. You should ask what the consequences would be if a particular decision became known to the public, your family, the media, or a government agency.

Long-term consequences test. The long-term and short-term consequences of a decision should be weighed against each other. This test helps avoid decisions that are expedient but could have negative long-term effects.

Examine-your-motives test. You should be sure that your decision benefits the company and others. It should not be primarily selfish in nature or designed to harm other people and their interest.

Inner-voice test. This is the test of conscience and moral values that have been instilled in most of us since childhood. If someone inside you says that the choice being contemplated may be wrong, it usually is.

It cannot be stressed enough that if a manager believes that a particular alternative is questionable or might not be acceptable within the organization's ethical policies, the manager should consult with his or her manager or with a staff specialist who is knowledgeable in that area for guidance in how to proceed.

Step 5: Evaluate the Alternatives and Select the "Best" Solution

The ultimate purpose of decision making is to choose the specific course of action that will provide the greatest number of desirable and the smallest number of undesirable consequences. After developing alternatives, managers can mentally test each of them by imagining that it has already been put into effect. They should try to foresee the probable desirable and undesirable consequences of each alternative. By thinking through the alternatives and appraising their consequences, managers will be in a better position to compare their choices. The usual way to begin is to eliminate alternatives that do not meet previously established decision criteria. The manager should evaluate each of the remaining alternatives based on the solution that meets the most criteria at the highest priority levels. More often than not, there is no clear choice.

Nonprogrammed decisions usually require the decision maker to choose a course of action without complete information about the situation. In making a decision, therefore, also consider the degree of risk and uncertainty involved in each alternative. No decision will be completely without risk; one alternative may simply involve less risk than the others.

The issue of time may make one alternative preferable to another, particularly if there is only a limited amount of time available, and the alternatives vary in how quickly they can be implemented. The manager should also consider the facilities, records, tools, and other resources that are needed and available for each alternative. It is critically important to judge different alternatives in terms of economy of effort and resources. In other words, managers should consider which action will give the greatest benefits and results for the least cost and effort.

In making a selection from among various alternatives, the manager should be guided by experience. Chances are that certain situations will reoccur, allowing managers to make wise decisions based on personal experience or the experience of another manager. Knowledge gained from experience is a helpful guide, the importance of which should not be underestimated; on the other hand, it is dangerous to follow experience blindly. When examining an earlier decision as a basis for choosing among alternatives, the manager should examine the situation and the conditions that prevailed at that time. It may be that conditions remain nearly identical, implying that the current decision should be similar to the previous one. More often than not, however, conditions have changed considerably and the underlying assumptions are no longer the same, indicating that the new decision probably should differ from the earlier one.

Managers admit that at times they base their decisions on intuition, defined as the ability to recognize quickly and instinctively the possibilities of a given situation. Some managers appear to have an unusual "intuitive" ability to solve problems satisfactorily by subjective means. A closer look, however, usually reveals that the so-called "intuition" is really experience or knowledge of similar situations that has been stored in the manager's memory.

Intuition may be particularly helpful in situations in which other solutions have not worked. If the risks are not too great, a manager may choose a new alternative because of an intuitive feeling that a fresh approach might bring positive results. Even if the hunch does not work out well, the manager benefits from trying something different. The manager will remember the new approach as part of his or her experience and can draw upon it in reaching future decisions.

Although a manager cannot shift personal responsibility for making decisions, the burden of decision making often can be eased by seeking the advice of others. The ideas and suggestions of employees, other managers, staff experts, technical authorities, and the manager's manager can be of great help in weighing facts and information. Seeking advice does not mean avoiding a decision; however, ultimately the manager decides what advice to accept and remains responsible for the outcome.

Many people believe that input from others can improve decision making. The following four guidelines can help managers decide whether to include groups in the decision-making process:

- If additional information would increase the quality of the decision, involve those who can provide that information.
- If acceptance of the decision is critical, involve those whose acceptance is important.
- If employees' skills can be developed through participation in decision making, involve those who need the development opportunity.

• If the situation is not life threatening and does not require immediate action, involve others because generally their varied perspectives and experiences will enhance the decision-making process.

In the scientific world, laboratory experimentation is essential and accepted. In supervision, however, experimentation to see what happens often is too costly in terms of people, time, and money. Nevertheless, sometimes a limited amount of testing and experimentation is advisable before making a final decision. For example, there are some instances in which testing provides employees with an opportunity to try out new ideas or approaches, perhaps of their own design. While experimentation may be valid from a motivational standpoint, it can, however, be a slow and relatively expensive method of reaching a decision.

When one alternative clearly appears to provide a greater number of desirable consequences and fewer unwanted consequences than any other alternative, the decision is fairly easy. However, the "best" alternative is not always so obvious. When two or more alternatives seem equally desirable, the choice may become a matter of personal preference. When no single alternative seems to be significantly stronger than any other, it might be possible to combine the positive aspects of the better alternatives into a composite solution. Sometimes none of the alternatives is satisfactory; all of them have too many undesirable effects and none will bring about the desired results. In this case, the manager should begin to think of new alternative solutions or perhaps even start all over again by attempting to redefine the problem.

A situation might arise in which the undesirable consequences of all the alternatives appear to be so overwhelmingly unfavorable that the manager feels that the best available solution is to take no action at all. This solution may be deceptive, however, as the problem will continue to exist if no action is taken. Taking no action is as much a decision as is taking a specific action, even though the manager may believe that an unpleasant choice has been avoided. The manager should visualize the consequences that are likely to result from taking action. Only if the consequences of inaction are more desirable should it be selected as the best solution.

Selecting the alternative that seems to be the best is known as optimizing. However, sometimes the manager makes a satisfying decision— selecting an alternative that minimally meets the decision criteria. A famous management theorist, Herbert Simon, once compared the procces to the difference between finding a needle in a haystack (satisfying) and finding the biggest, sharpest needle in the haystack (optimizing). A manager will rarely make a decision that is equally pleasing to everyone.

Step 6: Follow Up and Appraise the Consequences of the Decision

After a decision has been made and implemented, managers should evaluate the consequences. Follow up and appraisal of the results of a decision are actually part of the decision-making process. You should ask: "Did the decision achieve the desired results? If not, what went wrong? Why?" The answers to these questions can be of great help in similar future situations.

Follow-up and appraisal of a decision can take many forms, depending on the nature of the decision, timing considerations, costs, standards expected, personnel involved, and other factors. For example, a minor project-scheduling decision could easily be evaluated through a short written report or by the manager's observation or discussion with employees. A major decision involving the maintenance of complex equipment, however, will require close and time-consuming follow-up by the manager, technical, or other employees, and higher-level managers. This type of decision usually requires the manager to prepare numerous detailed written reports on equipment performance under varying conditions, which are compared closely with plans or expected standards for equipment maintenance.

The important point to recognize is that the task of decision making is not complete without some form of follow-up and appraisal of the actions taken. If the manager has established decision criteria or specific objectives that the decision should accomplish, it will be easier to evaluate the effects of the decision. If the results meet the objectives, the manager can feel reasonably confident that the decision was sound.

If the follow-up indicates that something has gone wrong or that the desired results have not been achieved, then the manager's decision-making process must begin all over again. This may even mean going back over each of the various steps of the decision-making process in detail. The manager's definition and analysis of the problem and the development of alternatives may have to be completely revised in view of new circumstances or data collected in the appraisal process. In other words, when follow-up and appraisal indicate that the problem has not been resolved satisfactorily, it is advisable to treat the situation as a new problem and go through the decision-making process from a completely fresh perspective.

In some situations, managers may feel they do not have enough time to go through the decision-making process outlined here. Frequently, a manager, a co-worker, or an employee approaches the manager, says, "Here's the problem," and looks to the manager for an immediate answer. Most problems do not require an immediate answer, however, and managers cannot afford to make decisions without considering the steps outlined here. Many managers get themselves into trouble by making hasty decisions.

When an employee brings up a problem, the manager should usually ask questions such as those listed below:

- How extensive is the problem? Does it need an immediate response? Is it safety related?
- Who else is affected by the problem? Should they be involved in this discussion?
- Have you (the employee) thought through the problem, and do you have an idea of what the end result should be?
- What do you recommend? Why?

This approach is a form of participative supervision that can help to develop the employee's analytical skills. With the additional information gained from the process, the manager can either think through the problem, apply the decision-making steps, or make a decision.

A word of caution here: during any stage of the process, managers should identify a specific time and then follow through when they tell other people that they "will get back to them." When managers fail to make a decision or give feedback by the specified time, they incur a serious breach of trust.

DECISION-MAKING STYLES

There are three basic decision-making styles: reflexive, reflective, and consistent. Let's take a closer look at each of these styles. *Reflexive decision makers* like to make quick decisions—"to shoot from the hip"—without taking the time to get all the information that may be needed and without considering all alternatives. On the positive side, reflexive decision-makers are decisive; they do not procrastinate. On the negative side, making quick decisions can be costly and wasteful when a decision is not the best possible alternative. Reflexive decision-makers may be viewed by employees as poor managers if they consistently make bad decisions. If you use a reflexive style, you may want to slow down and spend more time gathering information and analyzing alternatives. Following the steps in the decision-making process can help you develop those skills.

Reflective decision makers like to take plenty of time to make decisions, taking into account a considerable amount of information and analyzing several alternatives. On the positive side, the reflective types do not make quick decisions. On the negative side, they may procrastinate and waste valuable time and other resources. The reflective decision maker may be viewed as wishy-washy and indecisive. If you use a reflective style, you may want to speed up your decision making.

Consistent decision makers tend to make decisions without rushing or wasting time. They seem to know when they have enough information and alternatives to make a sound decision. Compared to decision makers using other styles, these decision makers tend to have the most consistent record of good decisions. They usually follow the decision-making steps discussed earlier.

GROUP DECISION MAKING

Decisions in organizations are increasingly being made by groups rather than by individuals. There seem to be at least two primary reasons for this. First, a group is likely to develop more and better alternatives than a single person, as indicated by the adage "two heads are better than one." Second, organizations are relying less on the historical idea that departments should be separate and independent decision units. To produce the best ideas and to improve their implementation, organizations are increasingly turning to teams that cut across traditional departmental lines. This requires the use of group decision-making techniques.

Advantages of Group Decision Making

Individual and group decisions each have their own set of strengths. Neither is ideal for all situations. Let's begin, therefore, by reviewing the advantages that group decision makers have over individuals.

More complete information. A group brings a range of experience and diverse perspectives to the decision-making process that an individual, acting alone, cannot.

More alternatives. Because groups have a greater quantity and diversity of information, they can identify more alternatives than could an individual.

Acceptance of solution. Many decisions fail because people do not accept the solution. If the people who will implement or be affected by a certain decision could participate in the decision-making process, they would be more likely to accept the decision and to encourage others to accept it.

Legitimacy. The group decision-making process is consistent with democratic ideals and therefore may be perceived as more legitimate than decision making by a single person.

Disadvantages of Group Decision Making

If groups are so good, where did the phrase, "A camel is a racehorse put together by a committee," originate? The answer, of course, is that group decision making has drawbacks. The major disadvantages are described below.

Time consuming. It takes time to assemble a group. In addition, the interaction that takes place once the group is in place is frequently inefficient. The result is that a group almost always takes more time to make a decision than does one individual.

Minority domination. Members of a group are never perfectly equal. They may differ in terms of rank in the organization, experience, knowledge about the problem, influence with other members, verbal skills, assertiveness, and the like. This creates the opportunity for one or more members to use their advantages to dominate others and impose undue influence on the final decision.

Pressures to conform. There are social pressures in groups. The desire of group members to be accepted and to be viewed as assets to the group can quash any overt disagreement and encourage conformity of viewpoints. This tendency of group members to withhold their individual views in order to appear to be in agreement is called groupthink and can result in bad decisions.

Ambiguous responsibility. Group members share responsibility for making decisions, but no one person is actually responsible for the final outcome. In an individual decision, it is clear who is responsible, but in a group decision, the responsibility of any single member is diluted.

When to Use Group Decision Making

In making decisions, when are groups better than individuals and vice versa? That depends on what you mean by "better." There are four criteria frequently associated with good decisions. First, the evidence indicates that, on average, groups make more *accurate* decisions than individuals. This does not mean, of course, that every group outperforms every individual. Rather, group decisions have been found to be more effective than those of the average member of the group; however, they seldom are as good as those of the best group member. Next, individual decision makers are *faster* than groups. Group decision processes are characterized by give and take, which consumes time.

Groups tend to do better than individuals in reaching *creative* decisions. This requires, however, that groups must avoid groupthink. They must encourage doubts about the group's shared views and challenges to favored arguments; they must avoid an excessive desire to give an appearance of consensus; and they must not assume that silence or abstention by members is a "yes" vote. Finally, group decisions typically result in greater *acceptance*. Because group decisions are made using input from more people, they are likely to result in solutions that more people will accept.

INCREASING EMPLOYEE INVOLVEMENT IN DECISION MAKING

The traditional view of decision making places the manager in the eminent position of primary decision maker. In today's complex work environment, it is unrealistic to expect one person to know all the answers. In addition, as employees continue to grow and take advantage of educational opportunities, it is smart to draw on their knowledge, creativity, and experience. When employees are involved effectively in decision making, the quality of decisions can be improved and an increased commitment to the organization can be achieved. This should not interfere with the authority of the manager, but rather promote teamwork, improve creativity, increase interaction, expand communications, and enhance overall organizational efficiency. Involving employees in decision making may earn the manager greater respect. A manager's decision-making ability can be improved if more employee ideas and suggestions are collected at the outset.

An effective FLM must learn to be a guardian of decisions instead of the maker of decisions. When possible, decisions should be delegated to employees at lower levels. Employees have a right to participate in decisions directly affecting them. The rationale is that employees possess valuable day-to-day knowledge of the job, and therefore, the organization benefits by allowing them to make certain decisions. The FLM oversees decision making to ensure that the group's decisions are in keeping with departmental goals, organizational objectives, and company policy. When employees make decisions, the organization gains because the most knowledgeable people make the decisions, the group gains by being included in the process, and individuals grow, increasing their potential and their long-term contributions to the organization.

Many managers have implemented *participative decision-making techniques* to boost productivity, improve employee relations, and increase the quality of decisions. Participative approaches invite decision sharing. Employees are made responsible for contributing opinions and information, and they are expected to participate in the decision-making process as much as possible. Participative managers do not disguise their power to make the final decisions, particularly when faced with crisis. They do, however, request and expect constant feedback, a practice that provides them with the best available information, ideas, suggestions, talent, and experience. The move toward participation is increasingly popular. Some organizations prefer traditional authoritarian methods for decision making; however, many organizations find themselves in transition and may wish to consider the many benefits of a participative approach. When employees participate in making decisions that affect them, they support those decisions more enthusiastically and try harder to make them work.

PRACTICAL PITFALLS TO AVOID WHEN MAKING DECISIONS

Many managers have a tendency to encounter one or more of a number of problems when making decisions. Some FLMs make all decisions into big or crisis decisions.

Pitfall 1: Making All Decisions into Big or Crisis Decisions

Everyone has run into the manager who treats every decision as if it were a life-and-death issue. These managers may spend two hours deciding whether to order one or two boxes of rubber bands. Some managers seem to delight in turning all decision situations into crisis situations. These approaches keep the employees confused; they have a hard time distinguishing between important and less important issues, crisis and non-crisis situations. As a result of this approach, the really important problems may not receive proper attention because the manager wastes time becoming bogged down in unimportant matters. This type of manager must learn to allocate an appropriate amount of time to each decision, based on its relative significance. Even when a true crisis does occur, such as the breakdown of a major piece of equipment or an accident, the manager must learn to remain calm and think clearly.

Pitfall 2: Failing to Consult Others

The advantage of consulting others in the decision-making process was discussed earlier in this chapter. Yet some managers are reluctant to seek advice, fearing it will make them look incompetent. Many managers, especially new ones, are under the impression that they should know all the answers and that to ask someone else for advice would be admitting a weakness. Successful managers place good sense and their reasoning ability ahead of their egos.

Pitfall 3: Never Admitting a Mistake

No one makes the best decision every time. If a manager makes a bad decision, it is best to admit it and do what is necessary to correct the mistake. The worst possible course is to try to force a bad decision into being a good decision.

Pitfall 4: Constantly Regretting Decisions

Some managers always want to change the unchangeable. Once a decision has been made and it is final, don't brood over it. Remember, very few decisions are totally bad; some are just better than others. A manager who spends all his or her time dreaming about "what if" will not have enough time or energy to implement decisions already made.

Pitfall 5: Failing to Utilize Precedents and Policies

Why reinvent the wheel? If a similar problem has arisen in the past, managers should draw on that experience. If a situation seems to recur constantly, it is usually useful to implement a policy covering it. For example, it is wise to have a policy covering priorities for vacation time. Managers should also keep abreast of current organizational policies, which can often help solve problems.

Pitfall 6: Failing to Gather and Examine Available Data

Some managers often ignore or fail to utilize available factual information. One common reason for this is that some degree of effort is normally required to gather and analyze data—it is easier to utilize only the data already on hand. A related problem is the need to separate the facts from gossip and rumor. The general tendency is to believe only what you want to believe and not to consider the facts.

Pitfall 7: Promising What Cannot Be Delivered

Managers sometimes make promises they know they can't keep and commitments when they don't have the necessary authority to do so. Managers may view such commitments and promises as ways of getting employees to go along with decisions. Failed commitments almost always come back to haunt the manager. The best approach is never to promise more than can be delivered.

Pitfall 8: Delaying Decisions Too Long

Many managers tend to put off making a decision "until we have more information." Timeliness is often critical and even good decisions can be ineffective if delayed too long. Managers rarely ever have all the information they would like. Good FLMs know when they have adequate information and then make decisions promptly.

SUMMARY

FLMs confront many decision situations, which can vary from the programmed type at one extreme to the nonprogrammed at the other. Decisions for routine, repetitive-type problems are usually made easier by the use of policies, procedures, standard practices, and the like. However, nonroutine decisions are usually one-time, unusual, or unique problems that require sound judgement and systematic thinking. Better decisions are more likely to occur when managers follow the guidelines for making decisions, get input from others, use group decision-making strategies when appropriate, and take steps to avoid decision-making pitfalls.

Chapter 12

Change and the Front-Line Manager

INTRODUCTION

It is a rare FLM who has the luxury to operate in a stable and predictable environment. The adjective many FLMs and other managers are increasingly using to describe their world is *chaotic*. Take a look at the experience of one FLM, Jerome Fisher. It has been a stressful couple of weeks for Jerome Fisher. Things had just begun to settle down after he reorganized his department into five-person work teams. Then, Jerome received word that a new team-based performance appraisal system would soon be introduced throughout the company. Jerome remembered the department's introduction to the computer system three years ago. The transition had been traumatic, to say the least. Now everyone would have to adjust to a new performance appraisal system. As he recalled the problems he had experienced during the previous changes in the department, Jerome wondered how to introduce this new change to make the transition less stressful for everyone. In today's work world, change is an everyday occurrence for managers like Jerome. The message is clear: "Change or else!"

The business landscape is not the same as it was just a few years ago. Change is everywhere. The organizations that FLMs find themselves in are not static but continually changing in response to a variety of influences coming from both outside and inside. Those companies that fail to change when required may likely find themselves out of business. For today's FLM, the challenge is to anticipate and help implement change processes on the front line so that organizational performance is enhanced. In this chapter, we shall examine the forces driving change in organizations and in the FLM's job, discuss employee reactions to change and how FLMs can overcome resistance to change, and highlight some inevitable behavioral reactions to change. The chapter concludes with a general model of change.

THE NATURE OF THE CHANGE PROCESS

Organization change is any substantive modification to some part of the organization. It involves movement from the present state of the organization to some future state. The future state may be a new strategy for the organization, changes in the organization's culture, introduction of new technology, and so on. Change can involve virtually any aspect of an organization including work schedules, departmentalization, span of management, machinery, organizational design, and employee selection. It is important to keep in mind that any particular change in an organization may have ripple effects. For example, when a company installed a new computerized production system at one of its plants, employees were required to learn to operate the new equipment, the compensation system was adjusted to reflect those newly acquired skills, the manager's span of management was altered, several related jobs were redesigned, the criteria for selecting new employees was changed, and a new quality control system was implemented.

FORCES OF CHANGE

Look around your office or organization and what do you see? Computers, copiers, fax machines, robots, and close-circuit TV sets were rare or nonexistent only a few short years ago. Look harder and you will probably notice that your company has changed in other, subtler, ways in order to respond to a host of new conditions and constituencies, such as government regulations, political activism, and criticism of big business. Some of these changes may not affect you personally, but many do.

It is hard to adjust to change. We tend to be the willing victims of inertia—comfortable with the status quo because we are used to it. If something threatens to "rock the boat," we often view it with suspicion and distrust. The accelerating rate of change makes change even more difficult to tolerate. Those who fail to adjust to it are condemning themselves to professional obsolescence. It is important to recognize that change is a natural part of life, and that change produces progress.

ORGANIZATIONS UNDER SIEGE

Intensifying global competition, increasing customer sophistication, demands for improved quality at lower prices, and a growing cynicism toward "big" business, government, and labor have worked to fuel a major attack on many of the venerable old institutions and organizations of the past. Government, universities, the military, financial institutions, major manufacturers, utilities, mainline churches, and not-for-profits have all become targets of scrutiny. Worldwide trends toward "downsizing" and "reengineering" have emerged in large organizations as a result of intense global competition and an attendant need for efficiency. These days, even experienced technicians, managers, and professionals are losing their jobs as organizations seek to "streamline" operations. These changes have led to considerable insecurity and stress among groups of employees who were protected from such pressures in the past.

WORKFORCE DIVERSITY

A related issue is workforce diversity. Workforce diversity is a powerful force for change in organizations. Workforce demographics are important contributing factors to workforce diversity. First, the workforce is witnessing an increased participation of females, and soon the majority of new workers will be female. Second, the workforce is becoming more culturally diverse than ever. Part of this is attributable to globalization, but U.S. demographics are changing as well. The participation of African-Americans and Hispanic-Americans is increasing at record rates. Third, the workforce is aging. There will be fewer younger workers and more middle-aged Americans working (Nelson & Quick, 2000).

A few years ago, Denny's, the restaurant chain, was a name synonymous with racism. In 1994, the company paid $544 million to settle two lawsuits brought by black customers who claimed some restaurants refused to seat or serve them. Advantica, Denny's parent company, undertook radical changes led by a new blunt-talking CEO in 1995. Because Denny's responded quickly, decisively, and sincerely, it weathered the crisis. Performance appraisals are now based on valuing diversity. A top manager who doesn't demonstrate concern for diversity can have up to 25 percent of his or her bonus withheld. Minorities now own 35 percent of the Denny's franchises. Nearly half of its officers and managers are minorities. The commitment to diversity has moved the company to the number two spot in Fortune's 1998 list of the 50 Best Companies for Asians, Blacks, and Hispanics (Faircloth, 1998).

TIME COMPRESSION

"It's in the mail," we used to say, knowing we could gain a few more days to complete a project. But first with overnight delivery services, then subsequently with fax machines and e-mail, the speed of communication has increased. Now we can be buzzed, beeped, paged, and prodded no matter where we are or what we are doing. As the exchange of messages has become faster and more efficient, people often feel that time has been compressed. FLMs and other managers are under considerable pressure to do more and more, faster and faster, and are beginning to experience negative stress. Stress is one of main reasons for employee failure.

COMPLYING WITH LAWS, STANDARDS, AND PROCEDURES

Most of us value "playing by the rules" and so try diligently to comply with laws, professional standards, regulations, and specified procedures. Staying in compliance becomes difficult, however, as these "rules" are constantly changing. This is a problem for many managers and employees these days: new statutes and administrative rules, new case law, new professional standards, and revised organizational policies and procedures are issued every day as the pace of change in the workplace accelerates.

No sooner do we implement one set of procedures than we find ourselves scrambling to respond to a new set of rules. Although employees and FLMs with years of experience have learned to adapt over time, the constant need to change their approach to work in response to more and more rules, laws, and standards can be stressful.

A TECHNOLOGY EXPLOSION

All of us have been affected by the explosion of new technology which has entered the workplace. Personal computers, fax machines, scanners, cellular telephones, graphics design software, the Internet, and other new wonders can be quite intimidating to those of us who still have trouble programming our VCRs! Yet new technologies enter the workplace daily, in wave after wave, version after version.

It has been said that if you understand your computer software, it is most likely obsolete, having already been surpassed by a newer version. Even the most sophisticated employees and managers are struggling to keep up with technology, use it effectively, and make cost-efficient decisions about its implementation. Technology also poses other problems. It is increasingly difficult to maintain the security of our technological investments and sensitive data. New technologies are wonderful, but they can be challenging and stressful as well.

THE FLM's JOB AND CHANGE

The old saying, "The one unchanging principle of life is the principle of change," contains an important element of truth: Change is an inevitable fact in the lives of FLMs and their organizations. For FLMs and their organizations, some facets of change are slow and nearly imperceptible, while others occur quite rapidly. In addition, the impact of change processes can vary from quite minor to truly substantial.

INTERNAL SOURCES OF CHANGE

Sources of change exist within the organization itself and often result in internal pressure for change. Examples include shifts in workers' attitudes toward their supervisor or their benefits package; budget adjustments; declining productivity; reorganizations; new employees; changes in key organizational personnel whose goals and values influence large populations of the organization; and implementation of new policies regarding overtime procedures, work schedules, or vacations. Changes in attitudes among employees (due to increased age or changes in job responsibilities) can result in changes in job satisfaction, attendance behavior, and commitment. Changes in top-level and other key individuals in an organization can alter the internal character of the organization. For example, if an incoming CEO or president emphasizes integrity, corporate ethics, and customer service to his or her staff, those concerns will come to be reflected in the creation of new programs, the restructuring of the organization, and the evolution of a different organizational culture. It is not unusual for individuals like FLMs to have input into these decisions.

EXTERNAL SOURCES OF CHANGE

External sources of change originate in the organization's environment. Specific examples of external change include evolving government regulations (e.g., new tax rates or new laws), changes in economic factors (e.g., interest rates or increase in minimum wage), and social changes (e.g., changing consumer desires, shifts in population, or new political trends). Ordinarily, changes of this kind have an indirect impact on the FLM, and there is very little that the FLM can do to influence them. It is important for today's FLM to understand that any of these features of the external environment can have profound positive or negative effects on an organization. The rise and fall of competitors has clear implications for organizational performance, as does the cooperativeness and competencies of suppliers. If the preferences of customers change as a result of changes in taste, the well-being of a product line can be affected. Recessions, periods of inflation, and upturns or downturns in the economy can have both direct and indirect influences on organizations. The education, talents, and attitudes of potential employees also play an important role in an organization's well-being. Changes in these facets of the labor force can lead to a shortage or surplus of qualified employees. Lastly, legislation can produce change. Federal legislation, such as the enforcement of the policies of the Equal Employment Opportunity Commission and the Federal Trade Commission, can alter the procedures an organization traditionally uses in its recruiting and marketing functions.

Regardless of the type of change, the FLM is responsible for helping to successfully implement the policies associated with that change. As a result, the FLM must deal with the frustrations and anxieties that usually accompany change and address some difficult questions: "Will the employees resist the change? When should my employees be informed of the change? Am I capable of implementing the change? What other changes will be necessary as a result of this change?"

PLANNED VERSUS UNPLANNED CHANGE

Organizational change is either planned well in advance or comes about as a reaction to unexpected events. Planned change is change that is designed and implemented in an orderly, systematic, and timely fashion by managers to move an organization, or a subsystem, to a new state. Planned change includes deliberately changing the organization's design, technology, tasks, people, information systems, and the like. Although managers try to follow a plan for change, it does not always move forward smoothly. The plan often hits roadblocks, causing managers to rethink their goal and plan. Unplanned change often results in piecemeal responses to events as they occur. Unplanned change occurs when pressures for change overwhelm efforts to resist the change. Such change may be unexpected by management and can result in uncontrolled, if not chaotic, effects on the organization. There is a greater potential for unplanned change to be poorly conceived and executed. Planned change is therefore almost always preferable to unplanned change.

Georgia-Pacific, a large forest products business, is an excellent example of an organization that recently went through a planned and well-managed change. When CEO A. D. Correll took over the company's leadership in 1991, he quickly became alarmed at the company's high accident rate: nine serious injuries per one hundred employees each year and twenty-six deaths during a five-year period. Even though the forest products business is inherently dangerous, Correll believed that the accident rate was far too high and began a major initiative to improve the situation. He and other top managers developed a multistage program intended to educate workers about safety, improve safety equipment in the plant, and eliminate a long-standing part of the company's culture that made injuries almost a badge of courage. Seven years later, Georgia-Pacific had the best safety record in the industry.

On the other hand, a few years ago, Caterpillar was caught flat-footed by a worldwide recession in the construction industry, suffered enormous losses, and took several years to recover. Had managers at Caterpillar anticipated the need for change earlier, they might have been able to respond more quickly. Similarly, Kodak recently announced plans to cut several thousand jobs, a reaction to sluggish sales and profits that had not been foreseen.

The importance of approaching change from a planned perspective is reinforced by the frequency of change in well-run organizations. Many companies implement some form of moderate change at least every year and major changes every four to five years. FLMs and other managers who sit back and respond only when necessary are likely to spend time and money hastily changing and rechanging things. It is more effective to anticipate the forces urging change and plan ahead to deal with them. Responsiveness to unplanned change requires tremendous flexibility and adaptability on the part of the organization. FLMs must be prepared to handle both planned and unplanned forms of change in the organizations.

EMPLOYEE REACTIONS TO CHANGE

How employees perceive a change greatly affects how they react to it. While many variations are possible, there are only four basic reactions. If employees clearly see that the change is not compatible with their needs and aspirations, they will resist the change. In this situation, the employees are certain that the change will make things worse. If employees cannot foresee how the change will affect them, they will resist the change or be neutral, at best. Most people shy away from the unknown. They often assume that the change may make things worse.

If employees see that the change is going to take place regardless of their objections, they may initially resist the change and then resignedly accept it. Although their first reaction is to resist, once the change appears inevitable, they often see no other choice than to go along with it. If employees see that the change is in their best interests, they will be motivated to accept it.

Obviously, it is critical for employees to feel confident that the change will make things better. It is the FLM's obligation to foster an accepting attitude. Note that three out of the four situations involve some form of resistance to change. Resistance to change is an emotional/behavioral response to real or imagined threats to an established work routine.

FLMs must understand resistance to change and learn techniques to overcome it.

UNDERSTANDING AND MANAGING RESISTANCE TO CHANGE

We tend to be creatures of habit. Many people find it difficult to try new ways of doing things. It is precisely because of this basic human characteristic that most employees are not enthusiastic about change in the workplace. This resistance is well documented. As one person once put it, "Most people hate any change that doesn't jingle in their pockets." No matter how technically or administratively perfect a proposed change may be, people make or break it.

Rare is the manager who does not have several stories about carefully cultivated changes that died on the vine because of employee resistance. It is important for managers to learn to manage resistance because failed change efforts are costly. These costs may include decreased employee loyalty, a lowered probability of achieving corporate goals, a waste of money and resources, and the difficulty of fixing the failed effort.

People resist change for many reasons. Resisting change does not necessarily mean that they will never accept it. In many cases, the change may be resisted because it was introduced improperly. The manager, by implementing drastic change, could have created feelings of insecurity in the employees. Perhaps the manager did not inform the employees about the change until the last minute. Sometimes the change is introduced properly but is still resisted. The manager may use resistance to change as a means of "taking the pulse" of the department. If minor change meets with resistance, it could indicate that other problems exist, such as problems with morale, commitment, or trust.

Individual and group behavior following an organizational change can take many forms, ranging from extremes of acceptance to active resistance. Resistance can be as subtle as passive resignation or as overt as deliberate sabotage. Resistance can also be immediate, or deferred. It is easiest for managers to deal with resistance when it is overt and immediate. For instance, a company proposes a change and employees quickly respond by voicing complaints, engaging in a work slowdown or threatening to go on strike. Although these responses may be damaging, their cause is clearly identifiable.

It is more challenging to manage resistance that is implicit or deferred. Implicit resistance is subtle—such as loss of loyalty to the organization, loss of motivation to work, increased errors or mistakes, or increased absenteeism due to "sickness"—and hence more difficult to recognize. Similarly, deferred resistance clouds the link between the source of the resistance and the reactions to it. For example, a change may produce what appears to be only a minimal reaction at the time it is initiated, but then resistance surfaces weeks, months, or even years later. In another type of deferred resistance, a single change that in and of itself might have had little impact can become the straw that breaks the camel's back. Reactions to change can build up and then explode in a response that seems totally out of proportion to the change it follows. The resistance, or course, has merely been deferred and stockpiled. What surfaces is a response to an accumulation of previous changes.

FLMs need to learn to recognize the manifestations of resistance to change both in themselves and in others if they want to be more effective in creating, supporting, and managing change. So why do people resist change? A number of specific reasons are discussed in the next few paragraphs.

PREDISPOSITION AGAINST CHANGE

Some people are predisposed to dislike change. This predisposition is highly personal and deeply ingrained. It is an outgrowth of how they learned to handle change and ambiguity as a child. Consider the hypothetical examples of Amy and Fred. Amy's parents were patient, flexible, and understanding. From the time Amy was weaned from a bottle, she was taught that there were positive compensations for the loss of immediate gratification. She learned that love and approval were associated with making changes. In contrast, Fred's parents were unreasonable and unyielding. They frequently forced him to comply with their wishes. They required him to take piano lessons even though he hated them. Changes were accompanied by demands for compliance. This taught Fred to be distrustful and suspicious of change. These learned predispositions ultimately affect how Amy and Fred handle change as adults.

HABITS

Habit is a wonderful thing for human beings. Can you imagine how difficult life would be without habits? Imagine if you had to think consciously about every little movement needed to drive an automobile. Would you ever make it to work in the morning? When we drive by habit our mind can think about other things, secure in the knowledge that our senses will warn us when something is wrong.

We do things by habit: routine household chores, dressing ourselves, greeting one another, sorting our mail, and so forth. Habits are easy and comfortable, freeing our minds to focus on other, more important things. Furthermore, habits are often difficult to change—reflect on a time when you or a friend tried to alter a morning routine or drop a bad habit. One very important reason we resist is because we do not want to change our safe, secure, habitual way of doing things.

LACK OF TRUST

Trust is a characteristic of high-performance teams in which team members believe in each other's integrity, character, and ability. FLMs who trust their employees make the change process an open, honest, and participative affair. Employees who trust management are more willing to expend extra effort and take chances with something different. Mutual mistrust, on the other hand, can doom an otherwise well-conceived change or project to failure.

SURPRISE AND FEAR OF THE UNKNOWN

When finding yourself in the presence of an unknown insect, many of us typically choose to kill it by swatting it or stepping on it. We typically rationalize, "Better safe than sorry." Fear is a natural reaction to the unknown. When innovative or radically different changes are introduced without warning, affected employees become fearful of the implications. Grapevine rumors fill the void created by a lack of official announcements, and employees often develop negative attitudes toward the change. They may also behave dysfunctionally—complaining, purposely working more slowly, or undermining department morale—if required to go through with the change. In these situations, employees let fear paralyze them into inaction. FLMs should therefore avoid creating situations in which employees are surprised and thus fear change. They can do this by keeping all affected employees adequately informed.

IGNORING CHANGE THROUGH SELECTIVE PERCEPTION

We are flooded every moment with information pouring into our brains from our sensory organs—our eyes, ears, nose, taste buds, and various touch and balance sensors. We cannot possibly attend to all of the information, so we screen out much of it through a process called "selective perception." This means that we pay attention to those sensations, which we judge to be important while ignoring the rest. Selective perception is a complex psychological process that occurs both intentionally and unconsciously.

How do we choose those messages to which we pay attention? When faced with messages signaling a change, we frequently attend to those that reinforce our belief in the status quo and maintain our present comfort level. In other words, too often we see only what we want to see, and hear only what we want to hear. Through selective perception, we frequently protect the status quo by filtering out troubling signals that a change is needed, or may be on its way.

Similarly, we often listen only to commentators or others with whom we agree or whose ideas resonate with our own. Dangerous messages, which somehow threaten our comfort level, are "tuned out" and ignored. The natural human tendency toward selective perception can harm our ability to deal with change. If we block out all information with which we disagree, we often miss clear signals that change is on the horizon. Thus when change occurs, we are surprised by it, unprepared for it, and afraid of it.

TOO MUCH DEPENDENCE ON OTHERS

One way to deal with the bombardment of information at work is to specialize. We tend to gravitate to our own spheres of interest and depend on others for information and insights outside our scope of knowledge. For example, when a car needs repairs, you may take it to a trusted mechanic rather than attempt to repair it yourself. The point is that everyone depends on certain people for advice and guidance. This dependence may serve you well, but only if the people on whom you rely are well informed—not if they give you misinformation or poor advice. Although you should not immediately become suspicious of all your advisors, you should recognize that too much dependence on others could become dangerous. FLMs and employees may resist change if they are advised to resist because the change may adversely affect them. Trusting in this advice, they may fail to understand for themselves the true nature of the situation and may be "blind sided" by the change when it occurs.

THREATS TO JOBS AND INCOME

Employees often fear that change may reduce their job security or income. New laborsaving equipment, for instance, may be interpreted as a signal that layoffs are imminent. When a potential change has the real possibility to cause employees harm, they are likely to resist it with all their might.

Changes in job tasks or established work routines often threaten employees. They worry that they won't be able to perform successfully, particularly where pay is closely tied to productivity. It is therefore important that managers consider any adverse effect employees might experience as a result of a proposed organizational change. If employees perceive that they will lose money, influence, clout, or status as the result of a change, managers can expect strong and active resistance. This resistance is not irrational but is aimed at protecting employee self-interest.

FLMs' ORIENTATION TO RESISTANCE TO CHANGE

FLMs can react to resistance to change in two ways. They can treat resistance as a problem to overcome or view it as a signal to get more information about the reasons for resistance. FLMs who view resistance as a problem to overcome may try to forcefully reduce it. Such coercive approaches often increase the resistance.

Alternatively, FLMs may see resistance as a signal that those responsible for the change need more information about the intended change. Those employees who will be affected by the change may have valuable insights about its effects. An alert FLM will involve the employees in diagnosing the reasons for the resistance. In this way, FLMs can use resistance to change as a tool to get needed information.

Should FLMs and other managers see the absence of resistance to change as a stroke of good fortune? Many reasons suggest that they should not. The absence of resistance is also a signal to managers. A change that is automatically accepted can be less effective than one that has been resisted and actively debated. The resisters play an important role by focusing manager's attention on potentially dysfunctional aspects of the proposed change.

MANAGING THE CHANGE PROCESS TO REDUCE RESISTANCE

Most changes are originated by middle or upper management. The changes are then passed down to the FLM—the link between management and employees—for successful implementation. In this process, the FLM is the person who must cope with employees' anxieties and fears about change. The environment created by the FLM can greatly affect employees' acceptance of change. Several suggestions for creating a positive environment for change are discussed in the following paragraphs.

BUILD TRUST

If employees trust and have confidence in the FLM, they are much more likely to accept changes; otherwise, they are likely to resist change vigorously. Trust cannot be established overnight: it is built over a period of time. The FLM's actions determine the degree of the employee's trust. Employees will trust an FLM they perceive to be fair, honest, and forthright. Employees will not trust a manager who they feel is always trying to take advantage of them. FLMs can go a long way toward building trust if they discuss upcoming changes with their employees and if they actively involve the employees in the change process.

OPENLY COMMUNICATE AND DISCUSS CHANGES

Communication about impending change is essential if employees are to adjust effectively. The details of the change should be provided, but equally important is the rationale behind the change. Employees want to know why change is needed. If there is no good reason for it, why should they favor the change? Fear of the unknown, one of the major barriers to change, can be greatly reduced by openly discussing any upcoming or current changes with the affected employees. An FLM should always begin by explaining the five W's and an H to the employees— What the change is? Why it is needed? Whom it will affect? When it will take place? Where it will take place? and How it will take place? During this discussion, the FLM should be as open and honest as possible. The more background and detail the FLM can give, the more likely it is that the employees will accept the changes. The FLM should also outline the impact of the changes on each of the affected employees. People are primarily interested in how change will affect them as individuals.

It is critical that FLMs give employees an opportunity to ask questions. This is the major advantage of an oral discussion over a written memo. Regardless of how thorough an explanation may be, employees will usually have questions that FLMs should answer to the fullest extent possible. When employees receive all the facts and get their questions answered, their resistance often fades. This explains why, for example, company officials at one organization allow their employees to review company profit and loss statements and answer their questions about the organization's performance. Improved communication is particularly effective in reducing problems resulting from unclear situations. For example, when the grapevine is active with rumors of cutbacks and layoffs, honest and open communication of the true facts can be a calming force. Even if the news is bad, a clear message often wins points and helps employees accept change. When communication is ambiguous and employees feel threatened, they often imagine scenarios that are considerably worse than the actual "bad news."

INVOLVE THE EMPLOYEES

Changes that are "sprung" on employees with little or no warning will likely result in resistance—simply as a knee-jerk reaction—until employees can assess how the change affects them. In contrast, employees who are involved in the change process better understand the need for change, and therefore, are less likely to resist it. Additionally, people who participate in making a decision tend to be more committed to the outcome than those who are not involved. Employee involvement in change can be extremely effective. It is difficult for individuals to resist a change when they participated in the decision and helped implement it. The psychology is simple: no one wants to oppose something that he or she has helped develop. It is useful to solicit employee ideas and input as early as possible in the change process. Don't wait until the last minute to ask the employees what they think about a change. When affected employees have been involved in a change at or near its inception, they will usually actively support the change.

PROVIDE REWARDS AND INCENTIVES

Employers can give employees rewards and incentives to help them see that supporting a change is in their best interests. One rather obvious—and quite successful—mechanism to facilitate change is rewarding people for behaving in the desired fashion. For example, employees who are required to learn to use new equipment should be praised for their successful efforts. In order to make incentives work effectively, employers should analyze the source of the resistance, and what might overcome that resistance. For example, employees may be afraid they won't be able to do a new task. FLMs could provide them with new skills training, or a short paid leave of absence to allow them to calm down, rethink their fears, realize that their concerns are unfounded. A difficult change can also have positive aspects. Layoffs can be viewed as opportunities for those who remain, allowing jobs to be redesigned to provide new challenges and responsibilities. Other incentives that can help reduce resistance include a pay increase, a new title, flexible work hours, or increased job autonomy.

MAKE SURE THE CHANGES ARE REASONABLE

The FLM should always do whatever is possible to ensure that any proposed changes are reasonable. Proposed changes that originate with upper management are sometimes totally unreasonable. When this is the case, it is usually because upper management is not aware of specific circumstances that make the changes unworkable. It is the FLM's responsibility to intervene in such situations and communicate the problem to upper management.

EDUCATE THE WORKFORCE

Sometimes people are reluctant to change because they fear what the future has in store. For example, fears about economic security may be put to rest by a few reassuring words from management. As part of educating employees about what organizational change means for them, top management must show considerable emotional sensitivity. Doing so makes it possible for people affected by a change to help make it work. Some companies have found that simply answering the question "What's in it for me?" can help to allay many fears.

AVOID THREATS

The FLM who attempts to implement change through the use of threats is taking a negative approach likely to decrease employee trust. A natural reaction is "This must be bad news if it requires a threat." Most people also dislike being threatened into accepting something. Even though threats may get results in the short term, they may be damaging to employees' morale and attitude over a longer period of time.

FOLLOW A SENSIBLE TIME SCHEDULE

As mentioned previously, most changes are passed down from upper management to the FLM for implementation. The FLM often has control or influence over when changes should be implemented, however. Some times are better than others. For example, the week before Christmas or the height of the vacation season would ordinarily not be good times to implement a major change. FLMs should rely on their valuable insights into the department and on their common sense when recommending a time schedule for implementing a change.

IMPLEMENT THE CHANGES IN A SENSIBLE MANNER

The FLM often has some choice about where changes will take place. When making these decisions, FLMs should rely on logic and common sense. For example, FLMs usually decide who will get a new piece of equipment. It would be sensible to introduce the equipment through those employees who are naturally more adaptable and flexible than others. If FLMs make it a point to know their employees, they usually will have a good idea as to which are more flexible. Another consideration in introducing changes is to implement them where possible in a way that minimizes their effects on interpersonal relationships. The FLM should avoid disturbing smoothly working groups or teams.

PROVIDE EMPATHY AND SUPPORT

Another strategy for overcoming resistance is providing empathy and support to employees who have trouble dealing with the change. Active listening is an excellent tool for identifying the reasons behind resistance and for uncovering fears. Expression of concern about the change can provide important feedback that FLMs can use to improve the change process. Emotional support and encouragement can help an employee deal with the anxiety that is a natural response to change. Employees who experience severe reactions to change can benefit from talking with a counselor. Some companies provide counseling through their employee assistance plans.

INEVITABLE REACTIONS TO CHANGE

In spite of attempts to minimize the resistance to change in an organization, some reactions to change are inevitable. Negative reactions may be manifested in overt behavior, or change may be resisted more passively. People show four basic identifiable reactions to change: disengagement, disidentification, disenchantment, and disorientation. FLMs can use interventions to deal with these reactions (Woodward & Bucholz, 1987).

Disengagement is psychological withdrawal from change. An employee appears to lose initiative and interest in the job. Employees who disengage may fear the change but take on the approach of doing nothing and simply hoping for the best. Disengaged employees are physically present but mentally absent. They lack drive and commitment, and they simply comply without real psychological investment in their work. Disengagement can be recognized by behaviors such as being hard to find or doing only the basics to get the job done. Typical disengagement statements include "No problem" or "This won't affect me."

The basic FLM strategy for dealing with disengaged individuals is to confront them with their reaction and draw them out, identifying concerns that must be addressed. Disengaged employees may not be aware of the change in their behavior and may need to be assured of the good intentions of the FLM. Helping them air their feelings can lead to productive discussions. Disengaged people seldom become cheerleaders for the change, but they can be brought closer to accepting and working with a change through open communication with an empathic FLM who is willing to listen.

Another reaction to change is disidentification. Individuals reacting in this way feel that their identity has been threatened by the change, and they feel very vulnerable. Many times they cling to a past procedure because they had a sense of mastery over it, and it gave them a sense of security. "My job is completely changed" and "I used to . . ." are verbal indications of disidentification. Disidentified employees often display sadness and worry. They may appear to be sulking and dwelling on the past by reminiscing about the old ways of doing things.

Disidentified employees often feel like victims in the change process because they are so vulnerable. FLMs can help them through the transition by encouraging them to explore their feelings and helping them transfer their positive feelings into the new situation. One way to do this is to help them identify what it is they liked in the old situation, as well as to show them how it is possible to have the same positive experience in the new situation. Disidentified employees need to see that work itself and emotion are separable—that is, that they can let go of old ways and experience positive reactions to new ways of performing their jobs.

Disenchantment is also a common reaction to change. It is usually expressed as negativity or anger. Disenchanted employees realize that the past is gone, and they are mad about it. They may try to enlist the support of other employees by forming coalitions. Destructive behaviors like sabotage and backstabbing may result. Typical verbal signs of disenchantment are "This will never work" and "I'm getting out of this company as soon as I can." The anger of a disenchanted performer may be directly expressed in organizational cultures where it is permissible to do so. This behavior tends to get the issues out in the open. More often, however, cultures view the expression of emotion at work as improper and unbusinesslike. In these cultures, the anger is suppressed and emerges in more passive-aggressive ways, such as badmouthing and starting rumors. One of the particular dangers of disenchantment is that it is quite contagious in the workplace.

It is often difficult to reason with disenchanted employees. Thus, the first step in managing this reaction is to bring these employees from their highly negative, emotionally charged state to a more neutral state. To neutralize the reaction does not mean to dismiss it; rather, it means to allow the individuals to let off the necessary steam so that they can come to terms with their anger. The second part of the strategy for dealing with disenchanted employees is to acknowledge that their anger is normal and that as their FLM you don't hold it against them. Sometimes disenchantment is a mask for one of the other three reactions, and it must be worked through to get to the core of the employee's reaction. Employees may become cynical about change. They may lose faith in the FLMs and other leaders of change.

A final reaction to change is disorientation. Disoriented employees are lost and confused and often unsure of their feelings. They waste energy trying to figure out what to do instead of how to do things. Disoriented individuals ask a lot of questions and become very detail oriented. They may appear to need a good deal of guidance and may leave their work undone until all of their questions have been answered. "Analysis paralysis" is characteristic of disoriented employees. They feel that they have lost touch with the priorities of the company, and they may want to analyze the change to death before acting on it. Disoriented employees may ask questions like "Now what do I do?" or "What do I do first?"

Disorientation is a common reaction among people who are used to clear goals and unambiguous directions. When change is introduced, it creates uncertainty and a lack of clarity. The FLM strategy for dealing with this reaction is to explain the change in a way that minimizes the ambiguity that is present. The information about the change needs to be put into a framework or an overall vision so that the disoriented individual can see where he or she fits into the grand scheme of things. Once the disoriented employee sees the broader context of the change, the FLM can plan a series of steps to help this employee adjust. The employee needs a sense of priorities.

FLMs need to be able to diagnose these four reactions to change. No single universal strategy can help all employees adjust because each reaction brings with it significant and different concerns. By recognizing each reaction and applying the appropriate strategy, it is possible to help even strong resisters work through a transition successfully.

THE LEWIN MODEL

Kurt Lewin, a noted organizational theorist, developed a model of the change process that has stood the test of time and continues to influence the way organizations manage planned change (Lewin, 1947). Lewin's model is based on the idea of force field analysis. Although force-field analysis may sound like something out of a *Star Trek* movie, it is a technique that can be used to analyze a change and help overcome resistance to it.

This model contends that a person's behavior is the product of two opposing forces; one force pushes toward preserving the status quo, and another force pushes for change. When the two opposing forces are approximately equal, current behavior is maintained. For behavioral change to occur, the forces maintaining status quo must be overcome. This can be accomplished by increasing the forces for change, by weakening the forces for status quo, or by a combination of these actions.

For FLMs, the first step in conducting a force-field analysis is to develop a list of all the forces promoting change and all those resisting change then determine which of the positive and which of the negative forces are the most powerful. The forces can be ranked in order of importance or by rate of strength. To facilitate the change, FLMs try to remove or at least minimize some of the forces acting against the change in order to tip the balance so that the forces furthering the change outweigh those hindering the change.

Lewin's change model suggests that every change requires employees to go through three steps:

- unfreezing—employees recognize the need for change
- changing or moving—employees begin trying to behave differently
- refreezing—the new behavior becomes part employees' moral behavior and procedures

In order for change to be fully implemented, the organization must help provide a way for the new behavior to become an established practice.

Unfreezing

In the unfreezing stage, employees must see the status quo as less than ideal. The FLM or other individual(s) responsible for implementing the change must spell out clearly to affected employees why the change is necessary. Allied Signal's CEO, Lawrence Bossidy, describes this step colorfully as the "burning platform theory of change":

When the roustabouts are standing on the offshore oil rig and the foreman yells, "Jump into the water," not only won't they jump but they also won't feel too kindly toward the foreman. There may be sharks in the water. They'll jump only when they themselves see the flames shooting up from the platform. . . . The leader's job is to help everyone see that the platform is burning, whether the flames are apparent or not. (Tichy & Charan, 1995)

In essence, unfreezing means overcoming fears about the change and other resistance to change. Organizations often accomplish unfreezing by eliminating the rewards for current behavior and showing that current behavior is not valued. Unfreezing on the part of individuals is an acceptance that change needs to occur. In essence, individuals surrender by allowing the boundaries of their status quo to be opened in preparation for change. The organization relies heavily on FLMs—as management's link to operating employees—to carry out this responsibility, for which they need good communication skills (see Chapter 4).

According to Ken Blanchard, a behavioral scientist, a major reason many efforts to change fail is that management does not consider the employees' point of view (Blanchard, 1992). Many changes require not only performing new tasks but also adopting new attitudes, such as a willingness to assume decision-making responsibility or a strong commitment to customers. Employees may have difficulty changing their attitudes, especially if they are unsure about management's sincerity.

Changing or Moving

When employees appreciate the need for a change and have received any necessary training, they are ready to begin altering their behavior.

It is practical to begin by attempting to make basic changes in employees' behavior, rather than trying to change their values. Values, by their very nature, are more resistant to change. To induce changes in behavior, FLMs and other managers should offer tangible and intangible rewards. As employees' attitudes become more positive, their values may shift as well.

The key to implementing change is to build on success. FLMs should determine those aspects of the change over which they have control and then try to carry them out successfully. An FLM should point out each success the group achieves along the way. For example, an FLM who has control over scheduling a change should establish reasonable deadlines. As employees meet each deadline, the FLM can praise their achievements. To be more specific, imagine that an accounting department is installing a new computer system. Instead of focusing simply on whether everyone is using the system properly, a manager can establish dates for setting up various pieces of equipment and teaching employees to operate different parts of the system. Then the FLM can note that the terminals arrived on time, that everyone learned how to log on and enter their passwords in a single training session, and so on. This positive reinforcement will help employees to change their behavior and their attitudes.

Refreezing

The change process is complete only when employees make the new behaviors, attitudes, and values part of their routine. In organizations that do not manage change effectively, FLMs may assume a change effort has succeeded simply because employees merely fulfill the basic requirements of a change without adjusting their routines or their attitudes. In such cases, backsliding is likely. Employees may revert to their old practices when the initial pressure for change eases, because new procedures are less comfortable than the old familiar ones. Changes in the reward structure may be needed to ensure that the organization is not rewarding the old behaviors and merely hoping for new behaviors.

Backsliding is a natural response to change, but it can become a problem unless the FLM acts to get everyone back on track. An FLM should remind employees about what they have achieved so far and what is expected of them in the future. It is important for the organization to continue to reinforce and reward employees for behavior that shows they have made the desired change.

Monsanto's approach to increasing opportunities for women within the company is an illustration of how to use the Lewin model effectively. First, Monsanto emphasized unfreezing by helping employees debunk negative stereotypes about women in business. This also helped overcome resistance to change. Second, Monsanto moved employees' attitudes and behaviors by diversity training in which differences were emphasized as positive, and supervisors learned ways of training and developing female employees. Third, Monsanto changed its reward system so managers were evaluated and paid according to how they coached and promoted women, which helped refreeze the new attitudes and behaviors.

Lewin's model proposes that for change efforts to be successful, the three-stage process must be completed. Failures in efforts to change can be traced back to one of the three stages. Successful change thus requires that old behaviors be discarded, new behaviors be introduced, and these new behaviors be institutionalized and rewarded.

SOME CONCLUDING THOUGHTS ON CHANGE

At the beginning of this chapter, front-line manager Jerome Fisher was faced with implementing another change in his unit. Because of uncertainties accompanying this change, he was not sure how the change would be accepted by his employees or how he should introduce the change to make it less stressful than previous changes. In introducing the new changes, Jerome should first concentrate on creating a positive environment. He should discuss the upcoming changes with his employees to solicit their ideas. At this time, Jerome should explain the five W's and H to them: What the change is; Why it is needed; Whom it will affect; When it will take place; Where it will take place; and How it will take place. Jerome should also make sure that the implementation of the change is realistic. He should be aware that the natural reaction of many of his employees will be to resist the change, and he should overcome much of this resistance by carefully explaining what the new changes will do and how they will affect each employee. Finally, it is important that the work climate be conducive to the change being introduced, implemented, and accepted.

REFERENCES

Blanchard, K. 1992. Six concerns in the change process. *Quality Digest* (June), 14, 62.

Faircloth, A. 1998. Guess who's coming to Denny's. *Fortune* (August 3), 95–108.

Lewin, K. 1947. Frontiers in group dynamics: Concepts, method and reality in social science. *Human Relations* (June), 5–41.

Nelson, D. L., & J. C. Quick. 2000. *Organizational behavior: Foundations, realities, and challenges.* Cincinnati, OH: South-Western College Publishing.

Tichy, N. M., & R. Charan. 1995. The CEO as coach: An interview with Allied Signal's Lawrence A. Bassidy. *Harvard Business Review* (March–April), 69–78.

Woodward, H., & S. Bucholz. 1987. *Aftershock: Helping people through corporate change.* New York: John Wiley.

Selected Bibliography

Austin, Mary Ruth. 1997. Managing change. *Manage* 49(1), 15–17.

Badaracco, Joseph L., Jr. 1997. *Defining moments: When managers must choose between right and right*. Boston: Harvard Business School Press.

Brannick, Michael T., Eduardo Salas, & Carolyn Prince (eds.). 1997. *Team performance assessment and measurement: Theory, methods, and applications*. Mahwah, NJ: Lawrence Erlbaum Associates.

Buckby, Simon, & Sathnam Sanghera. 1999. Setting great store by racial equality. *The Financial Times* (March 4), 11.

Buhler, Patricia M. 2000. Managing in the new millennium: Cultivating a staff. *Supervision* (February), 17–20.

Capelli, Peter. 1999. *The new deal at work: Managing the market-driven workforce*. Boston: Harvard Business School Press.

Caruth, Donald L. 2000. 11 characteristics of highly effective performance appraisals. *The Human Resource Professional* 13(1), 12.

Cole, Robert E. 1999. *Managing quality fads: How American business learned to play the quality game*. New York: Oxford University Press.

Crainer, Stuart. 1998. The 75 greatest management decisions ever made. *Management Review* 87(10), 16–21.

Evenson, Renee. 2000. Team effort: Beyond employees to team, beyond manager to coach. *Supervision* (February), 11–13.

Grote, Dick. 2000. Performance appraisal reappraised. *Harvard Business Review* 78(1), 21–30.

Henderson, Michael D. 1995. Operations management in health care. *Journal of Health Care Finance* 21(3), 44–48.

Hofstede, Geert. 1999. Problems remain, but theories will change: The universal and the specific in 21st century global management. *Organizational Dynamics* 27(1), 34–43.

Jackson, Susan E., & Marian N. Ruderman (eds.). 1995. *Diversity in work teams:*

Research paradigms for a changing workplace. Washington, DC: American Psychological Association.

Johnson, Spencer. 1999. *Who moved my cheese? An amazing way to deal with change in your work and in your life.* New York: G. P. Putnam's Sons.

Kanter, Rosabeth Moss. 1997. Lasting leadership lesson. *Sales & Marketing Management* 149(12), 22–25.

Kennedy, Marilyn Moats. 1998. The new rules. *Across the Board* 35(2), 51–52.

Kim, W. Chan, & Renee Mauborgne. 1997. Fair process: Managing in the knowledge economy. *Harvard Business Review* 75(4), 65–76.

Koch, Charles G. 1998. Empowering the entrepreneur within. *Chief Executive (U.S.)* (March), 46–50.

Korukonda, Appa Rao, John G. Watson, & T. M. Rajkumar. 1999. Beyond teams and empowerment: A counterpoint to two common precepts in TQM. *SAM Advanced Management Journal* 64(1), 29–37.

Lipnack, Jessica, & Jeffrey Stamps. 1999. Virtual teams: The new way to work. *Strategy & Leadership* 27(1), 14–20.

Luthans, Fred, & A. D. Stankovic. 1999. Reinforce for performance: The need to go beyond pay and even rewards. *The Academy of Management Executive* 13(2), 49–57.

Maddock, Richard C., & Richard L. Fulton. 1998. *Motivation, emotions, and leadership: The silent side of management.* Westport, CT: Quorum Books.

Managing in the info era: In the knowledge-based economy, workers will be valued for their ability to create, judge, imagine, and build relationships. 2000. *Fortune* 141(5), F-6+.

Markowich, Michael. 1995. Dinosauric management practices from Jurassic Park era. *HR Focus* 72(5), 1–4.

Mayers, Raymond Sanchez, Federico Souflee, Jr., & Dick J. Schoech. 1994. *Dilemmas in human services management: Illustrative case studies.* New York: Springer Publishing Co.

McGrath, Michael. 1999. Ten steps to better decisions. *Electronic Business* 25(3), 23.

Murphy, Kevin R., & Jeanette N. Cleveland. 1995. *Understanding performance appraisal: Social, organizational, and goal-based perspectives.* Thousand Oaks, CA: Sage Publications.

Nutt, Paul C. 1999. Surprising but true: Half the decisions in organizations fail. *The Academy of Management Executive* 13(4), 75–90.

O'Neil, Michael. 2000. Developing leaders. *Supervision* (March), 3–6.

Ostroff, Frank. 1998. *The horizontal organization: What the organization of the future actually looks like and how it delivers value to customers.* New York: Oxford University Press.

Pascarella, Perry. 1997 The manager as a true professional. *Management Review* 86(9), 47–49.

Pascarella, Perry, & Danah Zohar. 1998. Changing the thinking behind our thinking. *Management Review* 87(3), 56–59.

Pfeffer, Jeffrey, & John F. Veiga. 1999. Putting people first for organizational success. *The Academy of Management Executive* 13(2), 37–49.

Pollock, Ted. 2000. Boosting creativity. *Supervision* (March), 15–16.

Radin, Beryl A. 1998. The Government Performance and Results Act (GPRA):

Hydra-headed monster or flexible management tool? *Public Administration Review* 58(4), 307–317.

Rahim, M. Afzalur, Robert T. Golembiewski, & Kenneth D. McKenzie (eds.). 1999. *Current topics in management*, Vol. 4. Stamford, CT: JAI Press.

Schwarz, Robert M. 1994. *The skilled facilitator: Practical wisdom for developing effective groups*. San Francisco: Jossey-Bass.

Stamps, David. 1997. The self-organizing system. *Training* 34(4), 30–37.

Verespej, Michael A. 1998. Drucker sours on teams. *Industry Week* 247(7), 16–19.

Weaver, David A. 2000. Safety. *Supervision* (February), 13, 42.

Weston, Simon, & John Harper. 1998. The challenge of change. *Ivey Business Quarterly* 63(2), 78–82.

Index

About the Authors

RONALD R. SIMS is the Floyd Dewey Gottwald Professor of Business Administration at the College of William and Mary. He is the author or co-author of 17 books and more than 75 articles on a variety of organizational, change, and human resource management topics. His most recent books are *Keys to Employee Success in the Coming Decades*, co-edited with John G. Veres III (Quorum Books, 1999), *Reinventing Training and Development, Accountability and Radical Change in Public Organization*, and *Administration*.

JOHN G. VERES III is the Director of University Outreach at Auburn University, Montgomery. Since receiving his Ph.D. in Industrial/Organizational Psychology from Auburn University in June 1983, Dr. Veres' research interests have centered on job analysis, test validation, and issues in equal employment opportunity. Recent works include a 1998 *Journal of Applied Psychology* article entitled "Investigating Newcomer Expectations and Job-Related Outcomes," written with Buckley, Fedor, Wiese, and Carraher, and *Keys to Employee Success in the Coming Decades*, co-edited with Ronald R. Sims.

KATHERINE A. JACKSON is the Director of the Center for Business and Economic Development at Auburn University, Montgomery. She received a Doctor of Philosophy in Industrial and Organizational Psychology from Auburn University. Her primary interests include personnel administration and legislation, development of personnel selection procedures, performance feedback, and other human resources areas. Dr. Jackson's consulting experience has included job analysis, personnel selection, and test development and validation. She has managed projects with various classifications in numerous private and public sector organizations.

CAROLYN L. FACTEAU is Director of the Center for Government and Public Affairs at Auburn University, Montgomery. She received a Doctor of Philosophy in Industrial and Organizational Psychology from The University of Tennessee. Her primary interests include personnel assessment and selection, performance management, management development, and 360-degree feedback. Dr. Facteau has worked with both private and public sector organizations on projects involving 360-degree feedback; management development; entry level, promotional, and executive selection; performance management; survey design and administration; training; compensation; and team development.